D1263960

Advance praise for *A Guide to Bible Basics*

"Recently, I was reading through the stories about Joseph in Genesis with a group of adults. One of the members asked if Joseph was related to Abraham, and quickly another group member said he was not. I gently corrected her, and seizing a teachable moment, I invited the group to trace the lineage between Abraham and Joseph and discovered that most could not. What occurred to me was that while these adults, most of whom had been born and raised in the church, could tell stories about particular individuals in the Bible, they did not have an understanding of the overall story of the Bible and how the particular individuals related to one another. They needed Professor Mayfield's *Guide to Bible Basics*. This book is a treasure. It is no secret that many church members feel inadequate about their knowledge of the Bible. The truth is that many pastors feel the same way. In a remarkably accessible style, Professor Mayfield gives the reader a cogent overview of the whole of Scripture as well as each individual book. Through the careful work of the author, the reader gains a foundational and functional grasp of the Bible so that one may engage the Scripture with confidence and hope!"

—**RODGER NISHIOKA, Senior Associate Pastor,
Village Presbyterian Church, Prairie Village, Kansas**

"Everyone knows that the church in our culture faces a dreadful growth in biblical illiteracy wherein allusions to the Bible go increasingly unrecognized. Tyler Mayfield has written a terrific antidote to that illiteracy. His book-by-book, chapter-by-chapter introduction to the Bible provides easy access for fresh learning. With a generous use of charts, maps, outlines, and prompt questions, his book is user-friendly and pedagogically effective. I anticipate wide use of this book in congregations that 'want more Bible' and aim to advance biblical literacy that will in turn eventuate in a more knowing church."

—**WALTER BRUEGGEMANN, William Marcellus McPheeters
Professor Emeritus of Old Testament, Columbia Theological Seminary**

"Tyler Mayfield helps the reader build a scaffold for deeper understanding of the Bible and the setting into which it was written. This accessible and academically grounded resource for lay leaders, teachers, and new educators invites any student of Scripture to view a particular text through the larger arc of the biblical story."

—**REBECCA DAVIS, Associate Professor of Christian Education,
Union Presbyterian Seminary, and the 2018 ENRICH
Educator of the Year (Association of Presbyterian Church Educators)**

"This handy guide to the basic content of the Bible is a must for seminary students and for anyone seeking a way to organize the vast and diverse content of the Bible that is easy to retain. Dr. Mayfield breaks it all down with helpful synopses, outlines, charts, time lines, key concepts, places, names, and important quotations."

—**WILLIAM P. BROWN, William Marcellus McPheeters**
Professor of Old Testament, Columbia Theological Seminary

"In a time when the Bible is often invoked but without accurate knowledge of its actual content, Tyler Mayfield has provided an extremely helpful resource to introduce another generation to the basic content of the Bible. In a compact yet thorough volume, Mayfield walks readers through the whole Bible, with judicious chapter-by-chapter summaries for each book. With the Bible and this *Guide to Bible Basics* in tandem, readers will come to know—or rediscover—the key themes, people, places, and events in the biblical texts."

—**JOHN T. CARROLL, Harriet Robertson Fitts Memorial Professor**
of New Testament, Union Presbyterian Seminary

"This helpful text offers readers an overview of the content, context, and personalities found in Hebrew and Christian Scriptures. It is a valuable resource for Bible teachers and students, those who know a little or a lot about the people, places, and ideas found in specific books and stories. Professor Mayfield 'guides' us well."

—**BILL J. LEONARD, Professor Emeritus of Baptist Studies**
and Church History, Wake Forest University

A Guide to Bible Basics

Tyler D. Mayfield

WESTMINSTER
JOHN KNOX PRESS
LOUISVILLE · KENTUCKY

© 2018 Tyler D. Mayfield

First edition
Published by Westminster John Knox Press
Louisville, Kentucky

18 19 20 21 22 23 24 25 26 27—10 9 8 7 6 5 4 3 2 1

All rights reserved. No part of this book may be reproduced or transmitted in any form or by any means, electronic or mechanical, including photocopying, recording, or by any information storage or retrieval system, without permission in writing from the publisher. For information, address Westminster John Knox Press, 100 Witherspoon Street, Louisville, Kentucky 40202-1396. Or contact us online at www.wjkbooks.com.

Scripture quotations from the New Revised Standard Version of the Bible are copyright © 1989 by the Division of Christian Education of the National Council of the Churches of Christ in the U.S.A. and are used by permission.

Maps 1, 2, 3, 4, and 5 and the Chronological Outline were originally published in J. Maxwell Miller and John H. Hayes, *A History of Ancient Israel and Judah*, 2nd ed. (Louisville, KY: Westminster John Knox Press, 2006); maps 6 and 7 were originally published in M. Eugene Boring, *An Introduction to the New Testament: History, Literature, Theology* (Louisville, KY: Westminster John Knox Press, 2012).

Book design by Sharon Adams
Cover design by Mark Abrams

Library of Congress Cataloging-in-Publication Data

Names: Mayfield, Tyler D., 1980- author.
Title: A guide to Bible basics / Tyler D. Mayfield.
Description: Louisville, Kentucky : Westminster John Knox Press, 2018. |
  Includes bibliographical references and index. |
Identifiers: LCCN 2018025271 (print) | LCCN 2018029398 (ebook) | ISBN
  9781611648959 | ISBN 9780664263454 (pbk.)
Subjects: LCSH: Bible--Introductions.
Classification: LCC BS475.3 (ebook) | LCC BS475.3 .M3784 2018 (print) | DDC
  220.6/1—dc23
LC record available at https://lccn.loc.gov/2018025271

Most Westminster John Knox Press books are available at special quantity discounts when purchased in bulk by corporations, organizations, and special-interest groups. For more information, please e-mail SpecialSales@wjkbooks.com.

Contents

Maps and Chart

Acknowledgments

My gratitude begins with the Louisville Presbyterian Theological Seminary community. Thank you to my students David Annett, Shawn Harmon, Brittany Hesson, Brenda Holder, Megan McCarty, and Heather McIntyre, who met with me outside of class to talk about Bible content; Lucas Matthews and Timothy McNinch, who commented on early drafts; Daniel Van Beek, who provided tremendous amounts of perceptive editorial help near the end of the project; Cinda King, who offered thoughtful and detailed editorial feedback; and my fall 2017 Scripture I class for their insightful comments on an early draft. From the beginning, Dean Susan R. Garrett supported the project and provided New Testament book outlines.

Thank you to Bridgett Green, my editor at Westminster John Knox Press, who provided encouragement and astute comments throughout this project. It is nice to have a fellow biblical scholar as your editor.

Finally, this book is dedicated to my firstborn—my daughter, Livia. May the God of Sarah and Ruth, Mary and Priscilla, bless and keep you always.

Abbreviations

Acts	Acts of the Apostles	Lam	Lamentations
1–2 Chr	1–2 Chronicles	Lev	Leviticus
Col	Colossians	Mal	Malachi
1–2 Cor	1–2 Corinthians	Matt	Matthew
Dan	Daniel	Mic	Micah
Deut	Deuteronomy	Nah	Nahum
Eccl	Ecclesiastes	Neh	Nehemiah
Eph	Ephesians	Num	Numbers
Exod	Exodus	Obad	Obadiah
Ezek	Ezekiel	1–2 Pet	1–2 Peter
Gal	Galatians	Phil	Philippians
Gen	Genesis	Phlm	Philemon
Hab	Habakkuk	Prov	Proverbs
Hag	Haggai	Rev	Revelation
Heb	Hebrews	Rom	Romans
Hos	Hosea	1–2 Sam	1–2 Samuel
Isa	Isaiah	Song	Song of Songs
Jas	James	1–2 Thess	1–2 Thessalonians
Jer	Jeremiah	1–2 Tim	1–2 Timothy
Josh	Joshua	Zech	Zechariah
Judg	Judges	Zeph	Zephaniah
1–2 Kgs	1–2 Kings		

Introduction

This book invites us to become more familiar with the content of our Bibles. After all, most Americans own a Bible, maybe even two or three. We hear the Bible quoted in religious, cultural, and political discussions. We are ready to learn more about these stories. In addition to helping us read our Bibles more clearly, this book orients our reading so that we understand how particular biblical passages fit within the overall meaning of a book. Many biblical books are lengthy and complicated; even the shorter books are challenging to comprehend. My hope is that this book will be a guide for our Bible reading, that we will use this smaller book in order to organize and contextualize our reading of the larger book. This book can help us keep straight who's who and what's what. The structured information here can help us get a sense for the whole of the Bible and for the sections in the Bible that we wish to learn more about.

Nonetheless, this book should not be a substitute for reading the Bible. The best way to learn about the contents of the Bible is to read the Bible. There can be no good substitute for this activity. Yet I realize that reading such a dense and lengthy book can be overwhelming. The Bible I currently have on my desk is over two thousand pages in length, and it contains so many stories and names and places! How do we keep all that information organized?

A Guide to Bible Basics takes one step back from an ethical and theological concern for the Bible's relevance today. We want to examine the basic content of the Bible with the conviction that we first need some level of elementary comprehension of the Bible's stories, poetry, regulations, and teachings in order to imaginatively interpret them. We need biblical literacy. Interpreting the Bible requires the first step of knowing its content. What does the

Bible say? What are its narratives? How does the Bible speak about God and humanity? At the same time, this book does not strive to be exhaustive in its treatment of each biblical book. The reader will not find comprehensive lists of every single mention of a biblical character or place. In order to be useful, the book is selective in the content it presents.

This book is about the Christian Bible (Old and New Testaments). I write as a Christian and as a scholar of the Old Testament/Hebrew Bible. I hope that anyone who is curious about the Bible will find this book useful. Since the focus is content, I want to refrain from interpretive judgments as much as possible. As a result, this book does not introduce critical biblical scholarship, nor does it provide devotional readings of biblical passages.

WHAT IS THE BIBLE?

Christians use the word *Bible* to indicate both the Old Testament and the New Testament. As noted in the next section, different Christian traditions have different numbers of books included in their Bibles. As a Protestant, I open my Bible to find sixty-six books. My Catholic friend, however, finds almost a dozen additional books in her Bible. All Christians do not share the same Bible.

In addition, Christians share the Old Testament with Jews, who call it the *Tanakh*, or the *Bible*, or perhaps another name. To further complicate matters, Bible scholars often call this textual collection the *Hebrew Bible* in order to discuss this literature without demonstrating an expressly Christian or Jewish perspective. I will use the explicitly Christian designation *Old Testament*, since that is most familiar to Christians. Of course, just because something is labeled as "old" does not mean it is inferior or worthless when compared to something new.

The New Testament is not shared with Judaism. The number and arrangement of its books have been agreed upon by Christians for centuries.

WHICH BOOKS ARE IN THE BIBLE?

Each religious community has decided which books constitute its canon, its list of approved, inspired books—its sacred Scripture. Jews have a different canon from Christians. Even Christian communities have different canons from each other. I will discuss three of those canons here: Catholic, Protestant, and Orthodox.

The Christian Protestant canon contains sixty-six books: the Old Testament has thirty-nine books (the same books as in the Jewish canon but in a different order), and the New Testament has twenty-seven. The Christian Catholic canon contains all thirty-nine books from the Protestant Old Testament canon plus eleven additional books, then the twenty-seven New Testament books. Protestants often call these additional books found in Catholic Bibles the *Apocrypha*. The term is from Greek and means "hidden." Martin Luther, the Protestant Reformer, actually took these books from their place within the Catholic Bible and created a separate section with this title for his edition of the Bible. Eventually, many Protestant Bibles dropped this section altogether. Catholics call these same books *deuterocanonical*, another Greek term, which means "second canon." All Christians basically agree on the New Testament canon of twenty-seven books.

JEWISH CANON

Torah (Instruction)	*Nevi'im (Prophets)*	*Ketuvim (Writings)*
Genesis	Joshua	Psalms
Exodus	Judges	Proverbs
Leviticus	1–2 Samuel	Job
Numbers	1–2 Kings	Song of Songs
Deuteronomy	Isaiah	Ruth
	Jeremiah	Lamentations
	Ezekiel	Ecclesiastes
	Hosea	Esther
	Joel	Daniel
	Amos	Ezra
	Obadiah	Nehemiah
	Jonah	1–2 Chronicles
	Micah	
	Nahum	
	Habakkuk	
	Zephaniah	
	Haggai	
	Zechariah	
	Malachi	

PROTESTANT OLD TESTAMENT CANON

Pentateuch	*Historical Books*	*Poetry and Wisdom*	*Prophets*
Genesis	Joshua	Job	Isaiah
Exodus	Judges	Psalms	Jeremiah
Leviticus	Ruth	Proverbs	Lamentations
Numbers	1–2 Samuel	Ecclesiastes	Ezekiel
Deuteronomy	1–2 Kings	Song of Songs	Daniel
	1–2 Chronicles		Hosea
	Ezra		Joel
	Nehemiah		Amos
	Esther		Obadiah
			Jonah
			Micah
			Nahum
			Habakkuk
			Zephaniah
			Haggai
			Zechariah
			Malachi

CATHOLIC OLD TESTAMENT CANON

Pentateuch	*Historical Books*	*Poetry and Wisdom*	*Prophets*
Genesis	Joshua	Job	Isaiah
Exodus	Judges	Psalms	Jeremiah
Leviticus	Ruth	Proverbs	Lamentations
Numbers	1–2 Samuel	Ecclesiastes	Baruch
Deuteronomy	1–2 Kings	Song of Songs	Ezekiel
	1–2 Chronicles	Wisdom of Solomon	Daniel (with
	Ezra	Ecclesiasticus	additions)
	Nehemiah		Hosea
	Tobit		Joel
	Judith		Amos
	Esther (with		Obadiah
	additions)		Jonah
	1–2 Maccabees		Micah
			Nahum
			Habakkuk
			Zephaniah
			Haggai
			Zechariah
			Malachi

ORTHODOX OLD TESTAMENT CANON

Pentateuch	Historical Books	Poetry and Wisdom	Prophets
Genesis	Joshua	Psalms	Hosea
Exodus	Judges	Job	Amos
Leviticus	Ruth	Proverbs	Micah
Numbers	1–4 Kingdoms	Ecclesiastes	Joel
Deuteronomy	1–2 Chronicles	Song of Songs	Obadiah
	1–2 Esdras	Wisdom of Solomon	Jonah
	Nehemiah	Wisdom of Sirach	Nahum
	Tobit		Habakkuk
	Judith		Zephaniah
	Esther (with		Haggai
	additions)		Zechariah
	1–3 Maccabees		Malachi
			Isaiah
			Jeremiah
			Baruch
			Lamentations
			of Jeremiah
			Epistle of
			Jeremiah
			Ezekiel
			Daniel (with
			additions)

CHRISTIAN NEW TESTAMENT CANON

Gospels and Acts	Paul's Letters	General Letters and Revelation
Matthew	Romans	Hebrews
Mark	1–2 Corinthians	James
Luke	Galatians	1–2 Peter
John	Ephesians	1–3 John
Acts of the Apostles	Philippians	Jude
	Colossians	Revelation
	1–2 Thessalonians	
	1–2 Timothy	
	Titus	
	Philemon	

BIBLE TRANSLATIONS

The Old Testament was written primarily in Hebrew, although sections of Ezra and Daniel are in Aramaic, a closely related language. The New Testament was written in Greek. The Bibles we read today are translations. In fact, most Christians throughout history have only encountered the Bible through translation.

A Guide to Bible Basics uses the New Revised Standard Version (NRSV), a readable English translation completed by a committee of scholars including women and men representing Protestant, Roman Catholic, Eastern Orthodox, and Jewish communities of faith.

If you have only heard or read a certain translation, I recommend you try a different one. If you are accustomed to the King James Version, try the New Revised Standard Version. If you are familiar with the New Revised Standard Version, try the Common English Bible. For the names of biblical people and places, I follow the spelling of the New Revised Standard Version for ease of use. If you prefer to use a study Bible (a Bible with study notes at the bottom of the page) to help your understanding of specific passages, I recommend *The New Interpreter's Study Bible*, published by Abingdon Press, or *The Oxford Annotated Study Bible*, published by Oxford University Press. The notes in these two Bibles are written by reputable biblical scholars with commentary on historical, literary, and theological aspects of the text.

BIBLICAL TIME PERIODS

To provide an overview of the biblical story, I have divided it into nine time periods. For each period, I note some of the major events that are presented in the Bible as well as the biblical books that tell the story of the period. The biblical texts themselves have a more complicated history concerning their dating and editing. Therefore, I have organized the biblical books by the stories they present and when those stories most likely would have occurred, not by when the stories were written down.

Matriarchs and Patriarchs: 2000–1500 BCE

The biblical story begins with the creation of the world but quickly moves to the time period of the ancestors of the book of Genesis. These matriarchs and patriarchs include Abraham, Sarah, Hagar, Ishmael, Isaac, Rebekah, Jacob, Esau, Rachel, Leah, Zilpah, Bilhah, Dinah, Reuben, Simeon, Levi, Judah,

Tamar, Issachar, Zebulun, Dan, Naphtali, Gad, Asher, and Joseph. The story takes place mostly in Canaan, but by the end, Jacob's children are in Egypt.

Book: Genesis

Exodus and Wilderness: 1500–1200 BCE

The children of Jacob, the Israelites, are enslaved in Egypt. They are liberated with the help of their leader, Moses, and his siblings, Miriam and Aaron. The story continues with the Israelites' journey through the wilderness to Mount Sinai, where they receive divine instructions. Then the Israelites wander again through the wilderness as they prepare to enter the promised land.

Books: Exodus; Leviticus; Numbers; Deuteronomy

Promised Land and Judges: 1200–1000 BCE

With Joshua as their leader, the Israelites enter the land of Canaan and conquer various cities and peoples in order to occupy the land. They divide the promised land among the twelve tribes. A series of judges (e.g., Deborah, Gideon, and Samson) help deliver them from various oppressors.

Books: Joshua; Judges; Ruth

United Monarchy: 1000–922 BCE

The reigns of King Saul, King David, and King Solomon bring the monarchial state together.

Books: 1 and 2 Samuel; 1 Kings 1–11; 1 Chronicles 10–29; 2 Chronicles 1–9; Psalms

Divided Monarchy: 922–587 BCE

The sons of King Solomon divide the monarchy into two kingdoms: Israel in the north and Judah in the south. The northern kingdom of Israel survives until 722 BCE, when Samaria falls to the Assyrians. The southern kingdom of Judah survives until 587 BCE, when Jerusalem falls to the Babylonians.

Books: 1 Kings 12–22; 2 Kings 1–25; 2 Chronicles 10–36; Isaiah; Jeremiah; Ezekiel; Hosea; Amos; Jonah; Micah; Nahum; Habakkuk; Zephaniah

Babylonian Exile: 587–539 BCE

Some of the people of Judah are taken into captivity in Babylon. In exile, they have no temple and no monarchy.

Books: Lamentations; Ezekiel; Daniel 1–5, 7–8

Persian Period: 539–332 BCE

The people in Babylon are allowed to return home from exile and rebuild the Temple. Judah becomes a province of the Persian Empire.

Books: Ezra; Nehemiah; Esther; Daniel 6, 9–12; Joel; Haggai; Zechariah; Malachi

Hellenistic Period: 332–63 BCE

Alexander the Great conquers the area, and the Jews become increasingly under the influence of Hellenism.

Roman Period: 63 BCE–476 CE

The Romans take Jerusalem, and eventually Judea and Galilee come under the control of the Roman Empire. The events of the New Testament take place entirely during this period.

Books: New Testament

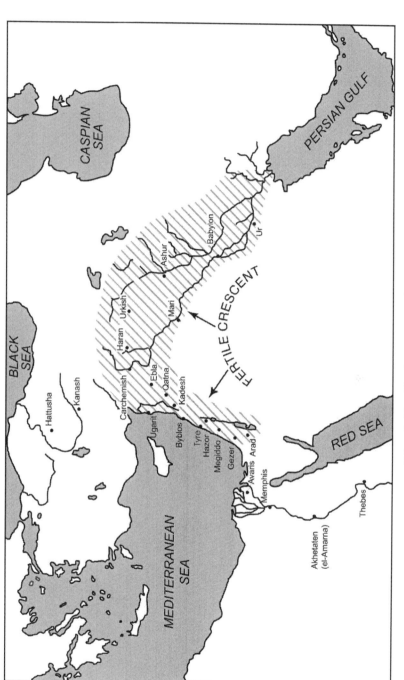

Map 1. Fertile Crescent with Egypt

(Originally published in J. Maxwell Miller and John H. Hayes, *A History of Ancient Israel and Judah*, 2nd ed. [Louisville, KY: Westminster John Knox Press, 2006], 8.)

1

The Pentateuch

The Greek word *Pentateuch* translates into English as "five scrolls" and is a standard Christian designation for the first five books in the Old Testament: Genesis, Exodus, Leviticus, Numbers, and Deuteronomy. Jews often refer to these same books as *Torah*, a Hebrew word meaning "instruction." These books are also referred to in both Judaism and Christianity as the *Five Books of Moses* in deference to the ancient tradition of Moses as the author.

PENTATEUCH CONTENT OUTLINE

The beginnings of humanity (Gen 1–11)
Abraham's story (Gen 12–25)
Jacob's story (Gen 26–36)
Joseph's story (Gen 37–50)
Israelites in Egypt (Exod 1–12)
Israelites delivered from Egypt (Exod 12–15)
Israelites in the wilderness (Exod 15–18)
Israelites at Sinai (Exod 19–40; Leviticus; Num 1–10)
Wilderness wanderings (Num 11–21)
Encampment on the Plains of Moab across the Jordan from Jericho (Num 22–36; Deuteronomy)

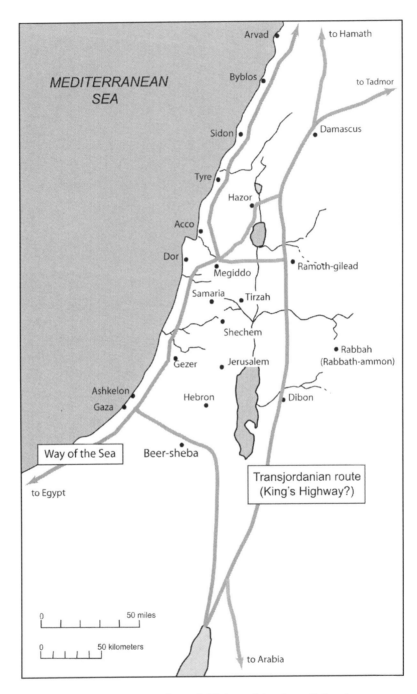

Map 2. Main Roads and Cities of Ancient Palestine

(Originally published in J. Maxwell Miller and John H. Hayes, *A History of Ancient Israel and Judah*, 2nd ed. [Louisville, KY: Westminster John Knox Press, 2006], 8.)

GENESIS

The English word *Genesis* is the Greek word for "origin" and was used to title this biblical book in the Septuagint, a Greek translation of the Old Testament from the original Hebrew that was produced in the third to second century BCE. In the Jewish tradition, the book is entitled *Bereshit*, which is the first Hebrew word in the book and means "in the beginning."

Synopsis

The book of Genesis tells a story of beginnings: the beginning of the world, of humanity, and of God's relationship with all creation. After the creation, the first human couple, Adam and Eve, disobeyed God, and the relationship between humans and God was immediately challenged. Their son Cain murdered their other son, Abel. Violence persisted, prompting God's decision to destroy the earth by a flood. After the flood, God promised never to destroy the earth or its creatures again and made a covenant with Noah and every living creature.

The book then turns from a more universal, worldwide perspective to focus on a single family. Abram/Abraham and his wife Sarai/Sarah made a journey to the land of Canaan, where God promised them land and numerous descendants. They traveled to Egypt and ventured through multiple Egyptian cities, encountering various leaders including the pharaoh of Egypt and the kings of Salem and Gerar. The story focuses on the divine promise to Abraham of a son; however, Sarah was barren. In her despair, she attempted to give Abraham a son through her Egyptian slave-girl, Hagar. Her plan succeeded, and Ishmael was born. However, God's promise was for Abraham's heir to come through Sarah. Finally, at an advanced age, Sarah bore a son and named him Isaac, the child of the promise. God asked Abraham to offer Isaac as a sacrifice. Abraham obeyed, but God provided a ram in Isaac's place. After Sarah's death and burial in Hebron, Abraham arranged a marriage between Isaac and Rebekah before marrying Keturah himself. Abraham died at 175 years old.

Isaac and Rebekah had twin sons, Esau and Jacob, who immediately engaged in sibling rivalry. Esau, the firstborn, sold his birthright to Jacob for a bowl of stew. Jacob tricked his father, Isaac, into giving him the blessing that was due Esau. Jacob had to leave home to escape Esau's anger. While away, Jacob had a dream at Bethel, encountered Rachel, and eventually married both Leah and Rachel, the daughters of Laban. Through these two sisters and their two slaves, Bilhah and Zilpah, Jacob had twelve sons and one daughter. Jacob became a wealthy man with large flocks and numerous slaves. Ultimately, Jacob and his family fled from Laban and his sons. Laban pursued

Jacob, and the two men made a covenant. After Jacob reconciled with Laban, he traveled to reconcile with his brother, Esau, sending presents in advance of their meeting. The night before he reached Esau, Jacob wrestled with a man (or God?) who dislocated Jacob's hip. After the brothers' reconciliation, they went in separate directions, with Jacob going to Succoth and Esau to Seir. Meanwhile, Jacob and Leah's daughter, Dinah, was raped by Shechem the Hivite, and her brothers took revenge on him and his city. The attention to Jacob ends with the birth of Benjamin and the deaths of Rachel and Isaac.

At this point, the focus of Genesis shifts to one of Jacob's sons. Joseph, the second to the youngest, dreamed of his brothers bowing down to him. These dreams, combined with his father's favoritism, caused great jealousy to arise in his brothers. They connived to get rid of Joseph, first throwing him in a pit and then selling him to a passing caravan. Joseph ended up in Egypt and rose to power in Pharaoh's administration as a trusted adviser after interpreting one of Pharaoh's dreams. When the famine predicted in Pharaoh's dreams arrived, ten of Joseph's brothers came to Egypt to buy grain. Joseph, whom they did not recognize, gave them the grain but demanded they return to Egypt with their youngest brother, Benjamin. Eventually, Joseph revealed himself to his brothers and brought all his family, including his father, to Egypt. As Jacob grew ill, he blessed Joseph's two sons, Ephraim and Manasseh, and offered final words to each of his own sons. Jacob died and was buried with Sarah, Abraham, and Isaac. Joseph forgave his brothers for their poor treatment of him. Joseph died in Egypt.

Content Outline

The Beginnings of Humanity

The world is created in six days	Genesis 1
The man and the woman are created	Genesis 2
The man and the woman listen to the serpent, disobey God, and are punished	Genesis 3
Cain kills Abel, his brother; Cain's descendants; Seth is born	Genesis 4
The ten generations from Adam to Noah	Genesis 5
God plans judgment via a flood; God instructs Noah to construct an ark	Genesis 6
Noah's family and pairs of animals board the ark; the flood begins	Genesis 7

Jacob's Story

Isaac passes Rebekah off as his sister to King Abimelech of Gerar	Genesis 26
Jacob tricks Isaac into blessing him instead of Esau	Genesis 27
Esau marries Ishmael's daughter; Jacob flees from Esau and dreams at Bethel	Genesis 28
Jacob encounters Rachel; Laban deceives Jacob; Jacob marries	Genesis 29
Leah, Rachel, Bilhah, and Zilpah bear children	Genesis 30
Jacob and his family flee from Laban; Laban pursues them; Laban and Jacob make a covenant	Genesis 31
Jacob prepares to meet Esau; Jacob wrestles at night at Peniel	Genesis 32
Esau and Jacob are reconciled	Genesis 33
Dinah is raped by Shechem; Simeon and Levi massacre the men of Shechem's city	Genesis 34
Jacob goes to Bethel; Rachel gives birth to Benjamin and dies; Isaac dies	Genesis 35
Descendants of Esau	Genesis 36

Joseph's Story

Joseph dreams and his brothers sell him; Joseph ends up in Potiphar's house	Genesis 37
Judah unknowingly has sex with his daughter-in-law, Tamar; she gives birth to twins	Genesis 38
Joseph refuses to have sex with Potiphar's wife; he goes to prison	Genesis 39
Joseph interprets the dreams of Pharaoh's cupbearer and baker while in prison	Genesis 40
Joseph interprets Pharaoh's dream and is promoted to a top position in Egypt	Genesis 41
Joseph encounters his brothers in Egypt; the brothers return to Canaan for Benjamin	Genesis 42

People

Adam and Eve—first couple
Cain, Abel, and Seth—sons of Adam and Eve
Noah and his unnamed wife—characters in the flood story
Shem, Ham, Japheth—sons of Noah and his wife
Terah—father of Abram/Abraham
Abraham (aka Abram)—husband of Sarai/Sarah; father of Ishmael and Isaac
Sarah (aka Sarai)—wife of Abraham; mother of Isaac
Lot—Abraham's nephew; Haran's son
Lot's unnamed wife and two daughters
Melchizedek—king of Salem
Hagar—Sarah's Egyptian slave-girl; Ishmael's mother
Abimelech—king of Gerar
Ishmael—Abraham and Hagar's son
Moab and Ben-ammi—sons of Lot and his two daughters
Isaac—Abraham and Sarah's son; father of Esau and Jacob
Rebekah—wife of Isaac; mother of Esau and Jacob; daughter of Bethuel the Aramean
Keturah—Abraham's wife
Esau—first son of Isaac and Rebekah
Jacob—second son of Isaac and Rebekah
Judith, Basemath, Adah, Oholibamah, Mahalath—the names of Esau's wives

Laban—Rebekah's brother; father of Rachel and Leah
Leah—Jacob's elder wife; daughter of Laban
Rachel—Jacob's younger wife; daughter of Laban
Zilpah—Leah's maid
Bilhah—Rachel's maid
Deborah—Rebekah's nurse
Reuben—Jacob and Leah's first son
Simeon—Jacob and Leah's second son
Levi—Jacob and Leah's third son
Judah—Jacob and Leah's fourth son
Issachar—Jacob and Leah's fifth son
Zebulun—Jacob and Leah's sixth son
Dinah—Jacob and Leah's daughter
Dan—Jacob and Bilhah's first son
Naphtali—Jacob and Bilhah's second son
Gad—Jacob and Zilpah's first son
Asher—Jacob and Zilpah's second son
Joseph—Jacob and Rachel's first son
Shechem—son of Hamor the Hivite
Benjamin—Jacob and Rachel's second son
Tamar—wife of Er, Judah's first son
Perez and Zerah—twin sons of Judah and Tamar
Potiphar—official in Pharaoh's court
Potiphar's unnamed wife
Pharaoh—king of Egypt
Asenath—daughter of Potiphera, wife of Joseph
Manasseh—Joseph's first son
Ephraim—Joseph's second son

Places

Garden of Eden—Adam and Eve's first habitat
Land of Nod—Cain settles here after killing his brother Abel
Mountains of Ararat—place where the ark lands after the flood subsides
Land of Shinar—where the Tower of Babel is built
Ur of the Chaldeans—Abraham and Terah's original homeland
Canaan—area that will become biblical Israel
Shechem—Abraham stops here and sets up an altar
Bethel—place associated with Abraham and Jacob
Egypt—Abraham and Sarah, as well as Joseph's brothers, journey here because of famine

Sodom and Gomorrah—cities destroyed by God
Gerar—Abraham and Sarah stop here; Isaac settles here
Wilderness of Paran—Ishmael's home
Land of Moriah—site of Abraham's near-sacrifice of Isaac
Beersheba—place associated with Abraham and Sarah
Hebron—place associated with Abraham and Sarah
Peniel—place associated with Jacob
Edom—place associated with Esau and his descendants
Goshen—area of Egypt associated with Joseph

Key Concepts

Creation—beginning of the world, of plants and animals and humanity
Flood—water covers the earth; Noah and his family survive in an ark
Noahic covenant—first covenant in the Bible between God and the world; rainbow is its sign
Tower of Babel—structure built by humans to reach the heavens
Promise of land and descendants—God's promise to Abraham, Isaac, and Jacob
Abrahamic covenant—made between God and Abraham; includes land and many descendants; circumcision is its sign
Circumcision—sign of the Abrahamic covenant between God, Abraham, and his descendants
Birthright—special inheritance given to the firstborn son
Chosen—God's election of Abraham and his family to be God's people

Important Quotations

"So God created humankind in his image, in the image of God he created them; male and female he created them." (Gen 1:27)

"And the Lord God commanded the man, 'You may freely eat of every tree of the garden; but of the tree of the knowledge of good and evil you shall not eat, for in the day that you eat of it you shall die.'" (Gen 2:16–17)

"This at last is bone of my bones and flesh of my flesh; this one shall be called Woman, for out of Man this one was taken." (Gen 2:23)

"Am I my brother's keeper?" (Gen 4:9)

"I have set my bow in the clouds, and it shall be a sign of the covenant between me and the earth." (Gen 9:13)

"Go from your country and your kindred and your father's house to the land that I will show you. I will make of you a great nation, and I will bless you, and make your name great, so that you will be a blessing." (Gen 12:1–2)

"The Lord said to Abraham, 'Why did Sarah laugh, and say, "Shall I indeed bear a child, now that I am old?" Is anything too wonderful for the Lord? At the set time I will return to you, in due season, and Sarah shall have a son.'" (Gen 18:13–14)

"Take your son, your only son Isaac, whom you love, and go to the land of Moriah, and offer him there as a burnt offering on one of the mountains that I shall show you." (Gen 22:2; God speaking to Abraham)

"Give me children, or I shall die!" (Gen 30:1; Rachel speaking to Jacob)

"Then the man said, 'You shall no longer be called Jacob, but Israel, for you have striven with God and with humans, and have prevailed.'" (Gen 32:28)

"But Esau ran to meet him, and embraced him, and fell on his neck and kissed him, and they wept." (Gen 33:4)

"Now Israel loved Joseph more than any other of his children, because he was the son of his old age; and he had made him a long robe with sleeves." (Gen 37:3)

"Even though you intended to do harm to me, God intended it for good, in order to preserve a numerous people, as he is doing today." (Gen 50:20)

Days of Creation in Genesis 1

1st day: light, darkness, day, night
2nd day: sky and sea
3rd day: dry land and plants
4th day: lights in the sky (stars), the greater light, the lesser light
5th day: living creatures in the waters, birds, sea monsters
6th day: living creatures on the earth, wild animals, humans
7th day: God rests

Life of Abram/Abraham

Abram before the Journey to Canaan

- Abram is mentioned for the first time in conjunction with his father, Terah, and his brothers, Nahor and Haran; there is no birth story (Gen 11:26–27)

- Abram takes Sarai as his wife; she is barren and without children (Gen 11:29–30)
- Abram journeys with his wife, father, and nephew from Ur to Haran (Gen 11:31)

Abram without Children

- God calls Abram to leave his father and go to the land of Canaan with his wife and nephew (Gen 12:1–9)
- Abram and Sarai journey to Egypt because of famine; Abram tells Pharaoh that Sarai is his sister (Gen 12:10–20)
- Abram separates from Lot when he comes out of Egypt and settles in Hebron (Gen 13)
- Abram rescues Lot from captivity and is blessed by Melchizedek (Gen 14)
- God makes a covenant with Abram, promising him land and descendants (Gen 15)

Abraham and Ishmael

- Abram has his first son, Ishmael, through Hagar; although Sarai devised this plan, she deals harshly with Hagar (Gen 16)
- God changes Abram's name to Abraham and Sarai's name to Sarah; God makes an everlasting covenant with Abraham, promising him land and descendants; the sign of this Abrahamic covenant is circumcision (Gen 17)
- Three men visit Abraham and promise Abraham and Sarah a son; Sarah laughs because of her old age (Gen 18:1–15)
- Abraham and God negotiate about the destruction of Sodom and Gomorrah (Gen 18:16–33)
- Abraham and Sarah journey to Gerar; Abraham tells King Abimelech that Sarah is his sister (Gen 20)

Abraham and Isaac

- At age 100, Abraham has a second son, Isaac, through Sarah; Abraham sends Hagar and Ishmael away (Gen 21:1–21)
- Abraham makes a covenant with Abimelech at Beersheba (Gen 21:22–34)
- God commands Abraham to sacrifice Isaac but provides a ram instead at the last moment (Gen 22)
- Abraham mourns Sarah and buries her (Gen 23)
- Abraham sends his servant back to his homeland to get Isaac a wife (Gen 24)
- Abraham marries Keturah and has six children with her (Gen 25:1–6)
- Abraham dies at age 175 (Gen 25:7–11)

Life of Jacob

Esau and Jacob at Home

- Jacob is born after his twin, Esau (Gen 25:19–28)
- Clever Jacob gets the birthright from Esau (Gen 25:29–34)
- Trickster Jacob gets the blessing from his father, Isaac, by disguising himself as Esau (Gen 27:1–29)
- Esau wants to kill Jacob, so Rebekah schemes to get Isaac to send Jacob away to find a wife (Gen 27:41–28:5)

Jacob Leaves Home

- Jacob dreams at Bethel (Gen 28:10–22)
- Jacob meets Rachel, daughter of his uncle Laban (Gen 29:1–14)
- Jacob works seven years for Rachel but is tricked into marrying Leah (Gen 29:15–25)
- Jacob works another seven years and marries Rachel (Gen 29:26–30)
- Jacob has children with Leah, Bilhah, Zilpah, and Rachel (Gen 29:31–30:24)
- Jacob acquires wealth, while Laban does not (Gen 30:25–43)
- Jacob flees from Laban; Laban pursues him; they make a covenant (Gen 31)
- Jacob begins his journey to meet his brother, Esau (Gen 32:1–21)
- Jacob wrestles with a man at Peniel, who changes Jacob's name to Israel (Gen 32:22–32)
- Jacob reconciles with Esau (Gen 33:1–17)
- Jacob returns to Bethel (Gen 35)

Jacob in Canaan

- Jacob settles in Canaan (Gen 37)
- Jacob mourns the "death" of his son Joseph (Gen 37)

Jacob in Egypt

- Jacob journeys to Egypt to see Joseph (Gen 46)
- Jacob settles in Goshen (Gen 46)
- Jacob requests to be buried with his ancestors (Gen 47)
- Jacob blesses Joseph's son (Gen 48)
- Jacob says his last words to his own sons (Gen 49)
- Jacob dies (Gen 49:33)
- Jacob is buried with his ancestors (Gen 50)

Jacob's Twelve Sons and One Daughter

Sons: Reuben, Simeon, Levi, Judah, Issachar, Zebulun, Benjamin, Dan, Naphtali, Gad, Asher, Joseph
Daughter: Dinah

EXODUS

The book of Exodus, the second book in the Hebrew Bible and the Christian Old Testament, continues the early story of the Israelites as they made their way out of Egyptian bondage and to Mount Sinai. The word *exodus* is from Greek and means "going out." It was used as the book's title first in the Septuagint, an early Greek translation of the Old Testament. In the Jewish tradition, the book is entitled *Shemot*, which means "names" and is one of the first Hebrew words in the book. The first half of Exodus contains narrative material; legal and instructional material is prevalent in the second half.

Synopsis

Exodus begins with notice of the death of Joseph and his brothers and of the multiplication of the Israelites in Egypt. A new Egyptian pharaoh, who did not know Joseph, began to oppress the Israelites and attempted to kill all the newly born male babies. The Hebrew midwives, Shiphrah and Puah, deceived Pharaoh and saved some babies. During this time of infanticide, Moses' mother hid her son in a basket on the river, where he was found by Pharaoh's daughter. Moses was raised as her adopted son with all the privileges of palace life. One day, Moses saw an Egyptian overseer beating a Hebrew; in an outrage, Moses murdered the Egyptian. When he learned that a fellow Hebrew had witnessed his action, Moses fled to Midian, where he met Jethro and his daughters. Moses married Jethro's oldest daughter, Zipporah. While working as a shepherd for his father-in-law, Moses received a divine call from a burning bush to return to Egypt to free the Israelites. Although he objected, God provided him with the power he would need.

Moses returned to Egypt and reunited with his brother, Aaron. Together they confronted Pharaoh about letting the Israelite slaves leave the country. Pharaoh refused, so God sent a series of ten plagues upon Egypt. Pharaoh did not listen until the last plague, when all the firstborn in Egypt, including his own son, were killed. Pharaoh conceded, and the Israelites left Egypt. Guided by a pillar of cloud by day and a pillar of fire by night, they made their way to the Sea of Reeds. Pharaoh changed his mind and pursued the Israelites. God divided the waters, and the Israelites crossed on dry land. The Egyptians followed in pursuit and drowned.

After the episode at the sea, the Israelites encountered other miracles, including bitter water that became sweet, bread from heaven, and water from a rock. Eventually, they reached Mount Sinai, where they were given the Ten Commandments, other laws, and instructions on building the tabernacle. God made a covenant with the people, which they quickly broke and had to renew after Moses descended the mountain and found them worshiping a golden calf. Finally, the people built the tabernacle, and God's glory filled it.

Content Outline

Israelites in Egypt

Pharaoh deals shrewdly with the Israelites and tries to kill every newborn boy	Exodus 1
Birth of Moses; Moses kills an Egyptian and flees to Midian	Exodus 2
Moses encounters a burning bush at Horeb; God reveals the divine name	Exodus 3
Moses objects to the call to free the Israelites from Egypt; God gives him powers	Exodus 4
Moses and Aaron confront Pharaoh; Pharaoh refuses to let the Israelites go free	Exodus 5
God ensures deliverance from Pharaoh; genealogy of Moses and Aaron	Exodus 6
Moses and Aaron confront Pharaoh again; first plague (water to blood)	Exodus 7
Second plague (frogs); third plague (gnats); fourth plague (flies)	Exodus 8
Fifth plague (pestilence upon livestock); sixth plague (boils); seventh plague (hail)	Exodus 9
Eighth plague (locusts); ninth plague (darkness for three days)	Exodus 10
Announcement of the tenth plague: death of the firstborn in Egypt	Exodus 11

Israelites Are Delivered from Egypt

Instructions for Passover; tenth plague; Israelites leave	Exodus 12
Festival of Unleavened Bread; God claims firstborn males; pillars of cloud and fire	Exodus 13
Israelites cross the Sea of Reeds; Egyptians pursue them and drown	Exodus 14
The Song of Moses and the Song of Miriam; bitter water becomes sweet	Exodus 15

Israelites in the Wilderness

Israelites complain; God provides manna and quail to eat	Exodus 16
God gives water from a rock; Joshua and the Israelites defeat the Amalekites	Exodus 17
Jethro and Moses reunite; Jethro gives advice	Exodus 18

Israelites at Sinai

The Israelites reach Sinai, where they are consecrated; God descends upon the mountain	Exodus 19
God speaks the Ten Commandments; God gives instructions for the altar	Exodus 20
Laws concerning slaves, violence against humans, and property	Exodus 21
Laws concerning restitution and miscellaneous social and religious laws	Exodus 22
Laws concerning justice and worship (sabbatical years, Sabbath, festivals)	Exodus 23
The people ratify the covenant; Moses goes up the mountain for forty days	Exodus 24
Instructions to construct the ark of the covenant, table for bread, and lampstand	Exodus 25
Instructions to construct the tabernacle	Exodus 26
Instructions to construct the altar and the court	Exodus 27

Instructions to make vestments for the priests	Exodus 28
Instructions for consecrating the priests and for the burnt offering	Exodus 29
Instructions to construct an incense altar and bronze basin	Exodus 30
Bezalel and Oholiab; laws about Sabbath	Exodus 31
The Israelites worship the golden calf; Moses is angered but intercedes with God on behalf of the people	Exodus 32
God commands the Israelites to leave Sinai, and Moses intercedes again	Exodus 33
Moses cuts two new tablets; another theophany; the covenant is renewed	Exodus 34
Construction of the tabernacle begins	Exodus 35
Construction of the tabernacle continues	Exodus 36
Construction of the ark of the covenant, table for bread, lampstand, and altar	Exodus 37
Construction of the burnt offering altar and court	Exodus 38
Making of the vestments for the priests; construction completed	Exodus 39
Tabernacle is set up and furnished; a cloud covers the tent of meeting, and God's glory fills the tabernacle	Exodus 40

People

Pharaoh—king of Egypt
Shiphrah—Hebrew midwife
Puah—Hebrew midwife
Unnamed Levite man and father of Moses (later identified as Amram in Exod 6:20)
Unnamed Levite woman and mother of Moses (later identified as Jochebed in Exod 6:20)
Moses—son of two Levites, brother of Aaron and Miriam
Unnamed sister of Moses (perhaps Miriam)—reunites baby Moses with his birth mother
Unnamed daughter of Pharaoh—takes baby Moses from the river

Jethro (aka Reuel)—priest of Midian; Moses' father-in-law

Zipporah—Moses' wife, from Midian

Gershom—Moses' first son by Zipporah

Aaron—Moses' brother, a Levite

Miriam—a prophet; Moses and Aaron's sister

Eliezer—Moses' second son by Zipporah

Nadab and Abihu—Aaron's sons

Bezalel and Oholiab—two craftsmen of the tabernacle

Joshua—Moses' assistant

Places

Egypt—place of the Hebrews' enslavement

Midian—place where Moses flees from Pharaoh; there he joins Jethro's household and marries Zipporah

Mount Horeb—mountain of God, where Moses encounters the burning bush

Goshen—region within Egypt where the Israelites live

Succoth—first place the Israelites stop after leaving Egypt

Marah—place in the wilderness where the water is bitter; *marah* means "bitter"

Elim—oasis in the wilderness where the Israelites find water

Wilderness of Sin—place where manna is provided

Rephidim—place where Moses gets water from the rock and the Israelites defeat the Amalekites

Mount Sinai—mountain at which Moses and the Israelites stop and receive a revelation

Key Concepts

Pharaoh's hardened heart—stubbornness created by God that denies the Israelites their freedom to leave Egypt

Plagues—various illnesses, pestilences, and other phenomena sent to inflict harm on Egypt and demonstrate God's power

Tabernacle—mobile sanctuary where God's presence dwells

Sinai—mountain where God appears to Moses and gives laws

Passover—annual festival in Israel to commemorate Israel's salvation from the death of the firstborn; first Passover occurs in Exodus 12

Festival of Unleavened Bread—annual festival in Israel in which Israelites eat unleavened bread for seven days to commemorate the exodus; first festival occurs in Exodus 23

Exodus—Israelites leave Egypt

Pillar of cloud and pillar of fire—symbols of God in nature that lead the people of Israel through the wilderness

Ten Commandments—God's laws given to Moses on Mount Sinai

Ark of the covenant—wooden coffer that symbolizes the presence of God and contains the Ten Commandments

Table for the bread of the presence—wooden table for the tabernacle

Lampstand—made of gold; provides light in the tabernacle

Ephod and breastplate—two pieces of clothing for the Israelite priests

Incense altar—wooden altar covered in gold in the tabernacle

Golden calf—idol created by Aaron using the Israelites' jewelry

Tent of meeting—another name for the tabernacle

Important Quotations

"Now a new king arose over Egypt, who did not know Joseph." (Exod 1:8)

"I AM WHO I AM." (Exod 3:14; God speaking to Moses)

"O my Lord, I have never been eloquent, neither in the past nor even now that you have spoken to your servant; but I am slow of speech and slow of tongue." (Exod 4:10)

"Then the LORD said to Moses, 'Go to Pharaoh; for I have hardened his heart and the heart of his officials, in order that I may show these signs of mine among them.'" (Exod 10:1)

"Sing to the LORD, for he has triumphed gloriously; horse and rider he has thrown into the sea." (Exod 15:21; Miriam's song after the exodus event and the first line of Moses' song in Exod 15:1)

"You have seen what I did to the Egyptians, and how I bore you on eagles' wings and brought you to myself. Now therefore, if you obey my voice and keep my covenant, you shall be my treasured possession out of all the peoples. Indeed, the whole earth is mine, but you shall be for me a priestly kingdom and a holy nation. These are the words that you shall speak to the Israelites." (Exod 19:4–6)

"You shall not oppress a resident alien; you know the heart of an alien, for you were aliens in the land of Egypt." (Exod 23:9)

"'But,' he said, 'you cannot see my face; for no one shall see me and live.' And the LORD continued, 'See, there is a place by me where you shall stand on the rock; and while my glory passes by I will put you in a cleft of the rock, and I will cover you with my hand until I have passed by; then I will take away my hand, and you shall see my back; but my face shall not be seen.'" (Exod 33:20–23)

"Moses came down from Mount Sinai. As he came down from the mountain with the two tablets of the covenant in his hand, Moses did not know that the skin of his face shone because he had been talking with God." (Exod 34:29)

Life of Moses in Exodus, Leviticus, Numbers, and Deuteronomy

Moses' Early Life in Egypt

- The infant Moses is hidden by his mother in a basket on the river (Exod 2)
- Moses is found by Pharaoh's daughter (Exod 2)
- Moses' sister gets a wet nurse for him (Exod 2)
- Moses is nursed by his birth mother, then brought to Pharaoh's daughter (Exod 2)
- Moses kills an Egyptian for beating a Hebrew and flees (Exod 2)

Moses in Midian and Horeb

- Moses flees to Midian and meets Reuel/Jethro and his daughters (Exod 2)
- Moses marries Zipporah and has a son, Gershom (Exod 2)
- Moses is called by God from a burning bush (Exod 3)

Moses Returns to Egypt

- Moses returns to Egypt with his wife and sons to speak to Pharaoh (Exod 4)
- Moses meets Aaron (Exod 4)
- Moses tells Pharaoh to "let my people go," but Pharaoh refuses (Exod 5)
- Moses goes to Pharaoh again and again, announcing the ten plagues (Exod 7–11)
- Moses and Israelites observe the first Passover (Exod 12)

Moses in the Wilderness

- Moses leads the people out of Egypt, and they cross the Sea of Reeds (Exod 13–14)
- Moses sings to God (Exod 15)
- Moses and Israelites journey through the wilderness toward Mount Sinai (Exod 15–18)

Moses at Mount Sinai

- Moses serves as mediator between God and people and receives the revelation (Exod 19–31)
- Moses is given the two tablets of the covenant (Exod 31)
- Moses descends, finds the people with the golden calf, and breaks the tablets (Exod 32)
- Moses makes new tablets and renews the covenant (Exod 34)
- Moses receives more instructions, including ones about the tabernacle (Exod 35–40)
- Moses receives instructions in the tent of meeting (Leviticus)
- Moses takes a census of the Israelites (Num 1)
- Moses receives more instructions (Num 2–10)

Moses in the Wilderness

- Moses and the Israelites leave Mount Sinai (Num 10)
- Moses and the Israelites wander in the wilderness (Num 11–25)
- Moses takes another census of the Israelites (Num 26)
- Moses is told that he will not enter the promised land (Num 27)
- Moses receives more instructions (Num 28–29)
- Moses and the Israelites arrive at the plains of Moab by the Jordan (Num 33)
- Moses gives a series of speeches and blessings (Deuteronomy)
- Moses dies and is buried (Deut 34)

Ten Plagues (Exod 7–12)

1. Water of the Nile turns to blood
2. Frogs
3. Gnats
4. Flies
5. Pestilence on livestock
6. Boils
7. Hail
8. Locusts
9. Darkness
10. Death of firstborn of humans and livestock

Ten Commandments (Exod 20)

1. You shall have no other gods before me.
2. You shall not make for yourself an idol.
3. You shall not make wrongful use of the name of God.
4. Remember the Sabbath day and keep it holy.
5. Honor your father and mother.
6. You shall not murder.
7. You shall not commit adultery.
8. You shall not steal.
9. You shall not bear false witness.
10. You shall not covet.

Note: Some religious traditions number the commandments differently. I have used the numbering familiar to most Protestants.

LEVITICUS

The book is structured as a series of divine speeches from God to Moses.

Synopsis

The book of Leviticus contains rules and regulations for the people, Israel, regarding both their daily lives and their ritual lives. The book instructs the people and the priests how to offer sacrifices, to establish the ritual worship life of the community, and to negotiate the boundaries of clean and unclean things.

Content Outline

Instructions for Sacrifices

Burnt offerings of cattle, sheep, or birds	Leviticus 1
Grain offerings	Leviticus 2
Sacrifice of well-being	Leviticus 3
Offerings for unintentional sins	Leviticus 4
More instructions on sin offerings and guilt offerings	Leviticus 5
Instructions to the priests about sacrifices	Leviticus 6
More instructions to the priests about sacrifices	Leviticus 7

Instructions for Worship

Ordination of priests	Leviticus 8
Aaron initiates sacrifice at Moses' command	Leviticus 9
Nadab and Abihu die after offering unholy fire before God	Leviticus 10

Regulations

Regulations concerning clean and unclean animals	Leviticus 11
Regulations concerning childbirth and purification	Leviticus 12
Regulations concerning skin diseases	Leviticus 13
Regulations concerning the cleansing of skin diseases	Leviticus 14
Regulations concerning male and female genital discharges	Leviticus 15

The Day of Atonement

Instructions for Yom Kippur, the Day of Atonement	Leviticus 16
Animal slaughters and the prohibition against consuming blood	Leviticus 17
Prohibited sexual relations	Leviticus 18
Holiness regulations	Leviticus 19
Penalties for violations of regulations	Leviticus 20
Regulations for priests	Leviticus 21
Priestly uncleanness, sacred donations, offerings	Leviticus 22
Festivals, Sabbath, Passover, Unleavened Bread, First Fruits, etc.	Leviticus 23
Instructions for the sacred lamp and bread; penalties for blasphemy	Leviticus 24
Sabbath and Jubilee	Leviticus 25
Blessings for obedience and curses for disobedience	Leviticus 26
Redemption of people and items consecrated to God	Leviticus 27

People

Moses—leader of Israelites
Aaron—priest; brother of Moses
Eleazar—priest; son of Aaron
Nadab and Abihu—Aaron's sons who offer unholy fire and are consumed by fire
Levites—priestly tribe among Israel
Ithamar—priest; brother of Nadab, Abihu, and Eleazar
Shelomith—member of the tribe of Dan

Key Concepts

Burnt offerings—sacrificed animals that were completely burned on the altar
Yom Kippur (Day of Atonement)—holy day for making atonement; described in Leviticus 16
Clean and unclean—categories for food, animals, and people
Passover—annual festival in Israel to commemorate Israel's salvation from the death of the firstborn
Sabbath—day of rest
Jubilee—restoration of land to its original owner every fifty years
Sabbatical year—every seventh year, when the land must rest completely
Priests and Levites—leaders of worship and ritual
Holiness—command for the Israelites to be holy because God is holy

Important Quotations

"Speak to all the congregation of the people of Israel and say to them: You shall be holy, for I the LORD your God am holy." (Lev 19:2)

"You shall not take vengeance or bear a grudge against any of your people, but you shall love your neighbor as yourself: I am the LORD." (Lev 19:18)

"Six days shall work be done; but the seventh day is a sabbath of complete rest, a holy convocation; you shall do no work: it is a sabbath to the LORD throughout your settlements." (Lev 23:3)

"Anyone who maims another shall suffer the same injury in return: fracture for fracture, eye for eye, tooth for tooth; the injury inflicted is the injury to be suffered." (Lev 24:19–20)

NUMBERS

The Greek Septuagint's title for the fourth book of the Old Testament comes from the many numbers and census lists in the book. The Hebrew tradition simply names the book after the first Hebrew word, *Bemidbar*, which in English is "in the wilderness." Indeed, the Israelites remain in the wilderness for the length of this book.

Synopsis

The book of Numbers contains narratives about the ancient Israelites as they leave Mount Sinai and begin to journey toward Canaan. Interspersed with these narratives are census lists and legal regulations concerning festivals and sacrifices. The opening chapters provide census data for the twelve tribes of Israel encamped at Sinai. One tribe, the Levites, and their leader, Aaron, are given special priestly roles in the community, including the care of the tabernacle.

Numbers then turns to various instructions and rules for the people's worship and daily life as they prepare to leave Sinai. When the Israelites departed from Sinai, they were led by a cloud. They complained to Moses and Aaron regarding the lack of food. Moses and Aaron sent spies into Canaan to gather information; the spies reported that the land was good but the people were strong. They attempted to take the land of Canaan but were defeated. They nevertheless defeated two small kingdoms along the way. The Moabite king sent the prophet Balaam to curse the Israelites, but he ended up blessing them.

The Israelites began to marry foreign women and worship foreign deities. In anger, God sent a plague and killed many of the Israelites. Numbers continues with another census of the Israelites and more stories of the wilderness experience. The daughters of Zelophehad inherited their father's property (no male heirs existed). Joshua was appointed as a successor to Moses. Some of the Israelites conquered and settled in the Transjordan area. The book concludes with the Israelites in the plains of Moab by the Jordan River at Jericho. They were finally ready to enter the promised land of Canaan.

Content Outline

In the Wilderness of Sinai

Census of the twelve tribes of Israel: 603,550 males	Numbers 1
The arrangement of the tribes in camps around the tent of meeting	Numbers 2

Wilderness Wanderings

Encampment on the Plains of Moab across the Jordan from Jericho

Balaam and his donkey see an angel	Numbers 22
Balaam's first and second oracles	Numbers 23
Balaam's third and fourth oracles	Numbers 24
Israelites worship foreign gods; Phinehas stops a plague through violence	Numbers 25
Census of the Israelites: 601,730 males	Numbers 26
The five daughters of Zelophehad inherit; Joshua's commissioning	Numbers 27
Offerings	Numbers 28
More offerings	Numbers 29
Vows	Numbers 30
Israelites go to war against Midian	Numbers 31
Reubenites and Gadites (and Manasseh tribe) settle in Transjordan	Numbers 32
Itinerary from Egypt to Canaan	Numbers 33
Boundaries of Canaan	Numbers 34
Levitical cities; cities of refuge	Numbers 35
Daughters of Zelophehad marry	Numbers 36

People

Moses—leader of the Israelites
Aaron—priest; not allowed to enter the promised land
Nadab, Abihu, Eleazar, Ithamar—Aaron's sons
Levites—tribe descended from Levi
Nazirites—group of people who separate themselves and devote themselves to God
Miriam—sister of Moses and Aaron
Korah, Dathan, Abiram—leaders of a revolt against Moses
Balaam—non-Israelite prophet
Phinehas—Aaron's grandson; ends plague through zealous violence
Mahlah, Noah, Hoglah, Milcah, Tirzah—daughters of Zelophehad

Moses' Cushite wife—according to Exod 2, Moses' wife, Zipporah, is a Midianite
Joshua—commissioned by Moses with authority
Caleb—one of twelve spies sent by Moses to Canaan
Balak—king of Moab

Key Concepts

Census—accounting of the tribes of Israel as commanded by God (Num 1 and 26)
Conquest—Israelites' conquering of the Transjordan (area east of the Jordan River)
Cities of refuge—places for people who accidently kill someone
Complaining in the wilderness—Israelites murmur against God as they travel
Spies—twelve people sent to Canaan to gather information on the land and people; they report that the land flows with milk and honey and that the people are strong
Offerings—book of Numbers gives instructions about various offerings such as burnt offerings, grain offerings, and sin offerings

Important Quotations

"The LORD bless you and keep you; the LORD make his face to shine upon you, and be gracious to you; the LORD lift up his countenance upon you, and give you peace." (Num 6:24–26)

"Has the LORD spoken only through Moses? Has he not spoken through us also?" (Num 12:2; Miriam and Aaron speaking against their brother, Moses)

"We came to the land to which you sent us; it flows with milk and honey, and this is its fruit. Yet the people who live in the land are strong, and the towns are fortified and very large." (Num 13:27–28; spies' report on Canaan)

"But the LORD said to Moses and Aaron, 'Because you did not trust in me, to show my holiness before the eyes of the Israelites, therefore you shall not bring this assembly into the land that I have given them.'" (Num 20:12)

"Why have you brought us up out of Egypt to die in the wilderness? For there is no food and no water, and we detest this miserable food." (Num 21:5)

"Balaam said to Balak, 'I have come to you now, but do I have power to say just anything? The word God puts in my mouth, that is what I must say.'" (Num 22:38)

DEUTERONOMY

The title for the fifth biblical book comes from the Septuagint. It is a Greek word meaning "second law," which is appropriate, as the book contains another set of laws spoken by Moses to the Israelites as they awaited entrance into the promised land. The Hebrew title, *Devarim*, means "words" and is taken from the book's opening phrase. The flashback nature of Deuteronomy may be confusing unless one understands the book as the recollections of Moses.

Synopsis

The book of Deuteronomy begins with a speech Moses gave to the Israelites at the border of the promised land in Moab and continues with several more speeches by Moses from this place. Moses recalled the events of the wilderness journey, repeating earlier materials from Exodus, Leviticus, and Numbers; he described the Israelites' journey from Mount Horeb (Deuteronomy's name for Mount Sinai) and into the wilderness; and he repeated the Ten Commandments. He recalled how although he asked to enter the promised land, God only allowed him to see it from afar. Moses sang a final song and offered a blessing on Israel. Moses died and was buried in Moab.

Content Outline

Moses' First Address

Command to leave Horeb and possess the land; leaders chosen; people rebel	Deuteronomy 1
Israelites in the wilderness; battle against Heshbon	Deuteronomy 2
Battle against Bashan; two and a half tribes settle in Transjordan	Deuteronomy 3
Statutes and ordinances	Deuteronomy 4

Moses' Second Address

Ten Commandments	Deuteronomy 5
Instructions to love God, not to follow other gods, and not to test God	Deuteronomy 6
Israel as a chosen people holy to God; obedience brings blessings	Deuteronomy 7

Instruction not to forget God, especially in times of prosperity	Deuteronomy 8
Israel's past disobedience and the consequences	Deuteronomy 9
New tablets of stone; general summary of the commandments	Deuteronomy 10
Admonition to obey the commandments	Deuteronomy 11
Ordinances about worship: one God at one place	Deuteronomy 12
Instructions not to worship other gods	Deuteronomy 13
Clean/unclean animals; tithing from fields and livestock	Deuteronomy 14
Regulations regarding the sabbatical year	Deuteronomy 15
Instructions to keep the Passover and festivals	Deuteronomy 16
Judicial decisions by priests and judges; monarchy's limitations	Deuteronomy 17
Priests and Levites; new prophet like Moses	Deuteronomy 18
Cities of refuge; laws regarding witnesses	Deuteronomy 19
Rules of war	Deuteronomy 20
Rules for murder, manslaughter, and marrying captive women; right of firstborn	Deuteronomy 21
Rules regarding property ownership and sexual relations	Deuteronomy 22
Community boundaries, sanitation rules, and other laws	Deuteronomy 23
Marriage and divorce laws; other laws	Deuteronomy 24
Levirate-marriage laws; other laws	Deuteronomy 25
First fruits and tithes	Deuteronomy 26
Instructions to build an altar on Mount Ebal; twelve curses	Deuteronomy 27
Obedience brings blessings; disobedience brings curses	Deuteronomy 28
Renewal of the covenant in the plains of Moab	Deuteronomy 29

God's faithfulness promised; life or death, blessing or curse—choose life	Deuteronomy 30
Joshua succeeds Moses; the law to be read every seven years	Deuteronomy 31
Song of Moses	Deuteronomy 32
Moses' blessing on the Israelites	Deuteronomy 33
Moses dies and is buried in Moab	Deuteronomy 34

Places

Mount Horeb—Deuteronomy's name for Mount Sinai
Plains of Moab—area east of the Jordan River
Mount Nebo—place from which Moses views the promised land
Mount Ebal—mountain in Israel near Shechem and Mount Gerizim

Key Concepts

Levirate marriage—marriage of a man to the wife of his deceased brother; their child is named after the deceased
Tithing—giving of a portion of one's income
Sabbatical year—every seventh year debts are canceled; Deuteronomy focuses on debts, Leviticus focuses on land
Cities of refuge—places for people who accidently kill someone
Promised land—land as promised to Israel by God as part of God's covenant with Abraham; Israelites are on the edge of the promised land at the end of the book of Deuteronomy
Worship regulations—laws pertaining to sacrifices and rituals
Blessings and curses—obedience to the laws leads to blessings; disobedience leads to curses
Ten Commandments—God speaks these laws on Mount Horeb

Important Quotations

"Hear, O Israel: The LORD is our God, the LORD alone. You shall love the LORD your God with all your heart, and with all your soul, and with all your might." (Deut 6:4–5)

"For you are a people holy to the LORD your God; the LORD your God has chosen you out of all the peoples on earth to be his people, his treasured possession." (Deut 7:6)

"So now, O Israel, what does the LORD your God require of you? Only to fear the LORD your God, to walk in all his ways, to love him, to serve the LORD your God with all your heart and with all your soul, and to keep the commandments of the LORD your God and his decrees that I am commanding you today, for your own well-being." (Deut 10:12–13)

"If you will only heed his every commandment that I am commanding you today—loving the LORD your God, and serving him with all your heart and with all your soul—then he will give the rain for your land in its season, the early rain and the later rain, and you will gather in your grain, your wine, and your oil; and he will give grass in your fields for your livestock, and you will eat your fill." (Deut 11:13–15)

"The LORD your God will raise up for you a prophet like me from among your own people; you shall heed such a prophet." (Deut 18:15)

"A wandering Aramean was my ancestor; he went down into Egypt and lived there as an alien, few in number, and there he became a great nation, mighty and populous. When the Egyptians treated us harshly and afflicted us, by imposing hard labor on us, we cried to the LORD, the God of our ancestors; the LORD heard our voice and saw our affliction, our toil, and our oppression. The LORD brought us out of Egypt with a mighty hand and an outstretched arm, with a terrifying display of power, and with signs and wonders; and he brought us into this place and gave us this land, a land flowing with milk and honey." (Deut 26:5–10)

"I call heaven and earth to witness against you today that I have set before you life and death, blessings and curses. Choose life so that you and your descendants may live." (Deut 30:19)

"Then Moses summoned Joshua and said to him in the sight of all Israel: 'Be strong and bold, for you are the one who will go with this people into the land that the LORD has sworn to their ancestors to give them; and you will put them in possession of it. It is the LORD who goes before you. He will be with you; he will not fail you or forsake you. Do not fear or be dismayed.'" (Deut 31:7–8)

"Never since has there arisen a prophet in Israel like Moses, whom the LORD knew face to face." (Deut 34:10)

Ten Commandments (Deut 5)

1. You shall have no other gods before me.
2. You shall not make for yourself an idol.
3. You shall not make wrongful use of the name of God.
4. Observe the Sabbath day and keep it holy.
5. Honor your father and mother.
6. You shall not murder.
7. You shall not commit adultery.
8. You shall not steal.
9. You shall not bear false witness.
10. You shall not covet.

Note: Some religious traditions number the commandments differently. I have used the numbering familiar to most Protestants.

2

The Historical Books

The Historical Books (Joshua, Judges, Ruth, 1 and 2 Samuel, 1 and 2 Kings, 1 and 2 Chronicles, Ezra, Nehemiah, and Esther) continue the story of the Pentateuch by telling of the Israelites' conquest of the land of Canaan, their intermittent alliances under the judges, the United Monarchy, the Divided Monarchy, the fall of the northern kingdom to the Assyrians, the fall of the southern kingdom to the Babylonians, and life back in Israel after the exilic period. They narrate then a major portion of the history of Israel and Judah, a history that occurs over more than seven hundred years.

In the Jewish canon, the books of Joshua, Judges, 1 and 2 Samuel, and 1 and 2 Kings constitute a section known as the Former Prophets. The books of Ruth, 1 and 2 Chronicles, Ezra, Nehemiah, and Esther are grouped in the Writings section of the Jewish Bible.

JOSHUA

Joshua is the first book in the Historical Books section of the Protestant Bible. It is named for its main character.

Synopsis

The book of Joshua begins where the book of Deuteronomy ends: Moses has died, and Joshua has been given charge of the Israelites and their final journey into the land of Canaan.

God told Joshua to possess the land, instructed him about preparing for the conquest, and assured him that God had already given the land to the

Israelites. Joshua sent two spies to Jericho to view the land. The spies met Rahab, the prostitute, who hid them from the king. In return for her gracious hospitality, the spies agreed to save her and her family when they returned to conquer the city of Jericho. The Israelites sanctified themselves and crossed the Jordan River on dry ground. At Gilgal, they set twelve stones from the Jordan as a memorial of the event. The Israelites circumcised themselves and celebrated Passover.

The Israelites conquered Jericho by marching around the city and blowing trumpets. They were not successful conquering the city of Ai because Achan had taken some of the plunder and hid it in his tent, though the instruction had been for everything to be destroyed completely. He and his family were stoned to death. The Israelites were then able to conquer Ai. Joshua built an altar on Mount Ebal and made a copy of the law of Moses. The Gibeonites, a neighboring people who were afraid of being captured and killed, tricked the Israelites into thinking they were from far away, so the Israelites made a treaty with them. The Israelites discovered the deception but kept the treaty and did not conquer them. Five kings who had heard about the treaty with the Gibeonites decided to attack them. The Israelites came to the defense of the Gibeonites. During the battle, God caused the sun to stand still so the Israelites could win. The Israelites defeated many peoples in the southern areas. The kings in the northern areas banded together to fight the Israelites, but the Israelites continued to prevail in the battles. The book provides a lengthy summary of the areas Joshua conquered and a brief mention of regions he did not.

The next section of Joshua details the allotment of the land to the tribes of Israel. Caleb received Hebron, and Joshua received his own town. Joshua also designated cities of refuge (places of safety for people who have killed without intent) and Levitical cities (cities for the Levite priests). Joshua encouraged the Israelites to obey the book of the law of Moses and not to worship other gods. Joshua made a covenant with the people at Shechem. Joshua died and was buried.

Content Outline

Preparations for Conquest

Joshua receives a command to proceed and makes preparations	Joshua 1
Joshua sends two spies to Jericho; Rahab helps them	Joshua 2

Conquest of the Land

Allocation of the Land

Levitical cities	Joshua 21
Transjordan tribes possess their land; memorial altar built and debated	Joshua 22

Joshua's Last Speeches

Joshua's speech	Joshua 23
Joshua's final speech and the covenant renewal; Joshua dies; Eleazar dies	Joshua 24

People

Joshua—leader of Israel after the death of Moses

Moses—although his death is announced in the first sentence of the book, he is mentioned throughout

Rahab—prostitute living in Jericho who hides the two Israelites spies and is saved from death when the Israelites conquer Jericho

King of Jericho—attempts to capture the two Israelites spies but is thwarted by Rahab

Achan—keeps some of the plunder that is supposed to be devoted to God, so the Israelites are not able to conquer Ai the first time

Gibeonites—Canaanite group that tricks the Israelites into making a treaty

King Adonizedek of Jerusalem—leader of the group of five southern kings who attack Gibeon and are defeated by the Israelites

King Jabin of Hazor—leader of the group of northern kings who attempt to band together to defeat Israel but are defeated

Eleazar—son of Aaron and nephew of Moses; priest who helped with the distribution of land

Caleb—Judahite and one of the spies in Numbers; receives Hebron from Joshua

Places

Shittim—place where the Israelites camp before they cross the Jordan River into the promised land

Jericho—city the Israelites spy on and eventually conquer after God makes its walls fall

Gilgal—first place the Israelites camp after they cross the Jordan River into the promised land

Ai—city captured by the Israelites on their second try

Gibeon—city whose people trick Joshua into making a treaty; sun stands still here during a battle

Jerusalem—first mention of this city by name in the Old Testament

Hebron—Caleb's inheritance, promised to him by Moses

Shechem—place where covenant renewal ceremony occurs

Key Concepts

Conquest—Israelites' conquering of the land of Canaan

Holy war—battles fought by the Israelites at God's command

Divine warrior—God's primary image in the book of Joshua

Cities of refuge—places for people who accidently kill someone

Devoted for destruction—idea that people and objects have been given completely by God to Israel

Land allotment—division of the conquered land among the tribes of Israel

Tribes—family groups of Israel named for the sons of Jacob; recipients of allotted land

Important Quotations

"I hereby command you: Be strong and courageous; do not be frightened or dismayed, for the LORD your God is with you wherever you go." (Josh 1:9; God speaking to Joshua)

"Now then, since I have dealt kindly with you, swear to me by the LORD that you in turn will deal kindly with my family. Give me a sign of good faith that you will spare my father and mother, my brothers and sisters, and all who belong to them, and deliver our lives from death." (Josh 2:12–13; Rahab's request to the Israelites spies)

"So Joshua defeated the whole land, the hill country and the Negeb and the lowland and the slopes, and all their kings; he left no one remaining, but utterly destroyed all that breathed, as the LORD God of Israel commanded." (Josh 10:40)

"Choose this day whom you will serve . . . ; but as for me and my household, we will serve the LORD." (Josh 24:15)

Life of Joshua

Joshua as Moses' Assistant

- No birth story
- Appears in Exodus, Numbers, and Deuteronomy as Moses' assistant

Joshua as Leader of the Israelites

- God tells Joshua to cross the Jordan (Josh 1)
- Joshua sends spies to Jericho and receives their report (Josh 2)
- Joshua leads Israelites to Jordan and crosses it (Josh 3)
- Joshua selects twelve men to set up twelve stones at Gilgal (Josh 4)
- Joshua circumcises the Israelites (Josh 5)
- Joshua leads the Israelites to conquer Jericho (Josh 6)
- Joshua deals with Achan, then conquers Ai (Josh 7–8)
- Joshua renews the covenant (Josh 8)
- Joshua makes a treaty with the Gibeonites (Josh 9)
- Joshua and warriors defeat a coalition of forces (Josh 10)
- Joshua defeats northern kings (Josh 11)
- Joshua defeats other kings (Josh 12)
- Joshua divides the land (Josh 13–21)
- Joshua gives a speech (Josh 23)
- Joshua renews the covenant (Josh 24)
- Joshua dies and is buried (Josh 24; Judg 2)

JUDGES

The book of Judges is named after the main characters of the book. Their work was not primarily legal in nature; rather, they were leaders who helped the tribes of Israel, mostly in military ways, before the establishment of the monarchy.

Synopsis

Judges contains the stories of the Israelite tribes between the time of the conquest of the land by Joshua and the establishment of the monarchy. These stories present a relatively consistent literary pattern:

1. The Israelites were unfaithful to God.
2. They were oppressed by a foreign people.

3. They cried out to God.
4. God sent a judge to deliver them from their oppression and to bring peace.
5. Peace only lasted for a certain period.
6. The Israelites again were unfaithful to God, and the cycle repeated.

The opening chapters of Judges link back to Joshua. These passages note that the Israelites had not conquered all of Canaan. They were still fighting. Othniel conquered the inhabitants of Debir and married his first cousin, Achsah, as a reward from his uncle, Caleb. The Israelites disobeyed God by worshiping other gods and marrying among other groups. God delivered them into the hands of a foreign power. The Israelites cried to God, and God sent Othniel, the first judge, to deliver them through war. The land had rest for forty years before the Israelites rebelled and came under Moabite oppression. God sent a deliverer in the left-handed man, Ehud. Ehud freed the Israelites from oppression by assassinating Eglon, the king of Moab. Ehud pulled a sword from his right thigh and drove it into the unprepared Eglon with his left hand. The land had rest for eighty years. Shamgar delivered Israel by killing six hundred Philistines.

The story in Judges then turns to the figure of Deborah. The Israelites did evil again, and God sold them into the hand of the Canaanites. They cried to God, and the prophet Deborah was raised up to judge Israel. She went into battle with the warriors and alongside the military leader, Barak. They defeated the Canaanites. Sisera, the Canaanites' army leader, fled but was killed by Jael, a Kenite woman, who drove a tent peg into his temple. Deborah and Barak sang a victory song, and Israel had peace for forty years.

Israel again did evil and was given into the hands of the Midianites. Gideon routed the Midianites with a very small army, proving God was responsible for the victory. After Gideon's death, the Israelites returned to worshiping foreign deities. Gideon's son Abimelech became ruler of Shechem and killed seventy of his rival brothers. His rule did not last long because of this crime, and he was killed in battle. Abimelech's skull was crushed by a woman who threw a stone from a tower, but before he died—not wanting to die at the hands of a woman—he asked one of his young men to kill him with a sword.

The book of Judges continues with mention of Tola and Jair, two judges of little significance, before noting that the Israelites fell into evil and under the oppression of the Ammonites. To lead the Israelites against these oppressors, the elders of Gilead brought back Jephthah, who had been disinherited by his family, to lead the battle. Jephthah attempted to negotiate with the king of Ammon, but his efforts failed. As he went into battle, Jephthah vowed that if God would give the Ammonites into his hands, he would sacrifice the first thing to greet him upon his return home. Jephthah won the battle. The first person to greet him upon his return was his daughter. Though she was his only child, Jephthah stayed true to his vow. He later battled against the Ephraimites.

The Israelites did evil again, and God gave them into the hand of the Philistines. Their deliverer this time was Samson, son of Manoah and his unnamed wife. Samson was raised as a nazirite. Samson married a Philistine woman and offered a riddle to the Philistines at the time of their wedding. His wife begged him to tell her the answer to the riddle, which she immediately shared with her people. When the townspeople revealed the correct answer to Samson, he killed thirty men and returned home without his new wife. Samson returned to Philistia to see his wife some time later and discovered she had been given away to another man by her father, who thought that Samson had rejected her. In his anger, Samson tied foxes' tails together and put a torch between their tails. As the foxes ran, they burned the Philistines' grain fields. The Philistines responded by burning Samson's wife and her father. The Philistines found and attacked Samson, but he killed a thousand men with the jawbone of a donkey. The Philistine leaders directed Delilah to discover what gave Samson his strength. Samson lied three times but ultimately told her about his nazirite vow to never cut his hair. While Samson slept, at Delilah's instruction, a man cut Samson's hair, and his strength left him. The Philistines captured him and gouged out his eyes. The final story of Samson is of his death. Samson was brought out of prison to perform for a crowd of Philistines, but instead he grasped the two main pillars of the house, pulling it down and killing himself and all the onlookers.

After the stories of Samson, the book of Judges abandons the pattern of unfaithfulness, oppression, repentance, and deliverance. The concluding stories are of Israel's decline. Micah stole eleven hundred pieces of silver from his mother, but when he returned them, she used some pieces to create an idol, and Micah created a shrine. Micah employed a traveling Levite as the priest of the shrine. The Danites came to Micah's house and took his priest and all his priestly elements, then settled in Laish.

Lastly, the book of Judges turns to the Benjaminites. Some members of this tribe raped a Judahite woman who was in the custody of a Levite. The Levite sliced her dead body into twelve pieces and sent them throughout Israel. This horrific action resulted in a gathering by the other tribes to attack the Benjaminites. The attack almost wiped out the entire tribe, but to survive, the Benjaminites captured wives from Shiloh.

Judges ends with this sentence: "In those days there was no king in Israel; all the people did what was right in their own eyes" (21:25).

Content Outline

Introduction

Major and Minor Judges

Conclusion: No King in Israel

Tribe of Dan explores and finds territory in the north	Judges 18
A Levite and his concubine at Gibeah	Judges 19
The tribes of Israel attack the tribe of Benjamin	Judges 20
The Benjaminites get new wives	Judges 21

People

Joshua—the leader of Israel after the death of Moses; his death is mentioned in chapters 1 and 2

Caleb—a leader of Israel; promises his daughter to the person who defeats Debir

Achsah—Caleb's daughter; marries Othniel after his victory over Debir and then asks her father for more land

Othniel—Caleb's younger brother; delivers Israel from Aram

Ehud—Benjaminite deliverer; left-handed assassin of King Eglon

King Eglon of Moab—defeats Israel and then is killed by Ehud

Shamgar—son of Anath; killed six hundred Philistines with an oxgoad

King Jabin of Canaan—reigned in Hazor

Deborah—prophet and judge; associated with song in Judges 5

Barak—military leader

Sisera—commander of King Jabin's army

Jael—wife of Heber; killer of Sisera

Gideon—son of Joash; judge

Abimelech—son of Jerubbaal/Gideon

Tola—son of Puah; deliverer

Jair—Gileadite; judge

Jephthah—Gileadite; son of a prostitute and a mighty warrior

Ibzan—judge

Elon—judge

Abdon—judge

Samson—judge; nazirite

Manoah—Samson's father

Unnamed wife of Manoah—Samson's mother

Delilah—Samson's lover

Micah—Ephraimite

Unnamed concubine of the Levite—raped by the inhabitants of Gibeah

Unnamed Levite—after the rape of his concubine, he cuts her into twelve pieces and sends her body parts throughout Israel

Places

Jerusalem—Jebusite town in the book of Judges that becomes the capital of the United Monarchy under David

Bochim—location of Israelites weeping because of their disobedience

Moab—neighboring nation east of the Dead Sea

Hazor—city in Canaan

Midian—neighboring nation

Shechem—important city in the north

Mizpah—Jephthah's home

Gaza—Philistine city

Timnah—city that Samson visits

Ephraim—northern hill country

Gibeah—city where the Levite and his concubine stay overnight and where the concubine is raped

Bethlehem—the Levite's town

Key Concepts

Judges—temporary leaders of Israel before the monarchy

Vows—Caleb and Jephthah make vows related to their daughters

Nazirites—people who take special vows not to drink wine or eat unclean food (e.g., Samson)

Conquest—Israelites' conquering of the land of Canaan

Deliverance—rescue and liberation of Israelites from the oppression of various military leaders and kings by a judge whom God sends

Important Quotations

"Then the Israelites did what was evil in the sight of the Lord and worshiped the Baals; and they abandoned the Lord, the God of their ancestors, who had brought them out of the land of Egypt. . . . So the anger of the Lord was kindled against Israel, and he gave them over to plunderers who plundered them. . . . Then the Lord raised up judges, who delivered them out of the power of those who plundered them. . . . But whenever the judge died, they would relapse and behave worse than their ancestors, following other gods, worshiping them and bowing down to them." (Judg 2:11–12, 14, 16, 19)

"But Jael wife of Heber took a tent peg, and took a hammer in her hand, and went softly to him and drove the peg into his temple, until it went down

into the ground—he was lying fast asleep from weariness—and he died."
(Judg 4:21)

"In those days there was no king in Israel." (Judg 18:1; 19:1)

"In those days there was no king in Israel; all the people did what was right in
their own eyes." (Judg 17:6; 21:25)

Judges and Oppressors

Judges	Oppressors
Othniel	Aram
Ehud	Moab
Shamgar	Philistines
Deborah	Canaan (Hazor)
Gideon	Midianites
Abimelech	No oppressor mentioned
Tola	No oppressor mentioned
Jair	No oppressor mentioned
Jephthah	Ammonites
Ibzan	No oppressor mentioned
Elon	No oppressor mentioned
Abdon	No oppressor mentioned
Samson	Philistines

RUTH

In the Christian Old Testament, the book of Ruth is located between the
books of Judges and 1 Samuel. This placement is likely based on the opening
line of the book, "In the days when the judges ruled . . . ," as well as the book's
concern with David's lineage. In the Jewish canon, Ruth is found in the third
and final section, Writings. The book is named after one of the story's central
characters.

Synopsis

A famine in Judah drove Elimelech, Naomi, and their two sons to Moab.
Elimelech died there. The two sons married Moabite women, Orpah and
Ruth. After a decade, both sons also died. Left with her two daughters-in-law
Naomi decided to return to her homeland of Bethlehem. She tried to persuade

Orpah and Ruth to remain in Moab and to remarry. Orpah initially resisted, but ultimately remained in Moab. Ruth, however, was adamant to stay with Naomi and accompany her back to Judah. When the two women arrived in Bethlehem, Naomi told the people to call her *Mara*, "bitter," because she left full and returned empty.

Ruth went into the field of Boaz, Naomi's relative by marriage, to glean grain. He invited her to stay in his fields, to follow closely behind his workers, and to glean from the standing sheaves. When Ruth returned to Naomi at the end of the day, Naomi explained to Ruth that Boaz was a close relative of Elimelech.

Naomi devised a plan for Ruth to approach Boaz at the threshing floor after a long day of work and a night of eating and drinking. The two women intended to persuade him to act as a kinsman redeemer for Ruth. Ruth followed the plan by going to the threshing floor and lying at Boaz's feet. When he awoke, she asked him, as her next of kin, to help her. Boaz agreed but stipulated that he must first speak to another relative who was more closely related to Ruth. Boaz and Ruth spent the night together, and Ruth returned to Naomi in the early morning with the news.

Boaz spoke with the next of kin at the city gate regarding a plot of land that belonged to Naomi. Boaz asked the man if he wanted to redeem the land. The man agreed to redeem it. Boaz then told him that redeeming the land also meant taking Ruth as his wife. The man then declined, and the two men sealed their agreement through a ritual of sandal exchange. The people at the gate witnessed the redemption and blessed Ruth and Boaz. Boaz took Ruth as his wife, and they had a son, Obed. Obed was the grandfather of David, the king. When people heard about the child, they blessed God because Naomi had received a grandson.

Content Outline

Journey to Moab; death of husbands and sons; Naomi and Ruth return to Bethlehem	Ruth 1
Ruth meets Boaz, Elimelech's relative, while gleaning grain in his fields	Ruth 2
Ruth goes to Boaz at night at the threshing floor and asks for his protection	Ruth 3
Boaz arranges the right of redemption, marries Ruth, and has a son	Ruth 4

People

Elimelech—Naomi's husband; name means "my God is king"
Naomi—Elimelech's wife; name means "pleasant"
Mahlon and Chilion—Elimelech and Naomi's sons
Orpah—Naomi's daughter-in-law and wife of Chilion
Ruth—Naomi's daughter-in-law and wife of Mahlon
Boaz—Elimelech's relative
Unnamed next-of-kin man—gives up his right to redeem Ruth
Obed—Ruth and Boaz's son
Jesse—Obed's son and Ruth and Boaz's grandson
David—King of Israel, Jesse's son, and Ruth and Boaz's great-grandson

Places

Bethlehem—home of Elimelech, Naomi, and Boaz; located south of Jerusalem in Judah
Moab—neighboring country on the east side of the Dead Sea; home of Ruth and Orpah

Key Concepts

Famine—inability to produce crops; the reason Elimelech and his family travel to Moab
Next of kin—relative with the ability to marry his deceased relative's wife
Gleaning sheaves—practice of gathering remaining grain after the initial harvest
Threshing floor—place to stomp and winnow grain
Redemption—Boaz acquires the land and all that belongs to his relative, including Ruth
City gate—place of legal decision making by the elders
Levirate marriage—next of kin marries the wife of his deceased kin, and their child is named after the deceased

Important Quotations

"Where you go, I will go; where you lodge, I will lodge; your people shall be my people, and your God my God." (Ruth 1:16)

"Call me no longer Naomi, call me Mara, for the Almighty has dealt bitterly with me. I went away full, but the LORD has brought me back empty." (Ruth 1:20–21)

"Then she fell prostrate, with her face to the ground, and said to him, 'Why have I found favor in your sight, that you should take notice of me, when I am a foreigner?'" (Ruth 2:10)

"I am Ruth, your servant; spread your cloak over your servant, for you are next-of-kin." (Ruth 3:9)

"Then the women said to Naomi, 'Blessed be the LORD, who has not left you this day without next-of-kin; and may his name be renowned in Israel!'" (Ruth 4:14)

"The women of the neighborhood gave him a name, saying, 'A son has been born to Naomi.' They named him Obed; he became the father of Jesse, the father of David." (Ruth 4:17)

1 SAMUEL

First Samuel is named after the prophet Samuel. His life is chronicled from birth to death, including his time as prophet and judge, and as the one to anoint Saul, the first king of Israel.

Originally, 1 Samuel and 2 Samuel were a single book, but they were divided at the point in the story when Saul died.

Synopsis

The opening chapters of the book focus on the special birth and remarkable childhood of the prophet Samuel. Hannah, Samuel's mother, was believed to be barren but became pregnant after vowing to give her child to God. Samuel was raised in the Shiloh temple with Eli, the priest. Samuel eventually prophesied against Eli and his household because of Eli's sons (Hophni and Phinehas) and their contemptuous treatment of the offerings.

The next several chapters focus on the ark of the covenant. The Philistines captured the ark during a battle with Israel. The ark brought misfortune to them, however, so they returned it to Israel, where it was placed at Kiriath-jearim, with Eleazar in charge. At this time, Samuel began to serve as judge over Israel. The people observed a time of fasting. The Philistines attacked again, but God thunderously gave the Israelites victory.

As Samuel grew old, the people requested a king to govern them like other nations. Samuel initially rejected the idea, but after consulting God, he conceded. While searching for his father's donkeys, Saul encountered Samuel. Samuel had been told by God to anoint Saul as the ruler over Israel. Samuel anointed Saul and sent him back to his home. Samuel summoned the people to Mizpah and drew lots to determine a king. The lot indicated Saul, but they could not find him because he was hiding among the baggage. A month later, Saul proved his ability to lead in a battle against the Ammonites. Samuel took Saul to Gilgal to renew the kingship. Samuel gave his farewell address, offering justification for his decisions and exacting judgment of the people's actions. Saul made several poor decisions. Instead of waiting for Samuel, he took the action of offering a sacrifice and inadvertently cursed his own son. God rejected Saul as king and instructed Samuel to anoint David as Saul's replacement.

The story then shifts to a series of encounters between David and Saul. Saul brought David into his court to play the lyre to sooth Saul's tormented spirit. Soon thereafter, David defeated the Philistine champion, Goliath. Saul attempted to kill David, causing David to flee from Israel. David and Jonathan, Saul's son, developed a friendship, and David married Saul's daughter, Michal. As Saul pursued David, David had the opportunity to kill Saul on several occasions but chose not to harm him. After the prophet Samuel died, Saul consulted a medium to hear from Samuel again. Samuel told Saul the kingdom was in David's control. During a battle, Saul tragically fell on his own sword and died. David continued to have military victories.

Content Outline

Stories about Samuel's Childhood

Samuel's birth to Hannah and Elkanah and his offering as a nazirite to God	1 Samuel 1
Hannah prays; Eli's sons treat offerings poorly; a man of God utters a prophecy against Eli's house	1 Samuel 2
Samuel receives a call and a prophecy about Eli; Samuel grows up and becomes a prophet	1 Samuel 3

Stories about the Ark

The Philistines defeat the Israelites and capture the ark of the covenant; Eli dies	1 Samuel 4

Stories about Saul

Stories about David and Saul

David leaves his parents with the king of Moab; Saul kills priests who helped David	1 Samuel 22
David defeats the Philistines at Keilah; Saul tries to capture David, but David escapes	1 Samuel 23
David spares Saul's life; David and Saul go their separate ways	1 Samuel 24
Samuel dies; David marries Nabal's widow, Abigail, and also Ahinoam	1 Samuel 25
David spares Saul's life again; they go their separate ways	1 Samuel 26
David lives in Philistia to avoid Saul; David raids towns	1 Samuel 27
Saul consults the medium of Endor to bring up Samuel; Samuel prophesies against Saul	1 Samuel 28
The Philistines ask David to part ways with them	1 Samuel 29
David attacks the Amalekites because they attacked his area and took his wives	1 Samuel 30
Saul dies in battle at Mount Gilboa	1 Samuel 31

People

Elkanah—father of Samuel; husband of Hannah and Peninnah
Hannah—mother of Samuel; Elkanah's wife
Peninnah—Elkanah's wife
Eli—priest at Shiloh; father of Hophni and Phinehas
Hophni—Eli's son; priest
Phinehas—Eli's son; priest
Samuel—son of Elkanah and Hannah; prophet, judge, priest; associated with Shiloh
Ichabod—son of Phinehas and his wife; name means "no glory"
Eleazar—priest in charge of the ark of the covenant
Joel—Samuel's first son
Abijah—Samuel's second son
Kish—Saul's father
Saul—first king of Israel; Kish's son; from the tribe of Benjamin
Jonathan—Saul's son; friend to David
Jesse—David's father; an Ephrathite of Bethlehem of Judah

David—second king of Israel; Jesse's youngest son
Eliab—David's brother; Jesse's firstborn son
Abinadab—David's brother; Jesse's second son
Shammah—David's brother; Jesse's third son
Goliath—Philistine champion from Gath; killed by David
Abner—commander of the Israelite army; Saul's cousin
Merab—Saul's oldest daughter
Michal—Saul's daughter; David's wife
Ahimelech—priest at Nob; gives bread and sword to David
Abiathar—son of Ahimelech; priest; escapes Saul's killing
Nabal—Calebite who is struck dead because of his treatment of David; Abigail's first husband
Abigail—Nabal's wife, then David's wife
Ahinoam—David's wife
Abishai—Joab's brother; David's nephew; one of David's soldiers
Achish—Philistine commander who hires David as his bodyguard

Places

Shiloh—central Israelite shrine
Ramah—Elkanah and Hannah's home
Beth-shemesh—place where the Philistines return the ark of the covenant
Kiriath-jearim—resting place of the ark for twenty years
Mizpah—gathering place; location of Saul's selection as king via lots
Gilgal—place where Saul's kingship is renewed after a battle
Gibeah—location associated with Saul
Bethlehem—David's hometown
Philistia—area on the Mediterranean coast; at war with Israel
Ziklag—town in southern Judah; also associated with the Philistines
Mount Gilboa—mountain in northern Israel; place of Saul's death

Key Concepts

Prophet—person who speaks a message from God to the people
Ark of God/ark of the covenant—symbol of God's presence
Judges—temporary leaders of Israel before the monarchy
Kingship—system of governance that Israel requests in order to be like other nations
Anointing—prophet's use of oil to appoint a ruler for Israel
War—Israel's fight against neighbors

Important Quotations

"Hannah prayed and said, 'My heart exults in the LORD; my strength is exalted in my God. My mouth derides my enemies, because I rejoice in my victory.'" (1 Sam 2:1)

"Speak, for your servant is listening." (1 Sam 3:10; Samuel as a boy speaking to God in the temple at Shiloh)

"But the LORD said to Samuel, 'Do not look on his appearance or on the height of his stature, because I have rejected him; for the LORD does not see as mortals see; they look on the outward appearance, but the LORD looks on the heart.'" (1 Sam 16:7)

"But David said to the Philistine, 'You come to me with sword and spear and javelin; but I come to you in the name of the LORD of hosts, the God of the armies of Israel, whom you have defied.'" (1 Sam 17:45)

"Then Jonathan made a covenant with David, because he loved him as his own soul." (1 Sam 18:3)

"This very day your eyes have seen how the LORD gave you into my hand in the cave; and some urged me to kill you, but I spared you. I said, 'I will not raise my hand against my lord; for he is the LORD's anointed.'" (1 Sam 24:10)

Life of Samuel

Samuel before Saul and Kingship

- Samuel is born (1 Sam 1)
- Samuel is offered as a nazirite (1 Sam 1)
- Samuel grows up in the presence of God (1 Sam 2)
- Samuel's call as a prophet (1 Sam 3)
- Samuel serves as judge (1 Sam 7)
- Samuel becomes old, appoints sons as judges (1 Sam 8)
- Samuel tells the people why they should not want a king (1 Sam 8)

Samuel and Saul

- Saul visits Samuel, who has already been told by God to anoint him king (1 Sam 9)
- Samuel anoints Saul as king (1 Sam 10)

- Samuel gathers the tribes together, draws lots to find a king, and teaches them about kingship (1 Sam 10)
- Samuel gives a farewell address (1 Sam 12)
- Samuel condemns Saul for sacrificing (1 Sam 13)
- Samuel tells Saul to attack the Amalekites (1 Sam 15)
- God tells Samuel that Saul is rejected as king (1 Sam 15)
- Samuel goes to Bethlehem and anoints David, a shepherd, as king (1 Sam 16)
- Samuel, David, and Saul are together; Saul falls into a prophetic frenzy (1 Sam 19)
- Samuel dies (1 Sam 25)
- The medium of Endor brings Samuel back for Saul (1 Sam 28)

Life of Saul

Saul's Life before David

- No birth story
- Saul is a handsome young man and taller than everyone else (1 Sam 9)
- Saul and Samuel meet, and Samuel anoints Saul as ruler over Israel (1 Sam 9–10)
- Saul falls into a prophetic frenzy to fulfill Samuel's prophecy (1 Sam 10)
- Saul is proclaimed king by drawing lots (1 Sam 10)
- Saul defeats the Ammonites in battle (1 Sam 11)
- Saul is made king at Gilgal (1 Sam 11)
- Saul offers the burnt offering instead of waiting for Samuel; Samuel condemns his kingship (1 Sam 13)
- Saul accidently curses his son Jonathan by making an impulsive oath (1 Sam 14)
- Saul fights against the Moabites, Ammonites, Edomites, Philistines, and Amalekites (1 Sam 14)
- Saul defeats the Amalekites but spares the king, against Samuel's command (1 Sam 15)
- God regrets making Saul king (1 Sam 15)
- An evil spirit torments Saul (1 Sam 16)

Saul and David

- Saul has David play the lyre to soothe him (1 Sam 16)
- Saul wants to know about the boy who killed Goliath (1 Sam 17)
- Saul places David over the armies but is jealous at his victories (1 Sam 18)

- Saul gives his daughter Michal to David (1 Sam 18)
- Saul attempts to kill David (1 Sam 19)
- Saul falls into a prophetic frenzy (1 Sam 19)
- Saul tells Jonathan of the plan to kill David (1 Sam 20)
- Saul has people and animals killed in Nob, the city of the priests, in search of David (1 Sam 22)
- Saul pursues David in the wilderness (1 Sam 23)
- Saul looks for David; David has an opportunity to kill Saul but does not (1 Sam 24)
- Saul pursues David; David has another opportunity to kill Saul but does not (1 Sam 26)
- Saul consults a medium to talk to Samuel (1 Sam 28)
- Samuel tells Saul that the kingdom will be torn out of his hand (1 Sam 28)
- Saul falls on his own sword in battle (1 Sam 31)

Life of David

See the section on 2 Samuel.

2 SAMUEL

The book of 2 Samuel is not about the prophet Samuel but features David as the key character. Originally, 1 Samuel and 2 Samuel were one book, but they were divided at the point in the story when Saul died.

Synopsis

The book of 2 Samuel begins with news of Saul's death and David's lament. The people of Judah named David their king; Abner named Ishbaal king of Israel in the north. This arrangement, of two separate kings, did not last long. Abner shifted his allegiance to David; David's commander, Joab, then killed Abner. Ishbaal was killed, and David was made king of all Israel. He established Jerusalem as his capital and brought the ark of God to reside there. David wanted to build a house for God, but God intended to make David a "house," that is, a kingdom and dynasty. David demonstrated his military might by defeating several peoples. He also brought Mephibosheth, Jonathan's son, into his household.

David sent for and lay with Uriah's wife, Bathsheba, then had Uriah killed in battle. Bathsheba then became David's wife. Nathan, the prophet, confronted David, who expressed remorse, but the child from the union of David and Bathsheba died. They had another child, Solomon. One of David's sons, Amnon, raped his half-sister, Tamar, but David refused to punish Amnon. Tamar's full brother, Absalom, had Amnon killed and then fled for his life. David forgave him for killing Amnon and brought him back to Jerusalem. Absalom usurped the throne from David, and David fled Jerusalem. David, however, had an inside source in Absalom's court named Hushai, who warned him of an attack. David defended himself, but Joab killed Absalom. David was greatly distressed by the death of Absalom but returned to the throne in Jerusalem just in time to squelch a revolt from Sheba.

The book ends with David making a deal with the Gibeonites and singing psalms. A list of David's warriors is also included. In the final story of 2 Samuel, David took a census of the people at God's urging. God then punished Israel for this action. God instructed David to buy the threshing floor of Araunah and to build an altar.

Content Outline

David Becomes King of Judah

David executes Saul's killer and laments Saul and Jonathan	2 Samuel 1
The people anoint David as king of Judah in Hebron; Ishbaal is anointed king of Israel	2 Samuel 2
Abner switches loyalties from the house of Saul to David; Joab kills Abner	2 Samuel 3
Ishbaal's captains kill him and bring his head to David in Hebron	2 Samuel 4

David as King of All Israel

David is made king of all Israel and moves the capital to Jerusalem	2 Samuel 5
David brings the ark of God to Jerusalem; Uzzah touches it and dies	2 Samuel 6
God will build David a kingdom; David prays	2 Samuel 7
David battles with the Philistines, Moabites, Arameans, and Edomites	2 Samuel 8

| David brings Mephibosheth, Jonathan's son, to his table in Jerusalem | 2 Samuel 9 |
| David fights the Ammonites, who have hired the Arameans to help | 2 Samuel 10 |

David's Personal Troubles

David lays with Bathsheba and has her husband, Uriah, killed in battle	2 Samuel 11
Nathan condemns David's behavior; the child of David and Bathsheba dies; Solomon is born	2 Samuel 12
Amnon rapes his half-sister, Tamar; Absalom has Amnon killed; Absalom flees	2 Samuel 13
A woman of Tekoa visits David; David forgives Absalom and brings him back	2 Samuel 14
Absalom attempts to become king; David flees Jerusalem	2 Samuel 15
David flees and encounters different people	2 Samuel 16
Absalom follows Hushai's advice and tries to kill David, but David learns of the plan	2 Samuel 17
David's army attacks Absalom's army; Joab kills Absalom; David mourns	2 Samuel 18
David returns to Jerusalem as king of all Israel; he is merciful to former enemies	2 Samuel 19
Sheba leads a revolt but is besieged and executed	2 Samuel 20

Epilogue

David makes a deal with the Gibeonites; he buries the bones of Saul and Jonathan	2 Samuel 21
David's psalm	2 Samuel 22
David's last words; list of David's warriors	2 Samuel 23
David takes a census of all Israel; God punishes David; David buys a threshing floor	2 Samuel 24

People

David—son of Jesse; second king of Israel
Ahinoam—David's wife
Abigail—Nabal's wife; David's wife
Abner—commander of Saul's army; son of Ner; killed by Joab
Ishbaal—Saul's son
Joab—commander of David's army; David's nephew
Amnon—David's first son; Ahinoam's son
Chileab—David's second son; Abigail's son
Absalom—David's third son; King Talmai of Geshur's daughter's son
Adonijah—David's fourth son
Shephatiah—David's fifth son
Ithream—David's sixth son; Eglah's son
Rizpah—Saul's concubine; daughter of Aiah
Michal—Paltiel's wife; David's wife
Mephibosheth—Jonathan's son
Rechab and Baanah—sons of Rimmon; killers of Ishbaal
Jebusites—inhabitants of Jerusalem before David takes it over
King Hiram of Tyre—sends cedar trees to Jerusalem and builds David a house
Uzzah—touches the ark of God to steady it and is struck dead by God
Obed-edom—Gittite; David brings the ark to his house first
Nathan—prophet who confronts David about Bathsheba
Jehoshaphat—David's recorder
Zadok and Ahimelech—priests under David
Seraiah—David's secretary
Bathsheba—Uriah's wife; David's wife; daughter of Eliam; mother of Solomon
Uriah—Hittite; Bathsheba's husband; soldier in David's army
Solomon—David and Bathsheba's son; his birth is mentioned in 2 Samuel
Tamar—Absalom's sister; David's daughter; Maacah's daughter
Jonadab—son of David's brother Shimeah
Ahithophel—David's counselor
Hushai—David's spy on Absalom
Ziba—servant of Mephibosheth
Amasa—Absalom's commander of the army when he rebels against David
Unnamed wise woman in Abel of Beth-maacah—brokers a deal with Joab to kill Sheba and spare her city
Araunah—Jebusite; owns a threshing floor that David buys to build an altar

Places

Gibeon—city in Benjamin
Hebron—David's capital when he is king of Judah
Tyre—city in Phoenicia
Jerusalem—David makes this city his capital by striking down the Jebusites
Israel—northern part of the kingdom, or the whole kingdom
Judah—southern part of the kingdom
Zela—final burial place for Saul and Jonathan

Key Concepts

House of Saul—Saul's family and supporters
House of David—David's family and supporters
Census—accounting of the people of Israel and Judah by David in obedience to God's command
Psalms—several songs are attributed to David in 2 Samuel
Kingship—system of governance that includes kings Saul and David

Important Quotations

"Your glory, O Israel, lies slain upon your high places! How the mighty have fallen!" (2 Sam 1:19)

"Then the people of Judah came, and there they anointed David king over the house of Judah." (2 Sam 2:4)

"There was a long war between the house of Saul and the house of David; David grew stronger and stronger, while the house of Saul became weaker and weaker." (2 Sam 3:1)

"So all the elders of Israel came to the king at Hebron; and King David made a covenant with them at Hebron before the LORD, and they anointed David king over Israel." (2 Sam 5:3)

"Your house and your kingdom shall be made sure forever before me; your throne shall be established forever." (2 Sam 7:16; God speaking to David)

"Nathan said to David, 'You are the man!'" (2 Sam 12:7; accusing David of misusing his power)

"The king [David] was deeply moved, and went up to the chamber over the gate, and wept; and as he went, he said, 'O my son Absalom, my son, my son Absalom! Would I had died instead of you, O Absalom, my son, my son!'" (2 Sam 18:33)

Life of David

Before His Kingship: David as Shepherd, Warrior, and Rival to Saul

- No birth story
- David is summoned to play the lyre to soothe King Saul (1 Sam 16)
- David slays Goliath (1 Sam 17)
- Saul puts David over the army (1 Sam 18)
- Jonathan, Saul's son, makes a covenant with David (1 Sam 18)
- Saul is jealous of David's battle victories and begins to watch him closely (1 Sam 18)
- Saul tries to kill David (1 Sam 18)
- All Judah and Israel love David (1 Sam 18)
- David marries Michal, Saul's daughter (1 Sam 18)
- Jonathan attempts to restore the relationship between Saul and David (1 Sam 19)
- Saul tries to kill David again; Michal helps David escape (1 Sam 19)
- Jonathan displays his loyalty to David (1 Sam 20)
- David lies in order to get bread and weapons (1 Sam 21)
- David pretends to be insane in Gath (1 Sam 21)
- David gathers a band of four hundred men together and sends his parents to Moab for protection (1 Sam 22)
- David attacks the Philistines and saves the city of Keilah (1 Sam 23)
- David escapes unharmed from Saul in the wilderness (1 Sam 23)
- David does not kill Saul but cuts the corner of his cloak (1 Sam 24)
- David asks Nabal for help, but Nabal refuses; God strikes Nabal dead (1 Sam 25)
- David takes Nabal's wife, Abigail, as his wife (1 Sam 25)
- David also marries Ahinoam of Jezreel (1 Sam 25)
- David does not kill Saul but takes his spear and water jar (1 Sam 26)
- David lives with the Philistines for over a year (1 Sam 27)
- The Philistines send David back (1 Sam 29)
- David fights against the Amalekites in retaliation for taking his wives (1 Sam 30)
- David learns of Saul's and Jonathan's deaths (2 Sam 1)
- David sings a lament (2 Sam 1)

David as King of Judah

- David is anointed king of Judah in Hebron (2 Sam 2)
- David has six sons by six women in Hebron (2 Sam 3)
- War breaks out between the house of Saul and the house of David (2 Sam 3)
- David mourns when Joab kills Abner (2 Sam 3)
- David receives the head of Ishbaal from Ishbaal's captains (2 Sam 4)

David as King of All Israel

- David is anointed king of all Israel (2 Sam 5)
- David moves the capital to Jerusalem by expelling the Jebusites (2 Sam 5)
- David fights against the Philistines (2 Sam 5)
- David brings the ark of God to Jerusalem with shouting and dancing (2 Sam 6)
- Michal rebukes David for exposing himself while dancing (2 Sam 6)
- God makes a covenant with David (2 Sam 7)
- David prays (2 Sam 7)
- David battles with the Philistines, Moabites, Arameans, and Edomites (2 Sam 8)
- David brings Mephibosheth, Jonathan's son, to Jerusalem (2 Sam 9)
- David fights the Ammonites, who have hired the Arameans to help (2 Sam 10)
- David lays with Bathsheba, the wife of Uriah (2 Sam 11)
- Bathsheba tells David that she is pregnant (2 Sam 11)
- David tries to manipulate Uriah into sleeping with Bathsheba (2 Sam 11)
- David has Uriah killed in battle (2 Sam 11)
- David is condemned by the prophet Nathan through a parable (2 Sam 12)
- David and Bathsheba's child dies (2 Sam 12)
- David consoles Bathsheba, and they have another child, Solomon (2 Sam 12)
- David fights against the Ammonites (2 Sam 12)
- David's son Amnon rapes his half-sister, Tamar (2 Sam 13)
- David is angry at Amnon but does not punish him (2 Sam 13)
- David's son Absalom kills Amnon to avenge his sister (2 Sam 13)
- An unnamed woman of Tekoa convinces David to bring Absalom home (2 Sam 14)
- David reconciles with Absalom after Absalom lives in Jerusalem for two years (2 Sam 14)
- Absalom usurps David's throne (2 Sam 15)
- David flees from Jerusalem into the wilderness (2 Sam 15)

- David receives loyalty from Ittai the Gittite, who goes with David into the wilderness (2 Sam 15)
- David tells Abiathar and Zadok to keep the ark of God in Jerusalem (2 Sam 15)
- David learns that Ahithophel conspired with Absalom against him (2 Sam 15)
- David sends Hushai back to Jerusalem to serve as a spy (2 Sam 15)
- David speaks with Ziba, Mephibosheth's servant, about Mephibosheth staying in Jerusalem (2 Sam 16)
- Shimei curses David for being a man of blood (2 Sam 16)
- Absalom tries to kill David based on Hushai's advice, but David learns the plot (2 Sam 17)
- David's army attacks Absalom's army (2 Sam 18)
- Joab, David's commander, kills Absalom (2 Sam 18)
- David mourns his son's death (2 Sam 18–19)
- David returns to Jerusalem as king of all Israel after the death of Absalom (2 Sam 19)
- David appoints Amasa as commander of the armies in place of Joab (2 Sam 19)
- David reunites with Mephibosheth (2 Sam 19)
- Sheba revolts against David and is murdered (2 Sam 20)
- Joab kills Amasa (2 Sam 20)
- David strikes a deal with the Gibeonites and hands over seven of Saul's sons to them (2 Sam 21)
- David buries the bones of Saul and Jonathan (2 Sam 21)
- David sings a psalm (2 Sam 22)
- David's last words (2 Sam 23)
- List of David's warriors (2 Sam 23)
- David takes a census of all Israel at God's initiative (2 Sam 24)
- God punishes Israel because David took a census (2 Sam 24)
- David buys Araunah's threshing floor (2 Sam 24)

David as an Old King

- David has Abishag as his attendant to serve him (1 Kgs 1)
- Adonijah, David's son, declares himself king without David knowing (1 Kgs 1)
- Bathsheba and Nathan go to David to convince him to declare Solomon as king (1 Kgs 1)
- David declares that Solomon will succeed him as king (1 Kgs 1)
- David's final words to Solomon (1 Kgs 2)
- David dies (1 Kgs 2)

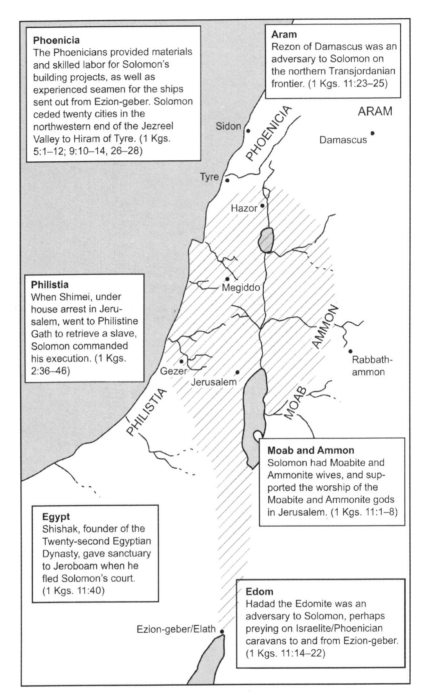

Phoenicia
The Phoenicians provided materials and skilled labor for Solomon's building projects, as well as experienced seamen for the ships sent out from Ezion-geber. Solomon ceded twenty cities in the northwestern end of the Jezreel Valley to Hiram of Tyre. (1 Kgs. 5:1–12; 9:10–14, 26–28)

Aram
Rezon of Damascus was an adversary to Solomon on the northern Transjordanian frontier. (1 Kgs. 11:23–25)

Philistia
When Shimei, under house arrest in Jerusalem, went to Philistine Gath to retrieve a slave, Solomon commanded his execution. (1 Kgs. 2:36–46)

Moab and Ammon
Solomon had Moabite and Ammonite wives, and supported the worship of the Moabite and Ammonite gods in Jerusalem. (1 Kgs. 11:1–8)

Egypt
Shishak, founder of the Twenty-second Egyptian Dynasty, gave sanctuary to Jeroboam when he fled Solomon's court. (1 Kgs. 11:40)

Edom
Hadad the Edomite was an adversary to Solomon, perhaps preying on Israelite/Phoenician caravans to and from Ezion-geber. (1 Kgs. 11:14–22)

Sidon
Damascus
ARAM
PHOENICIA
Tyre
Hazor
Megiddo
AMMON
Rabbath-ammon
Gezer
Jerusalem
MOAB
PHILISTIA
Ezion-geber/Elath

Map 3. Extent of Solomon's Kingdom

(Originally published in J. Maxwell Miller and John H. Hayes, *A History of Ancient Israel and Judah*, 2nd ed. [Louisville, KY: Westminster John Knox Press, 2006], 207.)

1 KINGS

Originally, 1 and 2 Kings were a single book. They were split into two books when the Hebrew Bible was translated into Greek. These books can be difficult to understand because after the reign of Solomon, the histories of Israel and Judah are narrated side by side without clear delineations.

Synopsis

In his old age, David was cared for by a beautiful woman named Abishag. Opportunistic Adonijah, David's fourth son, declared himself king with the support of several important people, including Joab, David's army commander, and Abiathar, a priest. Nathan the prophet heard this news and encouraged Bathsheba to remind David of his promise that Solomon would succeed him. Bathsheba did so, and David declared that Solomon would indeed be king. He sent for Zadok, another priest, and had him anoint Solomon as king. David gave final instructions to Solomon, including commands to follow God's law and admonitions about dealing with certain court personnel. David died after a forty-year reign.

After Solomon became king, he moved immediately to remove any rivals from power. David's son Adonijah asked to be given David's former attendant, Abishag, as his wife. Solomon had Adonijah killed. He also had Joab and Shimei killed, and he banished Abiathar to Anathoth. In a dream, God asked Solomon what he wanted, and Solomon requested a discerning mind. God gave him wisdom and riches. Two women came to Solomon arguing over a child, and Solomon was able to give a wise decision.

The text then turns to details concerning Solomon's officers, including the twelve officials over the twelve districts, his vast geographical kingdom, and his great wisdom.

Solomon prepared to build a house for God by renewing the treaty with King Hiram of Tyre and sending for timber from Tyre. He built the Temple, a three-room building that took seven years to complete, and then built a palace, which took an additional thirteen years. After completing the Temple, he gathered the leaders of Israel together and brought the ark of God into the Temple. Solomon gave a speech, prayed, and blessed the assembled people.

In addition to the Temple and the palace, Solomon completed other building projects, including a fleet of ships to import gold. The queen of Sheba visited him and marveled at his wisdom and wealth. Despite his success, Solomon had one problem: he loved foreign women who enticed him to worship foreign gods. God grew angry with Solomon and promised to tear the kingdom apart, leaving only one part of it to Solomon's son. God raised up several adversaries against Solomon, including Jeroboam. The prophet Ahijah prophesied that Jeroboam would receive ten tribes, and Solomon responded by attempting to kill Jeroboam. Jeroboam fled to Egypt. After forty years as king, Solomon died and was buried with his father, David. Rehoboam succeeded Solomon.

Rehoboam promised to be a stronger leader than his father, Solomon, so all the tribes, except Judah, decided to have Jeroboam rule over them. Jeroboam ruled over Israel from Shechem and established Bethel and Dan as rival sacrificial places to Jerusalem, with a golden calf in each city. A man of God came from Judah and condemned Jeroboam for his idolatry. Judgment came to Jeroboam through the sickness and death of his child Abijah. After a twenty-two-year reign, Jeroboam died. Meanwhile, Rehoboam reigned for seventeen years over Judah in Jerusalem. King Abijam succeeded Rehoboam as king of Judah and continued his father's evil practices. He was succeeded by his son Asa, who brought religious reform to Judah and made an alliance with Aram against Israel. Nadab reigned over Israel for two years before he was assassinated by Baasha, which began a second dynasty in Israel. Baasha's son Elah also reigned for two years before he was assassinated by Zimri, the commander of his chariots. Zimri's reign lasted only a week before he was usurped by Omri, the commander of the army. Omri reigned over Israel for twelve years and moved the capital to Samaria. All these kings of Israel were like their ancestor Jeroboam and did evil according to God.

Ahab, Omri's son, reigned for twenty-two years in Samaria. Ahab married Jezebel and erected an altar to Baal. Suddenly the prophet Elijah appeared in the story. He prophesied drought and went into the desert, where he was fed by ravens. Elijah traveled to Sidon and met the widow of Zarephath, who gave him food. Because of her generosity, she had food for herself during the drought. Elijah also raised her son back to life. Elijah went to Ahab and asked him to assemble the prophets of Baal at Mount Carmel. He proposed that they each call on the name of their god and that the one who answered with fire was the true God. The prophets of Baal tried and tried, but they could not get Baal to answer. Elijah called upon God, and God consumed the area with fire. Elijah seized all the prophets and killed them. Elijah prophesied that the drought would end. When Jezebel heard what Elijah had done to the prophets of Baal, she wanted to kill him. Elijah fled to the south through Beersheba to Mount Horeb, where he met God in the sound of silence. God told him to return home in safety. On the return trip, he found Elisha, who followed him.

The Arameans attacked Israel under King Ahab twice and lost both times. King Ahab wanted to take Naboth's vineyard, but Naboth refused to give his ancestral land away. Jezebel brought false charges against Naboth and had him stoned to death. Elijah condemned Ahab for this death, but Ahab repented and God declared punishment on Ahab's son, not Ahab. Israel and Judah wanted to go into battle against Aram and were instructed to proceed by Ahab's prophets. Only Micaiah prophesied disaster for them, so Ahab locked him in prison and proceeded to battle. Ahab was shot with an arrow and died in battle. Jehoshaphat reigned over Judah for twenty-five years before he died. Ahaziah, Ahab's son, reigned over Israel for two years and did evil things like his father and mother.

Content Outline

Solomon Becomes King

King David is old; Bathsheba wants her son to succeed David; Solomon is declared king	1 Kings 1
David gives final instructions to Solomon; David dies; Solomon has people killed	1 Kings 2
Solomon asks God for discernment; Solomon judges wisely for two women	1 Kings 3
Solomon's high officials, his vast kingdom, and his great wisdom	1 Kings 4
Solomon and King Hiram make a treaty; Hiram supplies cedar for the Temple	1 Kings 5
Solomon builds the Temple in seven years	1 Kings 6
Solomon builds his palace and other royal buildings	1 Kings 7
Solomon dedicates the Temple with sacrifices, a speech, a prayer, and a blessing	1 Kings 8
As he did with David, God promises Solomon a dynasty; Solomon's other building projects	1 Kings 9
Queen of Sheba visits Solomon and finds him wise; Solomon's wealth	1 Kings 10
Solomon worships other gods; God brings adversaries against him; Solomon dies	1 Kings 11

Divided Kingdom: Israel and Judah

Tribes other than Judah make Jeroboam their king; he makes two golden calves	1 Kings 12

Man of God condemns Jeroboam, but Jeroboam continues to build high places	1 Kings 13
Ahijah prophesies death for Abijah; Jeroboam dies; Rehoboam reigns	1 Kings 14
Abijam rules over Judah; Asa rules over Judah; Nadab reigns over Israel	1 Kings 15
Baasha, Elah, Zimri, Omri, and Ahab rule over Israel	1 Kings 16
Elijah prophesies drought; he visits a widow of Zarephath and brings her son back to life	1 Kings 17
Elijah confronts the prophets of Baal; drought ends	1 Kings 18
Elijah runs away from Jezebel; Elijah hears the sound of silence at Horeb; Elisha follows Elijah	1 Kings 19
Israel and the Arameans battle twice; a prophet judges Ahab	1 Kings 20
Ahab wants Naboth's vineyard; Jezebel has Naboth stoned to death; Elijah judges	1 Kings 21
Israel and Judah go to battle against Aram; Micaiah prophesies; Ahab dies; Jehoshaphat and Ahaziah reign	1 Kings 22

People other than Israelite or Judahite Kings

Associated with David and Solomon

Abishag—Shunammite; David's beautiful attendant in his old age

Adonijah—David's fourth son; Haggith's son; declares himself king without David's knowledge

Joab—David's nephew and army commander; supports Adonijah as king

Abiathar—priest in David's court; supports Adonijah

Zadok—priest in David's court; does not support Adonijah and anoints Solomon as king

Nathan—prophet; does not support Adonijah

Bathsheba—Solomon's mother; one of David's wives

Benaiah—Solomon's army commander; kills Adonijah, Joab, and Shimei for Solomon

Pharaoh's daughter—Solomon's wife

Pharaoh—king of Egypt; gave the Canaanite city of Gezer as a dowry to his daughter

Two unnamed women—bring a judicial case to Solomon

Azariah—high priest for Solomon; grandson of Zadok

King Hiram of Tyre—supplies cedar for the building of the Temple

Queen of Sheba—visits Solomon and recognizes his wisdom and wealth

Hadad the Edomite—Solomon's adversary

King Rezon of Aram—Solomon's adversary

Associated with the Divided Kingdom

Ahijah—prophet who says Jeroboam will rule over ten tribes from Shiloh

King Shishak of Egypt—Jeroboam flees to him; later attacks Jerusalem under Rehoboam

Man of God from Judah—condemns Jeroboam for sacrificing at Bethel

Abijah—Jeroboam's son who dies because of his father's idolatry

Jeroboam's wife—goes to the prophet Ahijah to ask about her son

Naamah the Ammonite—mother of Rehoboam

Maacah—daughter of Absalom; Abijam's mother; Asa's mother

King Benhadad of Aram—makes an alliance with Asa; attacks Israel during Ahab's reign

Jehu—son of Hanani; prophet; condemns Baasha

Jezebel—daughter of King Ethbaal of the Sidonians; wife of Ahab

Hiel of Bethel—rebuilds Jericho during the days of King Ahab and loses two sons because of it

Elijah the Tishbite—prophet

Widow of Zarephath—attends to Elijah during a drought; her son is resuscitated by Elijah

Obadiah—in charge of Ahab's palace; hides a hundred prophets from Jezebel

Prophets of Baal—unable to get Baal to respond; killed by Elijah

Elisha—Elijah's servant

Hazael—king of Aram

Unknown prophet—prophesies to Ahab about Israel's victory over the Arameans

Member of the company of prophets—condemns Ahab for not killing King Benhadad

Naboth—owner of a vineyard in Jezreel; stoned to death because of Jezebel's manipulations

Micaiah—son of Imlah; prophesies defeat for King Jehoshaphat and King Ahab

Azubah—daughter of Shilhi; mother of Jehoshaphat

Foreign Deities

Astarte—goddess of the Sidonians
Milcom/Molech—god of the Ammonites
Chemosh—god of the Moabites
Baal—god of the Canaanites

Places

Jerusalem—location of Solomon's reign
City of David—section of Jerusalem where the king's palace was
Anathoth—Abiathar's hometown, where he is banished from Jerusalem
Gibeon—major site for sacrifice; Solomon sacrifices here
Ezion-geber—site on the shore of the Red Sea where Solomon builds a fleet of ships
Egypt—where Jeroboam flees when Solomon attempts to kill him
Shechem—city that Jeroboam fortifies and makes his capital
Bethel—site where Jeroboam establishes a rival sacrificial place
Dan—site where Jeroboam establishes a rival sacrificial place
Shiloh—Ahijah the prophet's home
Tirzah—capital of the northern kingdom during the reigns of Jeroboam, Baasha, Elah, Zimri, and Omri
Ramah—city built by Baasha
Samaria—city made the new capital of Israel by Omri
Jericho—city rebuilt by Hiel during the days of Ahab
Wadi Cherith—place where Elijah lives east of the Jordan; ravens visit him there to feed him
Zarephath—city near Sidon where Elijah travels
Mount Carmel—location of the contest between Elijah and the prophets of Baal
Mount Horeb—where Elijah hears God in the sound of sheer silence
Jezreel—location of Naboth's vineyard

Key Concepts

Kingship—system of governance that includes King Solomon and his sons
Wisdom of Solomon—Solomon prays to God for wisdom to govern; he is known for this virtue
Wealth of Solomon—Solomon acquires great wealth in the form of tributes, building projects, and marriages

Solomon's temple—place of worship and sacrifice where God's presence dwells; Solomon builds the First Temple in Jerusalem
Prophet—person who speaks a message from God to the people
Baal worship—worship of a Canaanite deity

Important Quotations

"Give your servant therefore an understanding mind to govern your people, able to discern between good and evil; for who can govern this your great people?" (1 Kgs 3:9)

"People came from all the nations to hear the wisdom of Solomon; they came from all the kings of the earth who had heard of his wisdom." (1 Kgs 4:34)

"So the king [Jeroboam] took counsel, and made two calves of gold. He said to the people, 'You have gone up to Jerusalem long enough. Here are your gods, O Israel, who brought you up out of the land of Egypt.' He set one in Bethel, and the other he put in Dan." (1 Kgs 12:28–29)

"Then the word of the LORD came to him, saying, 'What are you doing here, Elijah?' He answered, 'I have been very zealous for the LORD, the God of hosts; for the Israelites have forsaken your covenant, thrown down your altars, and killed your prophets with the sword. I alone am left, and they are seeking my life, to take it away.'" (1 Kgs 19:9b–10)

Life of Solomon

Solomon and David

- Solomon is born to Bathsheba and David (2 Sam 12)
- Solomon is anointed by Zadok the priest as king at the Gihon (1 Kgs 1)
- Adonijah acknowledges Solomon as king, and Solomon allows him to go home (1 Kgs 1)
- Solomon receives final words from his father, David (1 Kgs 2)

Solomon Consolidates Power

- Solomon succeeds David as king when David dies (1 Kgs 2)
- Solomon has Adonijah killed (1 Kgs 2)
- Solomon banishes Abiathar, one of David's two priests, to Anathoth (1 Kgs 2)
- Solomon has Joab and Shimei killed (1 Kgs 2)

Solomon's Wisdom and Vast Kingdom

- Solomon asks for wisdom, and God promises wisdom and riches (1 Kgs 3)
- Solomon settles a judicial case between two women who claim the same child (1 Kgs 3)
- Solomon's high officials and twelve officials (1 Kgs 4)
- Solomon's vast kingdom and surpassing wisdom (1 Kgs 4)
- Solomon renews his father's covenant with King Hiram of Tyre (1 Kgs 5)

Solomon's Building Projects

- Solomon has timber brought from Tyre for building the Temple (1 Kgs 5)
- Solomon builds and furnishes the Temple (1 Kgs 6)
- Solomon builds his palace and other royal buildings (1 Kgs 7)
- Solomon dedicates the Temple (1 Kgs 8)
- Solomon's other building projects include cities and a fleet of ships (1 Kgs 9)

Solomon's Women and Decline

- Solomon is visited by the queen of Sheba, who finds him wise and wealthy (1 Kgs 10)
- Solomon loves foreign women, who lead him into idolatry (1 Kgs 11)
- God sends adversaries for Solomon because of his disobedience (1 Kgs 11)
- Jeroboam rebels against Solomon, and Solomon attempts to kill him (1 Kgs 11)
- Solomon dies after a forty-year reign over Israel (1 Kgs 11)

Kings of Israel (Northern Kingdom)

Name	Father	Mother	Length of reign
Jeroboam I	Nebat	Zeruah	22 years
Nadab	Jeroboam I		2 years
Baasha	Ahijah		24 years
Elah	Baasha		2 years
Zimri			7 days
Omri			12 years
Ahab	Omri		22 years
Ahaziah	Ahab		2 years
Jehoram	Ahab (brother of Ahaziah)		12 years

Jehu	Jehoshaphat (son of Nimshi)	28 years
Jehoahaz	Jehu	17 years
Joash/Jehoash	Jehoahaz	16 years
Jeroboam II	Joash	41 years
Zechariah	Jeroboam II	6 months
Shallum	Jabesh	1 month
Menahem	Gadi	10 years
Pekahiah	Menahem	2 years
Pekah	Remaliah	20 years
Hoshea	Elah	9 years

Kings (and Queen) of Judah (Southern Kingdom)

Name	Father	Mother	Length of reign
Rehoboam	Solomon	Naamah	17 years
Abijam	Rehoboam	Maacah	3 years
Asa	Abijam	Maacah	41 years
Jehoshaphat	Asa	Azubah	25 years
Jehoram	Jehoshaphat		8 years
Ahaziah	Jehoram	Athaliah	1 year
Athaliah	Ahab of Israel?		7 years
Jehoash/Joash	Ahaziah	Zibiah	40 years
Amaziah	Jehoash/Joash	Jehoaddin	29 years
Azariah/Uzziah	Amaziah	Jecoliah	52 years
Jotham	Azariah	Jerusha	16 years
Ahaz	Jotham		16 years
Hezekiah	Ahaz	Abi	29 years
Manasseh	Hezekiah	Hephzibah	55 years
Amon	Manasseh	Meshullemeth	2 years
Josiah	Amon	Jedidah	31 years
Jehoahaz	Josiah	Hamutal	3 months
Jehoiakim	Josiah	Zebidah	11 years
Jehoiachin	Jehoiakim	Nehushta	3 months
Zedekiah	Josiah	Hamutal	11 years

Chart 1. Chronological Outline of the Kings of Israel and Judah

Judah	Israel
Rehoboam (926–910)	Jeroboam (927–906)
Abijam/Abijah	
(909–907)	Nadab (905–904)
Asa (906–878 [866])	Baasha
	(903–882 [880])
	Elah (881–880)
	Zimri (seven days)

Four Decades of Hostilities (927–879 B.C.E.)

Solomon's death and the Israelite rebellion against Rehoboam's rule resulted in two minor kingdoms—Israel in the north and Judah in the south. Hostilities between the two kingdoms drained their strength, and the effective domain of both kingdoms combined probably consisted of little more than the hill country west of the Jordan. Sheshonq, biblical Shishak and founder of Egyptian Dynasty 22, conducted a military campaign into Syria-Palestine early in Rehoboam's reign. Phoenician sailor-merchants were exploring the Mediterranean shores.

Judah	Israel
	Omri (879–869)
Jehoshaphat (877–853)	
	Ahab (868–854)
Jehoram (852–841)	Ahaziah (853–852)
	Jehoram (851–840)
Ahaziah (840)	

The Omride Era (879–840 B.C.E.)

Israel emerged strong under Omri and Ahab and enjoyed a period of prosperity and international prominence that probably exceeded that of Solomon. Good commercial relations with the Phoenicians were enhanced by Ahab's marriage to Jezebel, daughter of the king of Sidon. Judah under Jehoshaphat was a close ally of Israel—possibly little more than a vassal. Assyria began to expand westward under Ashurnasirpal and Shalmaneser III.

Judah	Israel
Athaliah (839–833)	Jehu (839–822)
Joash/Jehoash	
(832–803 [793])	Jehoahaz (821–805)
Amaziah	Joash (804–789)
(802–786 [774])	
Uzziah/Azariah	Jeroboam II
(785–760 [734])	(788–748)
Jotham (759–744)	

The Jehu Dynasty (839–748 B.C.E.)

Related palace coups brought new rulers to the thrones of both Israel and Judah and initiated a period of mutual weakness. Urartu emerged strong, extended its domain into northern Syria, and even threatened Assyria. Momentarily free of Assyrian pressure, Aramaean kings of Damascus, Hazael and Ben-hadad, made deep inroads into Israelite and Judean territory. Assyrian armies were active in the region again toward the end of the 9th century, during the reign of Adad-nirari III but probably led by the energetic Assyrian governor Shamshi-ilu. Both Israel and Judah enjoyed a brief period of recovery during the reign of Jeroboam II. It was at this time also that the Cushite Dynasty 25 came to power in Egypt.

(Originally published in J. Maxwell Miller and John H. Hayes, *A History of Ancient Israel and Judah*, 2nd ed. [Louisville, KY: Westminster John Knox Press, 2006], 222–23.)

Judah	Israel	Under Assyrian Rule (745–627 B.C.E.)
	Zechariah (six months)	Under Tiglath-pileser III (744–727), Assyria entered a new phase of conquest and consolidation of the resulting empire. By the end of his reign, all of the peoples of Syria-Palestine, including Israel and Judah, were under the Assyrian yoke. Tiglath-pileser's immediate successors continued the momentum, and eventually overpowered even the Cushite dynasty in Egypt. Attempts to rebel against Assyrian rule resulted in the annihilation of Israel and annexation of its territories. Judah managed to survive as an Assyrian vassal through the reign of Ashurbanipal (668–627), at which time a close alliance existed between Assyria and Egypt, and Egypt gradually assumed administrative control of Syria-Palestine. For a brief period following the death of Ashurbanipal, Egypt alone controlled Syria-Palestine.
	Shallum (one month)	
Jehoahaz/Ahaz I (743–728)	Menahem (746–737)	
	Pekahiah (736–735)	
	Pekah (734–731)	
Hezekiah (727–699)	Hoshea (730–722)	
Manasseh (698–644)		
Amon (643–642)	**Fall of Samaria (722)**	
Josiah (641–610)		

Under Babylonian Rule (605–586 B.C.E.)

Jehoahaz II (three months)
Jehoiakim (608–598)
Jehoiachin (three months)
Zedekiah (596–586)

Destruction of Jerusalem (586)

The Assyrian Empire declined rapidly after Ashurbanipal's death, while Babylon emerged strong under the energetic rule of Nabopolassar. The Babylonians and Medes joined forces to conquer the Assyrian capital Nineveh in 612, and the Assyrians made a last unsuccessful stand at Carchemish in 605. Soon the Babylonians were masters of Syria-Palestine. Judean resistance led eventually to the Babylonian destruction of Jerusalem and the exile of King Zedekiah in 586.

Life of Elijah

- Elijah prophesies a drought for Israel (1 Kgs 17)
- Elijah moves to the Wadi Cherith, and ravens bring him food (1 Kgs 17)
- Elijah goes to Zarephath to visit a widow, who prepares food for him (1 Kgs 17)
- Elijah brings the widow's son back to life (1 Kgs 17)
- Elijah and the prophets of Baal have a contest at Mount Carmel (1 Kgs 18)
- Elijah runs away from Jezebel because she threatens to kill him (1 Kgs 19)
- Elijah hears the sound of silence at Mount Horeb (1 Kgs 19)
- Elijah is told by God to anoint kings (1 Kgs 19)
- Elisha becomes Elijah's servant (1 Kgs 19)
- Elijah condemns Ahab for taking Naboth's life and vineyard (1 Kgs 21)
- Elijah condemns Ahaziah to death for consulting other gods (2 Kgs 1)
- Elijah calls fire from heaven to kill messengers (2 Kgs 1)
- Elijah ascends to heaven in a whirlwind (2 Kgs 2)

2 KINGS

This book was originally connected to 1 Kings as a unified whole. The reason for the story's division at this point—in the middle of the reign of Ahaziah—is not clear. Perhaps the transition from Elijah's ministry to Elisha's ministry provides a good reason to create the division here. The entire book deals with the divided monarchy, that is, the Israelite and Judahite kingdoms, with their histories intertwined into a complicated narrative. A key question to ask in the reading of 2 Kings is: Are we dealing with the northern kingdom of Israel or the southern kingdom of Judah?

Synopsis

The book of 2 Kings begins with a focus on the prophet Elijah and then on his successor, Elisha. Elijah condemned King Ahaziah of Israel for turning to a foreign god after an injury. The king sent messengers to Elijah, and Elijah called down fire from heaven upon each group of messengers. Ahaziah died and was succeeded by his brother, Jehoram of Israel. Elijah was taken up to heaven in a whirlwind, and Elisha picked up Elijah's mantle and continued his prophetic ministry. He purified bad water for a city and cursed young boys who mocked him.

During Jehoram's reign, King Mesha of Moab stopped supplying Israel with sheep and wool. Consequently, Israel and Judah attacked Moab. In an act of desperation, King Mesha sacrificed his oldest son, and Israel withdrew from battle. Several miracles performed by Elisha follow: he provided a supply of oil to a widow in debt; he raised the Shunammite's son back to life; he purified a pot of stew so the company of prophets could eat it; he fed one hundred people with a little food; he cured Naaman, an Aramean, of leprosy; and he caused a submerged iron ax head to float on water. The Arameans attempted to attack Elisha, but they were thwarted. They laid siege to Samaria but soon fled, because God caused them to hear the sound of chariots and a great army coming to attack.

While Jehoram (also known as Joram) of Israel was reigning, King Jehoram (same name but different person!) of Judah began to reign and battled with the Edomites. Then Ahaziah reigned over Judah for one year.

In Israel, Jehu was anointed king even though Jehoram was still king. Jehu killed Jehoram of Israel, Ahaziah of Judah, and Jezebel, Ahab's wife. Jehu then killed Ahab's descendants, Ahaziah of Judah's relatives, and the worshipers of Baal. Because of this bloodshed, God allowed parts of Israel to come under foreign control. Jehu died. After Jehu's death, Jehoahaz reigned over Israel for seventeen years and warred with Aram. His son, Jehoash of Israel, reigned for sixteen years. It was during his reign that Elisha died.

Queen Athaliah, Ahaziah's mother, reigned over Judah because Ahaziah of Judah only had a baby son, who was hidden from the queen for six years. The priest Jehoiada killed Queen Athaliah and anointed the child, Joash, king. Joash (also known as Jehoash) reigned for forty years over Judah and restored the Temple.

Jeroboam, Zechariah, Shallum, Menahem, Pekahiah, Pekah, and Hoshea reigned over Israel in the north. These kings represented five different dynasties. As the Israelite kings before them, they did evil in the sight of God. The Israelite kingdom was attacked and captured by the Assyrians. The Assyrians settled different peoples in the cities of Israel.

In Judah, there were several long kingships: Amaziah for twenty-nine years, Azariah for fifty-two years, Jotham for sixteen years, Ahaz for sixteen years, and Hezekiah for twenty-nine years. Hezekiah's reign is discussed at length because Assyria, after defeating Israel in the north, attacked Judah in the south during Hezekiah's kingship. Hezekiah consulted the prophet Isaiah about his options, and Isaiah prophesied that Sennacherib, the Assyrian king, would return home and fall by the sword in his own land. Hezekiah prayed to God, and the Assyrians were struck down by an angel of God. Sennacherib went home and was assassinated by his sons.

After Hezekiah's death, his son, Manasseh, reigned for fifty-five years. He rebuilt the altars his father had destroyed. Manasseh's son, Amon, also reigned and did evil in the sight of God. His servants killed him. The people placed eight-year-old Josiah on the throne. As an adult, Josiah initiated religious reforms based on the book of the law, which had been discovered in the Temple. Before he began his reforms, he consulted Huldah, who prophesied against him and the community for their disobedience.

After Josiah's death, Jehoahaz reigned for a short period of time before the Egyptian pharaoh made Jehoahaz's brother, Jehoiakim, king. Jehoiakim eventually became the vassal of Babylon, the new empire that had recently defeated Egypt. His son, Jehoiachin, became king, but Babylon attacked Jerusalem and took Jehoiachin and other leaders along with treasures back to Babylon. Zedekiah, Jehoiachin's uncle, was placed on the throne by the king of Babylon. He reigned for eleven years before he rebelled against Babylon. The rebellion led to the fall and capture of Jerusalem and the exile of Zedekiah. Zedekiah was blinded. Gedaliah was appointed governor of Judah. The new king of Babylon released Jehoiachin from prison and allowed him to dine at the king's table.

Content Outline

Elisha's Ministry

Elijah denounces Ahaziah for inquiring of a foreign god; Ahaziah dies	2 Kings 1
Elijah ascends to heaven; Elisha receives the spirit of Elijah and performs miracles	2 Kings 2
Jehoram reigns; Israel and Judah battle against Moab; Mesha sacrifices his son	2 Kings 3
Elisha performs four miracles	2 Kings 4
Elisha cures Naaman from Aram of leprosy; Gehazi's personal gain leads to leprosy	2 Kings 5
Aram tries to attack Elijah; Aram lays siege to Samaria	2 Kings 6
Aram flees from the area, and the people plunder their camp	2 Kings 7
Ben-hadad of Aram dies; Jehoram reigns over Judah; Ahaziah reigns over Judah	2 Kings 8
Jehu is anointed king of Israel; Jehu kills Joram of Israel, Ahaziah of Judah, and Jezebel	2 Kings 9
Jehu kills Ahab's descendants, Ahaziah's relatives, and followers of Baal; Jehu loses land and dies	2 Kings 10

Athaliah reigns over Judah; Joash/Jehoash is anointed king; the priest Jehoiada kills Athaliah	2 Kings 11
Jehoash restores the Temple and pays votive gifts to Aram; Jehoash dies	2 Kings 12

Fall of the Northern Kingdom of Israel

Jehoahaz reigns over Israel; Jehoash reigns over Israel; Elisha dies	2 Kings 13
Amaziah of Judah reigns and battles against Edom and Israel; Jeroboam II reigns over Israel	2 Kings 14
Azariah reigns with leprosy over Judah; Zechariah, Shallum, Menahem, Pekahiah, Pekah reign over Israel	2 Kings 15
Ahaz reigns over Judah; Ahaz forms an alliance with Assyria against Israel and Aram	2 Kings 16
The Israelites are attacked by Assyria and exiled because of the people's sin	2 Kings 17

Fall of the Southern Kingdom of Judah

Hezekiah reigns; Assyria invades Judah	2 Kings 18
Hezekiah asks Isaiah to intercede; Hezekiah prays; Assyria is defeated	2 Kings 19
Hezekiah gets sick, welcomes Babylonian envoys, and dies	2 Kings 20
Manasseh reigns over Judah; Amon succeeds his father to reign over Judah	2 Kings 21
Josiah reigns over Judah; high priest Hilkiah discovers the book of the law	2 Kings 22
Josiah institutes religious reforms; Josiah dies; Jehoahaz reigns but is taken to Egypt	2 Kings 23
Jehoiakim rebels against King Nebuchadnezzar of Babylon; Jehoiachin reigns; Jerusalem is taken captive; Zedekiah reigns	2 Kings 24
Siege of Jerusalem; Temple burned; Gedaliah made governor; Jehoiachin freed from captivity	2 Kings 25

People other than Israelite or Judahite Kings

Elijah—prophet; Tishbite; taken up into heaven by a chariot

Elisha—prophet; receives a double portion of Elijah's spirit

Mesha—king of Moab; supplies sheep and wool to Israel, but rebels during Jehoram's reign

Unnamed king of Edom—fights with Israel and Judah against Moab

Gehazi—Elisha's servant

Unnamed wife of a member of the company of prophets—recipient of a miracle performed by Elisha

Shunammite woman—shelters Elisha, who brings her son back to life; sojourns and has her land restored by the king

Naaman—commander of the army of the king of Aram; leprous

Naaman's unnamed wife—told by her servant about the prophet Elisha

Unnamed Israelite servant of Naaman's wife—tells Naaman's wife about the prophet Elisha

Ben-hadad—king of Aram

Hazael—king of Aram; father of Ben-hadad

Jehu—commander of the Israelite army; kills Jehoram to become the tenth king of Israel

Athaliah—mother of Ahaziah of Judah; granddaughter of Omri of Israel

Zimri—commander of the Israelite army

Jezebel—killed by Jehu

Jehosheba—King Jehoram's daughter and King Ahaziah's sister; hides Joash for six years

Jehoiada—priest and husband of Jehosheba

Zibiah—mother of Jehoash

Jehoaddin—mother of Amaziah, king of Judah

Jonah—son of Amittai; prophet

Jecoliah—mother of Azariah

Pul/Tiglath-pileser—king of Assyria

Jerusha—mother of Jotham

Rezin—king of Aram; forms a coalition with Israel against Assyria

Uriah—priest; builds a new altar for Ahaz

Shalmaneser—king of Assyria; is paid tribute by Hoshea of Israel

Abi—daughter of Zechariah; mother of Hezekiah

Sennacherib—king of Assyria

Rabshakeh—Assyrian diplomat

Eliakim—in charge of the palace for Hezekiah

Isaiah—prophet; son of Amoz; consulted by Hezekiah

Merodachbaladan—son of Baladan; king of Babylon; sends envoys to King Hezekiah

Hephzibah—mother of Manasseh

Meshullemeth—mother of Amon; daughter of Haruz

Jedidah—mother of Josiah; daughter of Adaiah

Hilkiah—high priest during Josiah's reign; finds book of the law in the Temple

Shaphan—secretary during Josiah's reign

Huldah—prophet; wife of Shallum; consulted by Josiah's officials

Pharaoh Neco—king of Egypt; kills Josiah at Megiddo

Hamutal—mother of Jehoahaz and Zedekiah; daughter of Jeremiah of Libnah

Zebidah—mother of Jehoiakim; daughter of Pedaiah

Nebuchadnezzar—king of Babylon

Nehushta—mother of Jehoiachin; daughter of Elnathan

Mattaniah—original name of Zedekiah; king of Judah

Nebuzaradan—captain of the bodyguard for Nebuchadnezzar

Seraiah—chief priest of Zedekiah

Gedaliah—son of Ahikam; appointed governor of Judah by the king of Babylon

Ishmael—son of Nethaniah; assassinates Gedaliah

Evilmerodach—king of Babylon

Foreign Deities

Baalzebub—god of Ekron

Baal—god of the Canaanites

Asherah—goddess

Key Concepts

Kingship—system of governance that includes the kings of Israel and Judah

Divided Monarchy—division of Israel into a northern and southern kingdom after the death of Solomon

Israel—northern kingdom

Judah—southern kingdom

Exile—forced removal of the people out of Jerusalem and Judah to live with their captors in Babylon

Important Quotations

"As they continued walking and talking, a chariot of fire and horses of fire separated the two of them, and Elijah ascended in a whirlwind into heaven. Elisha kept watching and crying out, 'Father, father! The chariots of Israel and its horsemen!' But when he could no longer see him, he grasped his own clothes and tore them into two pieces." (2 Kgs 2:11–12)

"He went up from there to Bethel; and while he was going up on the way, some small boys came out of the city and jeered at him, saying, 'Go away, baldhead! Go away, baldhead!' When he turned around and saw them, he cursed them in the name of the Lord. Then two she-bears came out of the woods and mauled forty-two of the boys." (2 Kgs 2:23–24)

"He did what was evil in the sight of the Lord." (statement found in many of the kings' stories in 2 Kings)

"The high priest Hilkiah said to Shaphan the secretary, 'I have found the book of the law in the house of the Lord.' When Hilkiah gave the book to Shaphan, he read it. . . . When the king heard the words of the book of the law, he tore his clothes." (2 Kgs 22:8, 11)

"The king of Babylon struck them down and put them to death at Riblah in the land of Hamath. So Judah went into exile out of its land." (2 Kgs 25:21)

Life of Elisha

- Elisha leaves home and becomes Elijah's servant (1 Kgs 19)
- Elisha witnesses Elijah's ascent to heaven in a whirlwind (2 Kgs 2)
- Elisha purifies bad water and curses small boys for jeering at him (2 Kgs 2)
- Elisha prophesies for Jehoram of Israel and Jehoshaphat of Judah (2 Kgs 3)
- Elisha provides a supply of oil to a widow in debt (2 Kgs 4)
- Elisha raises the Shunammite's son back to life (2 Kgs 4)
- Elisha purifies a pot of stew so that the company of prophets can eat it (2 Kgs 4)
- Elisha feeds a hundred people with only a little food (2 Kgs 4)
- Elisha cures Naaman, an Aramean, of leprosy (2 Kgs 5)
- Elisha causes a submerged iron ax head to float on water (2 Kgs 6)
- Elisha helps the king of Israel against the Arameans (2 Kgs 6–7)
- Elisha prophesies about King Ben-hadad (2 Kgs 8)
- Elisha tells a prophet to anoint Jehu as king (2 Kgs 9)
- Elisha dies (2 Kgs 13)

1 CHRONICLES

The books of 1 Chronicles and 2 Chronicles were originally one. The name of the book comes from Jerome and his Latin Vulgate translation. In the Hebrew canon, the book is named *Dibre Hayyamim*, which means "the matters of the days." Chronicles is the last book in the Jewish canon. Using genealogies, 1 Chronicles tells an abbreviated version of the biblical story starting with Adam, the first human, and running through Saul, the first king. Then the book focuses on David's reign. First Chronicles covers material from Genesis through 2 Samuel, although from a different theological perspective.

Synopsis

"Adam, Seth, Enosh, Kenan, Mahalalel . . ." The book of 1 Chronicles continues in this fashion for nine chapters, presenting a long genealogy that begins with Adam, the first person, and continues through to the community that existed after the Babylonian exile. The genealogy digresses briefly to explore the family of Saul, the first king. Chapter 10 begins with Saul's death in battle and continues with statements about his unfaithfulness to God; however, his reign is not the focus of this telling.

David is the subject of the remainder of the book. He was anointed king of Israel and established Jerusalem as the capital. A list of all his warriors and supporters demonstrated his widespread support. David brought the ark to Jerusalem and into the tent. He had thirteen children and defeated the Philistines. God established a covenant with David. David secured his kingdom by defeating various neighboring nations in multiple battles.

David wanted to build a temple for God and made preparations for it. He bought a threshing floor and set an altar where the temple would be built. Ultimately, he charged Solomon, his son, with building it. He gave the building plans to Solomon and received offerings from all the tribal leaders to construct the temple. He also provided construction materials. David made Solomon king. David died at the conclusion of the book.

Content Outline

Genealogies

Descendants from Adam to Jacob as well as Esau	1 Chronicles 1
Descendants from Israel to Caleb	1 Chronicles 2
Descendants of David and Solomon	1 Chronicles 3

Descendants of Judah and Simeon	1 Chronicles 4
Descendants of Reuben, Gad, and Manasseh	1 Chronicles 5
Descendants of Levi	1 Chronicles 6
Descendants of Issachar, Benjamin, Naphtali, Manasseh, Ephraim, and Asher	1 Chronicles 7
Descendants of Benjamin	1 Chronicles 8
People of Jerusalem's postexilic community; genealogy of King Saul	1 Chronicles 9

Stories about Saul

Saul and his sons die in battle with the Philistines; Saul's unfaithfulness to God	1 Chronicles 10

David Becomes King

David anointed king of all Israel; David establishes the capital in Jerusalem; David's warriors	1 Chronicles 11
More of David's warriors	1 Chronicles 12

Stories about the Ark

Ark of the covenant brought up	1 Chronicles 13
David has children and defeats the Philistines	1 Chronicles 14
Ark brought to Jerusalem	1 Chronicles 15
Ark brought into the tent; David sings praises	1 Chronicles 16

Davidic Covenant

God's covenant with David; David prays	1 Chronicles 17

David's Military Exploits

David defeats the Philistines, Moab, Zobah, Damascus, and Edom	1 Chronicles 18
David defeats the Ammonites and Arameans	1 Chronicles 19
David defeats the Ammonites and Philistines	1 Chronicles 20

David and the Temple

David takes a census; God sends a plague; David buys a threshing floor and builds an altar	1 Chronicles 21
David makes preparations to build the Temple; David tells Solomon to build it	1 Chronicles 22
List of Levites during David's time	1 Chronicles 23
David's priests	1 Chronicles 24
David's musicians	1 Chronicles 25
David's gatekeepers, treasurers, officers, and judges	1 Chronicles 26
David's army, tribal leaders, other officials	1 Chronicles 27
David gives Solomon the plans for the Temple	1 Chronicles 28
David and leaders give offerings to build the Temple; Solomon reigns; David dies	1 Chronicles 29

Content Unique to 1 Chronicles Compared to 2 Samuel

Preparations to bring the ark to Jerusalem; list of Levites (1 Chr 15)
Stories about David's preparations for the Temple (1 Chr 22)
David's speech to Solomon (1 Chr 22)
Levitical priestly lists (1 Chr 23)
David's priests, musicians, gatekeepers, army leaders, and other officials (1 Chr 24–27)
David's instructions to Solomon (1 Chr 28)
Offerings to build the Temple (1 Chr 29)

2 CHRONICLES

Second Chronicles was originally connected to 1 Chronicles as one biblical book. It tells the story of Solomon's reign and the Divided Monarchy with a focus on the kingdom of Judah. Much of this material is covered in 1 and 2 Kings.

Synopsis

Second Chronicles begins with Solomon's request to God for wisdom and God's gift of both wisdom and wealth. Solomon occupied himself with building the Temple. He prepared for construction by making an alliance with the king of Tyre. He built the temple and produced all the furnishings for it. He brought the ark into the Temple and made sacrifices to God. After Solomon dedicated the Temple, the glory of God filled it as a sign of God's acceptance. The queen of Sheba visited Solomon and commented on his wealth. At the end of his life, Solomon had accumulated great wealth.

After Solomon's death, the kingdom was divided by rivals to the throne—Jeroboam and Rehoboam, Solomon's son. Second Chronicles focuses on the almost uninterrupted line of Judahite rulers. Most prominent among these were Asa, Jehoshaphat, Joash, Hezekiah, and Josiah. The kings attempted to reform their kingdom. Many of the kings' reigns displayed a pattern of early faithfulness that was rewarded but that was followed by unfaithfulness, which led to judgment and/or death.

The book ends with the fall of Jerusalem and the words of Cyrus of Persia concerning the rebuilding of the temple in Jerusalem.

Content Outline

Solomon's Reign

Solomon asks God for wisdom; God gives wisdom and wealth	2 Chronicles 1
Solomon prepares to build the Temple and sends word to King Huram of Tyre	2 Chronicles 2
Solomon builds the Temple	2 Chronicles 3
Temple furnishings	2 Chronicles 4
Solomon brings the ark of the covenant to the Temple	2 Chronicles 5
Solomon dedicates the Temple with a speech and prayer	2 Chronicles 6
The glory of God fills the Temple; God appears to Solomon at night	2 Chronicles 7
Solomon's other building projects and activities	2 Chronicles 8
The queen of Sheba visits Solomon; Solomon's great wealth; Solomon dies	2 Chronicles 9

Divided Monarchy

Rebellion of Jeroboam against Rehoboam leads to two kingdoms	2 Chronicles 10
Rehoboam reigns in Jerusalem with priests' support; he marries and has children	2 Chronicles 11
Egypt attacks Rehoboam because he abandoned the ways of God; Rehoboam dies	2 Chronicles 12
Abijah reigns over Judah; war breaks out between Abijah and Jeroboam of Israel	2 Chronicles 13
Asa, Abijah's son, reigns; Ethiopians attack but are defeated	2 Chronicles 14
Asa's religious reforms	2 Chronicles 15
Asa makes an alliance with Aram; Hanani rebukes Asa; Asa's foot disease and death	2 Chronicles 16
Jehoshaphat, Asa's son, reigns	2 Chronicles 17
Jehoshaphat makes an alliance with King Ahab of Judah; Micaiah prophesies doom	2 Chronicles 18
Jehoshaphat's religious reforms	2 Chronicles 19
The Moabites and Ammonites attack Jehoshaphat; he prays, and God brings victory	2 Chronicles 20
Jehoram reigns; Elijah's letter of judgment; Jehoram's disease and death	2 Chronicles 21
Ahaziah, Jehoram's youngest son, reigns; Ahaziah dies; Athaliah takes the throne	2 Chronicles 22
Joash, Ahaziah's son, reigns at age seven; Athaliah is murdered	2 Chronicles 23
Joash restores the Temple; Joash is idolatrous; Joash dies	2 Chronicles 24
Amaziah, Joash's son, reigns; he defeats the Edomites and Judah; Amaziah dies	2 Chronicles 25
Uzziah, Amaziah's son, reigns; Uzziah's leprosy; Uzziah dies	2 Chronicles 26

Jotham, Uzziah's son, reigns	2 Chronicles 27
Ahaz, Jotham's son, reigns; he is defeated by Aram and Israel; Oded the prophet	2 Chronicles 28

Monarchy Reunited

Hezekiah, Ahaz's son, reigns; he restores the Temple and worship	2 Chronicles 29
Hezekiah invites all Israel and Judah to celebrate Passover	2 Chronicles 30
Hezekiah's religious reforms	2 Chronicles 31
King Sennacherib of Assyria attacks Judah but is defeated; Hezekiah's great riches	2 Chronicles 32
Manasseh, Hezekiah's son, reigns; Amon's reign	2 Chronicles 33
Josiah, Amon's son, reigns; Josiah finds a book of the law; Huldah's declaration	2 Chronicles 34
Josiah celebrates Passover; Josiah killed in battle against Egypt	2 Chronicles 35
Jehoahaz, Jehoiakim, Jehoiachin, and Zedekiah reign; Jerusalem falls; Cyrus liberates the exiles	2 Chronicles 36

Content Unique to 2 Chronicles Compared to 1 and 2 Kings

Rehoboam abandoned the law and then humbled himself (2 Chr 12:1, 12)
Abijah's speech (2 Chr 13:4–12)
Asa's religious reforms; Azariah's speech; Asa's response (2 Chr 14:3–14; 15:1–15)
Hanani, the prophet, rebukes Asa (2 Chr 16:7–10)
Jehoshaphat's reign (2 Chr 17:2–19)
Jehoshaphat's judicial reforms (2 Chr 19)
Jehoshaphat's battle against the Moabites and Ammonites (2 Chr 20:1–30)
Elijah's letter to Jehoram (2 Chr 21:12–15)
Amaziah defeats the Edomites (2 Chr 25:5–16)
Uzziah's reign (2 Chr 26:5–20)
Hezekiah's reforms (2 Chr 29:3–26; 30:1–27)
Hezekiah's blessings of wealth (2 Chr 32:25–30)
Manasseh repents (2 Chr 33:10–17)

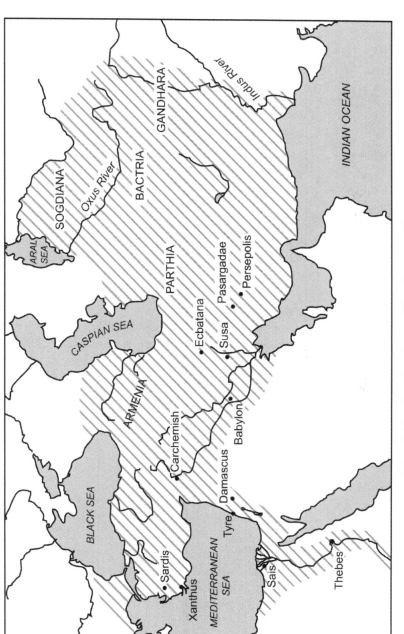

Map 4. Persian Empire and Its Greatest Extent

(Originally published in J. Maxwell Miller and John H. Hayes, *A History of Ancient Israel and Judah*, 2nd ed. [Louisville, KY: Westminster John Knox Press, 2006], 504.)

EZRA

Like 1 and 2 Chronicles, Ezra and Nehemiah originally formed one book called Ezra. In today's Bible, they are two separate books. Ezra is named after a main character in the narrative. The book focuses on the return of the exiles from Babylon and the rebuilding of the Temple.

Synopsis

God stirred the spirit of the Persian king, Cyrus, who declared that the exiles would be allowed to leave Babylon and return home to Judah, where they could rebuild the temple in Jerusalem. The people prepared themselves for the journey home, and Cyrus gave them the temple vessels to take with them. A long list of returning exiles is included at this point in the book.

Upon their return to Jerusalem, Jeshua and Zerubbabel led them to rebuild the altar, begin to offer sacrifices, and lay the foundation for the Temple. Some of the local people who did not go into exile, as well as the officials, did not want the Temple to be rebuilt. They delayed construction for several years until the prophets Haggai and Zechariah told the people to start rebuilding again. Opposition to rebuilding arose a second time. The Jews claimed they had permission from Cyrus to reconstruct the Temple many years before. A letter was written to King Darius of Persia to see if the returned exiles had permission to rebuild. Darius found the decree from Cyrus and told the people who opposed the building that the Jews could indeed rebuild the Temple. The Temple was completed and dedicated; the people celebrated Passover.

The story then turns to Ezra, a scribe and priest, who returned from Babylonia with a letter from King Artaxerxes of Persia. The letter gave Ezra the authority to investigate how the community in Judah was doing in regard to following the law. Ezra was also given the power to set up judges. He was accompanied to Judah by twelve large families. Before arriving in Jerusalem, Ezra noticed that there were no Levites among the group, so he requested Levites from a nearby town. The group fasted and prayed for God's protection while they journeyed toward Jerusalem. Ezra learned about the mixed marriages between the Israelites and "the peoples of the lands" and went into public mourning. He prayed, sharing his deep shame as well as gratitude for God's provision. The people swore to send all of the foreign wives and children away.

Content Outline

Exiles Return and Rebuild

Cyrus's edict concerning exiles returning to Jerusalem to rebuild; exiles return	Ezra 1
List of returning exiles, including priests, Levites, and temple servants	Ezra 2
Returning exiles rebuild the altar to sacrifice, lay the foundation of the Temple, and praise God	Ezra 3
Local people object to rebuilding the Temple, and the work is delayed for years	Ezra 4

Rebuilding of the Temple

Haggai and Zechariah initiate the rebuilding again	Ezra 5
Darius decrees that the Jews can rebuild the Temple; the Temple is dedicated; Passover is celebrated	Ezra 6

Ezra Returns to Jerusalem

Ezra comes to Jerusalem; Artaxerxes sends a letter with Ezra, giving him authority	Ezra 7
Family heads with Ezra; fasting and prayer; temple gifts; journey to Jerusalem	Ezra 8
Ezra mourns because Israelites took foreign wives; Ezra prays	Ezra 9
Ezra declares that the men must separate from their foreign wives and children; some obey	Ezra 10

People

Cyrus—king of Persia
Jeremiah—prophet who prophesied a seventy-year exile
Nebuchadnezzar—king of Babylon who took Judah into exile
Mithredath—treasurer
Sheshbazzar—prince of Judah
Jeshua—son of Jozadak; Zadokite priest; rebuilt the altar
Zerubbabel—son of Shealtiel; governor; rebuilt the altar

Darius—king of Persia
Ahasuerus/Xerxes—king of Persia
Artaxerxes—king of Persia
Rehum—royal deputy
Shimshai—scribe
Haggai—prophet
Zechariah—prophet; son of Iddo
Tattenai—governor of the province Beyond the River
Ezra—son of Seraiah; priest and scribe
Shecaniah—son of Jehiel; tells Ezra that the Israelites will send away their foreign wives

Places

Persia—empire that defeated the Babylonians and released the exiles
Jerusalem—place of the new temple
Babylonia—location of the exile

Key Concepts

Herald—messenger of the king
Edict—royal decree or statement
Second Temple—temple rebuilt after the Babylonian exile
Exiles—people who went to Babylon after the conquest of Judah
People of the land—probably refers to the people who did not go into exile
Mixed marriages—marriages between Jewish men and foreign women

Important Quotations

"Thus says King Cyrus of Persia: The LORD, the God of heaven, has given me all the kingdoms of the earth, and he has charged me to build him a house at Jerusalem in Judah." (Ezra 1:2)

"And they sang responsively, praising and giving thanks to the LORD, 'For he is good, for his steadfast love endures forever toward Israel.' And all the people responded with a great shout when they praised the LORD, because the foundation of the house of the LORD was laid." (Ezra 3:11)

"The people of Israel, the priests and the Levites, and the rest of the returned exiles, celebrated the dedication of this house of God with joy." (Ezra 6:16)

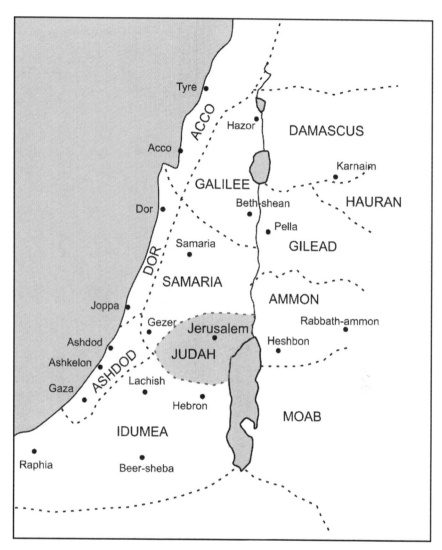

**Map 5. Persian Province of Judah among Other Provinces
beyond the River**

(Originally published in J. Maxwell Miller and John H. Hayes, *A History of Ancient
Israel and Judah*, 2nd ed. [Louisville, KY: Westminster John Knox Press, 2006], 530.)

"This Ezra went up from Babylonia. He was a scribe skilled in the law of
Moses that the LORD the God of Israel had given; and the king granted
him all that he asked, for the hand of the LORD his God was upon him."
(Ezra 7:6)

"For they have taken some of their daughters as wives for themselves and
for their sons. Thus the holy seed has mixed itself with the peoples of the
lands, and in this faithlessness the officials and leaders have led the way."
(Ezra 9:2)

"So now let us make a covenant with our God to send away all these wives
and their children, according to the counsel of my lord and of those who
tremble at the commandment of our God; and let it be done according to
the law." (Ezra 10:3)

NEHEMIAH

The book is titled after the main character. It focuses primarily on the rebuilding of the walls of Jerusalem and the repopulating of the city.

Synopsis

Nehemiah, a cupbearer in the king's court in Persia, learned from his brother
that the returned exiles in Jerusalem were in trouble. The city walls and gates
were destroyed. After fasting and praying, Nehemiah asked the king to send
him to Jerusalem to rebuild the walls of the city. After making the journey,
Nehemiah inspected the walls by night and found them in total disarray. He
exhorted the officials and priests to help him rebuild the walls, which they
agreed to do. Some of the governors accused him of rebelling against the king
of Persia by rebuilding the walls, but Nehemiah assured them that God would
give him success.

In the process of rebuilding the walls, some opposition and threats
occurred. Nehemiah appointed troops to guard the builders, and many of the
builders worked with a weapon in one hand. The people began to complain
about the government, and Nehemiah had to act as a negotiator to gain relief.
He served as governor in Judah for twelve years. His enemies, Tobiah and
Sanballat, tried to lure Nehemiah away from the city so that they could harm
him, but he refused to go. They hired the prophet Shemaiah to trick Nehemiah into hiding in the Temple, but Nehemiah realized that Shemaiah was a
false prophet. Finally, the walls were completed.

Nehemiah gave his brother, Hanani, control over Jerusalem and populated the city with the returned exiles. Ezra stood and read from the book of the law of Moses while the people listened. He declared a holy day of celebration. The people celebrated the Festival of Booths for the first time since the days of Joshua.

Soon thereafter, the people held a fast day. Ezra prayed, mentioning God's care for them in the past and complaining about their current situation as slaves in their own land. The people made a firm agreement to observe the commandments and to support the Temple.

The people agreed to move 10 percent of the population into the city of Jerusalem, with the others staying in their towns and villages. They dedicated the walls and established certain temple duties. Finally, the foreigners were separated from Israel.

Nehemiah came back to Jerusalem later and found the Temple and the Levites were not functioning properly, so he changed some of the activities and corrected some of the Sabbath violations. Nehemiah also condemned the people who were married to foreign women and expelled one of them from the community.

Content Outline

Israelites fast; Ezra prays; firm agreement is made	Nehemiah 9
List of people who signed the agreement; terms of the agreement	Nehemiah 10
List of the 10 percent of the people who moved to Jerusalem	Nehemiah 11
List of priests and Levites; dedication of the walls	Nehemiah 12
Foreigners are separated from Israel; Nehemiah's reforms	Nehemiah 13

People

Nehemiah—son of Hacaliah; cupbearer of the Persian king
Hanani—brother of Nehemiah
Artaxerxes—king of Persia
Unnamed queen of Persia
Asaph—keeper of the king's forest
Sanballat—governor of Samaria
Tobiah—governor of Ammon
Geshem—king of Kedar
Shallum's daughters—only women mentioned as repairers of the city walls
Shemaiah—prophet hired by Tobiah and Sanballat to trick Nehemiah
Hananiah—commander of the citadel
Ezra—scribe and priest
Eliashib—priest appointed over the chambers of the Temple

Places

Susa—Persian city
Jerusalem—city whose walls and gates were rebuilt
Judah—Nehemiah's homeland

Key Concepts

Mixed marriages—marriages between Jewish men and foreign women
Exile—period when the Babylonians took many Israelites into captivity
Temple walls—physical, protective walls around the city that were destroyed by the Babylonians
Passover—Jewish festival

Important Quotations

"They replied, 'The survivors there in the province who escaped captivity are in great trouble and shame; the wall of Jerusalem is broken down, and its gates have been destroyed by fire.'" (Neh 1:3)

"Then I said to them, 'You see the trouble we are in, how Jerusalem lies in ruins with its gates burned. Come, let us rebuild the wall of Jerusalem, so that we many no longer suffer disgrace.'" (Neh 2:17)

"So the wall was finished on the twenty-fifth day of the month Elul, in fifty-two days. And when all our enemies heard of it, all the nations around us were afraid and fell greatly in their own esteem; for they perceived that this work had been accomplished with the help of our God." (Neh 6:15–16)

"They told the scribe Ezra to bring the book of the law of Moses, which the LORD had given to Israel. Accordingly, the priest Ezra brought the law before the assembly, both men and women and all who could hear with understanding. This was the first day of the seventh month. He read from it facing the square before the Water Gate from early morning until midday, in the presence of the men and the women and those who could understand; and the ears of all the people were attentive to the book of the law." (Neh 8:1b–3)

"Now the leaders of the people lived in Jerusalem; and the rest of the people cast lots to bring one out of ten to live in the holy city Jerusalem, while nine-tenths remained in the other towns. And the people blessed all those who willingly offered to live in Jerusalem." (Neh 11:1–2)

"Now at the dedication of the wall of Jerusalem they sought out the Levites in all their places, to bring them to Jerusalem to celebrate the dedication with rejoicing, with thanksgivings and with singing, with cymbals, harps, and lyres." (Neh 12:27)

"In those days also I saw Jews who had married women of Ashdod, Ammon, and Moab; and half of their children spoke the language of Ashdod, and they could not speak the language of Judah, but spoke the language of various peoples. And I contended with them and cursed them and beat some of them and pulled out their hair; and I made them take an oath in the name of God, saying, 'You shall not give your daughters to their sons, or take their daughters for your sons or for yourselves.'" (Neh 13:23–25)

ESTHER

Esther is the last book in the Historical Books section of the Protestant Bible. It is named after its main character, a Jewish woman who becomes a Persian queen.

Synopsis

King Ahasuerus gave a lavish banquet that lasted half a year, followed by a smaller banquet that lasted a week. There was much drinking during this banquet. Ahasuerus called Queen Vashti to come before him so that the officials and people of Susa could see her beauty. Vashti refused to come. In humiliation, he consulted the sages, who advised him to banish her for disobeying him.

Ahasuerus searched for another queen. Esther, a Jewish woman who, after the death of her parents, had been adopted by her cousin, Mordecai, was brought into the court. Esther won the favor of Hegai, the eunuch in charge of the king's harem, and was brought to the king. The king loved her more than all the other women and made her queen, not knowing she was a Jew. Ahasuerus gave a banquet in her honor. Mordecai learned of a plot by two eunuchs to kill the king and told Esther, who then told the king. Both men were hanged. Haman received a promotion to high official in the court of Ahasuerus. Mordecai refused to bow down to Haman. Haman learned that Mordecai was a Jew and devised a plan to kill all Jews throughout the kingdom. Haman convinced the king to write letters to the provinces with the order that all the Jews should be killed. Mordecai learned of the plan and mourned. He told Esther that she was in the position to influence the king. Esther decided to fast before approaching the king about the matter.

Esther held a banquet and invited both Ahasuerus and Haman. When the king asked about her request, she invited them both to another banquet the following day. Meanwhile, Haman was still upset at Mordecai and asked his advisers and wife what he should do. They told him to construct gallows and tell the king to have Mordecai hanged the next day.

In the middle of the night, the king could not sleep and asked that the record books be read to him. When he heard about Mordecai's earlier help with the assassination plot by the two eunuchs, he decided to honor Mordecai. He asked Haman how exactly he should go about honoring someone who had performed a favorable deed toward the king. Haman, thinking the king wished to honor him, answered that the person should receive royal robes, a horse, and a royal crown; he should then be paraded around the open city square. The king immediately responded that Haman should quickly do all of this for the Jew Mordecai. Haman complied, then returned to his home humiliated.

At the banquet, Esther made the request to the king for her people to be spared. When the king asked who had devised the plan to kill the Jews, Esther pointed to Haman. The king became very angry and left the banquet. When he returned, he saw Haman at the couch where Esther was reclining and assumed he was assaulting her. The king ordered Haman to be hanged on the gallows prepared for Mordecai. Esther received the house of Haman and gave it to Mordecai. Esther also requested that the king write to the provinces of the kingdom declaring that the Jews could defend themselves against any attacking forces.

Over the next two days, the Jews struck down their enemies. They established the Festival of Purim to celebrate the end of the fighting.

Content Outline

People

Ahasuerus—king of Persia
Vashti—queen of Persia
Mehuman, Biztha, Harbona, Bigtha, Abagtha, Zethar, and Carkas—seven eunuchs who assist the king
Carshena, Shethar, Admatha, Tarshish, Meres, Marsena, and Memucan—seven sages of the king
Hegai—king's eunuch; in charge of the king's harem in Susa
Mordecai—son of Jair; Benjaminite
Hadassah/Esther—Jewish woman; Mordecai's cousin; daughter of Abihail; becomes Persian queen
Shaashgaz—king's eunuch; in charge of the king's concubines
Bigthan and Teresh—two of the king's eunuchs who conspire to assassinate the king
Haman—son of Hammedatha, the Agagite; an official who wants to get rid of the Jews
Hathach—king's eunuch who attends to Esther
Zeresh—Haman's wife

Places

Susa—one of the capitals of Persia

Key Concepts

Laws of the Persians and the Medes—known to be unalterable laws
Purim—Jewish festival that celebrates victory over the Jews' enemies

Important Quotations

"Mordecai had brought up Hadassah, that is Esther, his cousin, for she had neither father nor mother; the girl was fair and beautiful, and when her father and her mother died, Mordecai adopted her as his own daughter." (Esther 2:7)

"The king loved Esther more than all the other women; of all the virgins she won his favor and devotion, so that he set the royal crown on her head and made her queen instead of Vashti." (Esther 2:17)

"So, having been told who Mordecai's people were, Haman plotted to destroy all the Jews, the people of Mordecai, throughout the whole kingdom of Ahasuerus." (Esther 3:6b)

"For if you keep silence at such a time as this, relief and deliverance will rise for the Jews from another quarter, but you and your father's family will perish. Who knows? Perhaps you have come to royal dignity for just such a time as this." (Esther 4:14)

"Then Queen Esther answered, 'If I have won your favor, O king, and if it pleases the king, let my life be given me—that is my petition—and the lives of my people—that is my request.'" (Esther 7:3)

"Haman son of Hammedatha the Agagite, the enemy of all the Jews, had plotted against the Jews to destroy them, and had cast Pur—that is 'the lot'—to crush and destroy them; but when Esther came before the king, he gave orders in writing that the wicked plot that he had devised against the Jews should come upon his own head, and that he and his sons should be hanged on the gallows. Therefore these days are called Purim, from the word Pur. Thus because of all that was written in this letter, and of what they had faced in this matter, and of what had happened to them." (Esther 9:24–26)

3

The Poetic Books

The Poetic Books—Job, Psalms, Proverbs, Ecclesiastes, and the Song of Songs—are grouped together not because they tell a coherent story but because of their abundant use of poetry. These five books stand outside of the basic chronological framework of Genesis to Esther, that is, the story that originates with the beginning of the world and ends during the Persian period. Furthermore, they are not prophetic books. The category is based on genre: it is difficult to find a common literary or theological theme shared by all five other than their use of poetry.

JOB

The biblical book is named after its main character.

Synopsis

Job, a man with ten children, many animals, and many servants, was blameless and upright. One day, God and Satan were conversing. God pointed to Job as an example of a righteous person. Satan suggested that Job only feared God because God had protected and blessed him. God agreed to test Job. Job lost all his property and even his children through human and natural forces. Job responded by mourning and worshiping, but not by sinning or charging God with any wrongdoing. Satan convinced God to allow Job to suffer more, and Job developed sores all over his body. His wife suggested he should curse God, but Job did not sin amid his troubles. Three friends heard of Job's situation and traveled to be with him in his troubles and suffering.

After a week of sitting with his friends in silence, Job finally spoke to curse the day of his birth. His friends took turns speaking to Job, and Job replied to each. The friends accused Job of wrongdoing, suggested his troubles were punishment for his sin, and called him to recognize that God's ways were not understandable to humans. The friends presented traditional understandings of God's actions in the world and the presence of suffering. Job replied by noting the dejected situation of his life. He could not find peace; he hated his life. Wicked people went unpunished, but Job, who was guiltless, lost everything.

Finally, God answered Job from a whirlwind with an extended series of questions about Job's participation in creation and control of nature. Job responded by acknowledging that God could do all things and that Job had talked about things he could not understand. Job repented.

In the closing verses of the book, God told Job's friends they were wrong and that Job was right about God. The friends were instructed to take sacrifices to Job and were told that Job would pray for them. Job did so, and God accepted his prayer. God restored Job's fortunes twofold. Job again had ten children and many animals. After a long life, Job died.

Content Outline

Job and his household; Satan and God talk; Job loses property and children	Job 1
Satan and God talk again; Job is inflicted with sores; three friends visit him	Job 2
Job curses the day of his birth	Job 3
Eliphaz's first speech	Job 4–5
Job replies to Eliphaz	Job 6–7
Bildad's first speech	Job 8
Job replies to Bildad	Job 9–10
Zophar's first speech	Job 11
Job replies to Zophar	Job 12–14
Eliphaz's second speech	Job 15
Job replies to Eliphaz	Job 16–17
Bildad's second speech	Job 18
Job replies to Bildad	Job 19
Zophar's second speech	Job 20

Job replies to Zophar	Job 21
Eliphaz's third speech	Job 22
Job replies to Eliphaz	Job 23–24
Bildad's third speech	Job 25
Job replies to Bildad	Job 26–27
Job's speech about wisdom	Job 28
Job's speech	Job 29–31
Elihu's speeches	Job 32–37
God answers out of the whirlwind	Job 38–40
Job responds	Job 40
God answers again	Job 40–41
Job responds	Job 42
Job's friends are humiliated; Job's fortunes and family are restored; Job dies	Job 42

People

Job—main character; blameless and upright man
Job's seven unnamed sons—killed when a wind causes a house to fall on them
Job's three unnamed daughters—killed when a wind causes a house to fall on them
Heavenly beings—literally "sons of God"; present themselves to God
Satan—literally "the Accuser"; converses with God
Sabeans—people from southern Arabia
Chaldeans—people from Mesopotamia
Job's unnamed wife—encourages Job to curse God
Eliphaz the Temanite—Job's friend
Bildad the Shuhite—Job's friend
Zophar the Naamathite—Job's friend
Elihu—son of Barachel the Buzite

Places

Land of Uz—Job's homeland and the setting of the entire book

Key Concepts

Suffering—major theme that describes the travails of the righteous
Friendship—Job's friends sit with him and offer him advice
Poetry—primary literary form of the book of Job

Important Quotations

"Naked I came from my mother's womb, and naked shall I return there; the LORD gave, and the LORD has taken away; blessed be the name of the LORD." (Job 1:21)

"Then his wife said to him, 'Do you still persist in your integrity? Curse God, and die.'" (Job 2:9)

"Let the day perish in which I was born, and the night that said, 'A man-child is conceived.'" (Job 3:3)

"Think now, who that was innocent ever perished? Or where were the upright cut off? As I have seen, those who plow iniquity and sow trouble reap the same." (Job 4:7–8)

"I am a laughingstock to my friends; I, who called upon God and he answered me, a just and blameless man, I am a laughingstock." (Job 12:4)

"I know that my Redeemer lives, and that at the last he will stand upon the earth." (Job 19:25)

"Who is this that darkens counsel by words without knowledge? . . . Where were you when I laid the foundation of the earth? Tell me, if you have understanding." (Job 38:2, 4; God speaking to Job)

"I know that you can do all things, and that no purpose of yours can be thwarted. 'Who is this that hides counsel without knowledge?' Therefore I have uttered what I did not understand, things too wonderful for me, which I did not know." (Job 42:2–3)

"I had heard of you by the hearing of the ear, but now my eye sees you." (Job 42:5)

"And the LORD restored the fortunes of Job when he had prayed for his friends; and the LORD gave Job twice as much as he had before." (Job 42:10)

PSALMS

The Hebrew title for this collection of 150 individual psalms is *Tehillim*, which means "praises." The musical poems offer praise to God as well as lament and thanksgiving. The Septuagint provided the eventual English title through its title, *Psalmoi*, a Greek word meaning "instrumental songs."

Synopsis

The book of Psalms has no plot to summarize, no narrative to recall. It is a collection of 150 prayers and songs that give praise to God, Zion, and the king; give thanks to God and ask God for deliverance; announce trust in God; and petition God. The psalms are both communal and individual prayers.

Content Outline

Happy are those who delight in God's instructions	Psalm 1
"I have set my king on Zion, my holy hill"	Psalm 2
I have many foes, but God is a shield around me	Psalm 3
Answer me in my distress	Psalm 4
"Lead me, O Lord, in your righteousness because of my enemies"	Psalm 5
Healing and deliverance from illness	Psalm 6
"Lift yourself up against the fury of my enemies"	Psalm 7
"How majestic is your name in all the earth"	Psalm 8
"When my enemies turned back, they stumbled and perished before you"	Psalm 9
"Why, O Lord, do you stand far off?"	Psalm 10
Trust and refuge in God who dwells in the holy temple	Psalm 11
"Help, O Lord, for there is no longer anyone who is godly"	Psalm 12
"How long, O Lord? Will you forget me forever?"	Psalm 13
Fools say there is no God	Psalm 14
The blameless shall dwell in God's temple	Psalm 15

"In your presence there is fullness of joy; in your right hand are pleasures forevermore"	Psalm 16
"Guard me as the apple of the eye"	Psalm 17
Thanksgiving for victory	Psalm 18
"The heavens are telling the glory of God"	Psalm 19
"The LORD answer you in the day of trouble!"	Psalm 20
"In your strength the king rejoices, O LORD, and in your help how greatly he exults!"	Psalm 21
"My God, my God, why have you forsaken me?"	Psalm 22
"The LORD is my shepherd, I shall not want"	Psalm 23
"Lift up your heads, O gates! . . . that the King of glory may come in"	Psalm 24
"Make me to know your ways, O LORD; teach me your paths"	Psalm 25
"Vindicate me, O LORD, for I have walked in my integrity"	Psalm 26
"The LORD is my light and my salvation; whom shall I fear?"	Psalm 27
"Hear the voice of my supplication, as I cry to you for help"	Psalm 28
"The voice of the LORD is powerful; the voice of the LORD is full of majesty"	Psalm 29
"O LORD my God, I cried to you for help, and you have healed me"	Psalm 30
"You are indeed my rock and my fortress"	Psalm 31
"Happy are those whose transgression is forgiven, whose sin is covered"	Psalm 32
"For the word of the LORD is upright, and all his work is done in faithfulness"	Psalm 33
"I sought the LORD, and he answered me, and delivered me from all my fears"	Psalm 34
"Contend, O LORD, with those who contend with me"	Psalm 35
"Transgression speaks to the wicked deep in their hearts"	Psalm 36
"Trust in the LORD, and do good; so you will live in the land, and enjoy security"	Psalm 37

"O LORD, do not rebuke me in your anger"	Psalm 38
"And now, O LORD, what do I wait for? My hope is in you"	Psalm 39
"I waited patiently for the LORD; he inclined to me and heard my cry"	Psalm 40
"Happy are those who consider the poor; the LORD delivers them in the day of trouble"	Psalm 41
"As a deer longs for flowing streams, so my soul longs for you, O God"	Psalm 42
"Vindicate me, O God, and defend my cause against an ungodly people"	Psalm 43
"Rise up, come to our help. Redeem us for the sake of your steadfast love."	Psalm 44
"In your majesty ride on victoriously for the cause of truth and to defend the right"	Psalm 45
"God is our refuge and strength, a very present help in trouble"	Psalm 46
"God is king over the nations; God sits on his holy throne"	Psalm 47
"Great is the LORD and greatly to be praised in the city of our God"	Psalm 48
Do not trust in riches, for the rich will die	Psalm 49
Offer God a sacrifice of thanksgiving	Psalm 50
"Create in me a clean heart, O God, and put a new and right spirit within me"	Psalm 51
"The righteous will see, and fear, and will laugh at the evildoer"	Psalm 52
"Fools say in their hearts, 'There is no God'"	Psalm 53
"Save me, O God, by your name, and vindicate me by your might"	Psalm 54
It is not my enemy who taunts me, but my friend	Psalm 55
"Be gracious to me, O God, for people trample on me"	Psalm 56
"He will send from heaven and save me, he will put to shame those who trample on me"	Psalm 57

"O God, break the teeth in their mouths; tear out the fangs of the young lions, O LORD"	Psalm 58
"Deliver me from my enemies, O my God"	Psalm 59
"O God, you have rejected us, broken our defenses. . . . Now restore us."	Psalm 60
"Lead me to the rock that is higher than I"	Psalm 61
"For God alone my soul waits in silence; from him comes my salvation"	Psalm 62
"O God, you are my God, I seek you, my soul thirsts for you"	Psalm 63
"Hear my voice, O God, in my complaint; preserve my life from the dread enemy"	Psalm 64
"By awesome deeds you answer us with deliverance, O God of our salvation"	Psalm 65
"Make a joyful noise to God, all the earth; sing the glory of his name"	Psalm 66
"May God be gracious to us and bless us and make his face to shine upon us"	Psalm 67
"Let God rise up, let his enemies be scattered; let those who hate him flee before him"	Psalm 68
"Save me, O God, for the waters have come up to my neck"	Psalm 69
"Be pleased, O God, to deliver me. O LORD, make haste to help me."	Psalm 70
"In you, O LORD, I take refuge; let me never be put to shame"	Psalm 71
"Give the king your justice, O God, and your righteousness to a king's son"	Psalm 72
"Truly God is good to the upright, to those who are pure in heart"	Psalm 73
"O God, why do you cast us off forever?"	Psalm 74
"We give thanks to you, O God; we give thanks; your name is near"	Psalm 75
"His abode has been established in Salem, his dwelling place in Zion"	Psalm 76

"I will call to mind the deeds of the Lord; I will remember your wonders of old"	Psalm 77
God's guidance and the people's distrust	Psalm 78
"O God, the nations have come into your inheritance; they have defiled your holy temple"	Psalm 79
"Restore us, O God; let your face shine, that we may be saved"	Psalm 80
"Sing aloud to God our strength; shout for joy to the God of Jacob"	Psalm 81
"Rise up, O God, judge the earth; for all the nations belong to you"	Psalm 82
"Fill their faces with shame, so that they may seek your name, O Lord"	Psalm 83
"How lovely is your dwelling place, O Lord of hosts!"	Psalm 84
"Lord, you were favorable to your land; you restored the fortunes of Jacob"	Psalm 85
"Incline your ear, O Lord, and answer me, for I am poor and needy"	Psalm 86
"The Lord loves the gates of Zion more than all the dwellings of Jacob"	Psalm 87
"But I, O Lord, cry out to you; in the morning my prayer comes before you"	Psalm 88
"You said, 'I have made a covenant with my chosen one, . . . my servant David'"	Psalm 89
"Lord, you have been our dwelling place in all generations"	Psalm 90
"You who live in the shelter of the Most High, who abide in the shadow of the Almighty"	Psalm 91
"It is good to give thanks to the Lord, to sing praises to your name"	Psalm 92
"The Lord is king, he is robed in majesty"	Psalm 93
"O Lord, you God of vengeance, you God of vengeance, shine forth!"	Psalm 94

"O come, let us sing to the LORD; let us make a joyful noise to the rock of our salvation!"	Psalm 95
"O sing to the LORD a new song; sing to the LORD, all the earth"	Psalm 96
"The LORD is king! Let the earth rejoice"	Psalm 97
"O sing to the LORD a new song, for he has done marvelous things"	Psalm 98
"The LORD is king; let the peoples tremble!"	Psalm 99
"Make a joyful noise to the LORD, all the earth"	Psalm 100
"I will sing of loyalty and of justice; to you, O LORD, I will sing"	Psalm 101
"Hear my prayer, O LORD; let my cry come to you"	Psalm 102
"Bless the LORD, O my soul, and all that is within me, bless his holy name"	Psalm 103
"O LORD, how manifold are your works!"	Psalm 104
"O give thanks to the LORD, call on his name"	Psalm 105
"Both we and our ancestors have sinned"	Psalm 106
"O give thanks to the LORD, for he is good; for his steadfast love endures forever"	Psalm 107
"Be exalted, O God, above the heavens, and let your glory be over all the earth"	Psalm 108
"Help me, O LORD my God! Save me according to your steadfast love"	Psalm 109
"The Lord is at your right hand; he will shatter kings on the day of his wrath"	Psalm 110
"Great are the works of the LORD, studied by all who delight in them"	Psalm 111
"Happy are those who fear the LORD, who greatly delight in his commandments"	Psalm 112
"He raises the poor from the dust, and lifts the needy from the ash heap"	Psalm 113

"Judah became God's sanctuary, Israel his dominion"	Psalm 114
"Not to us, O Lord, not to us, but to your name give glory"	Psalm 115
"I love the Lord, because he has heard my voice and my supplications"	Psalm 116
"Praise the Lord, all you nations! Extol him, all you peoples!"	Psalm 117
"O give thanks to the Lord, for he is good; his steadfast love endures forever"	Psalm 118
"Happy are those whose way is blameless, who walk in the law of the Lord"	Psalm 119
"In my distress I cry to the Lord, that he may answer me"	Psalm 120
"I lift up my eyes to the hills—from where will my help come?"	Psalm 121
"I was glad when they said to me, 'Let us go to the house of the Lord!'"	Psalm 122
"Have mercy upon us, O Lord, have mercy upon us"	Psalm 123
"If it had not been the Lord who was on our side . . ."	Psalm 124
"Those who trust in the Lord are like Mount Zion, which cannot be moved"	Psalm 125
"When the Lord restored the fortunes of Zion, we were like those who dream"	Psalm 126
"Unless the Lord builds the house, those who build it labor in vain"	Psalm 127
"Happy is everyone who fears the Lord, who walks in his ways"	Psalm 128
"May all who hate Zion be put to shame and turned backward"	Psalm 129
"I wait for the Lord, my soul waits, and in his word I hope"	Psalm 130
"O Israel, hope in the Lord from this time on and forevermore"	Psalm 131
"O Lord, remember in David's favor all the hardships he endured"	Psalm 132

"How very good and pleasant it is when kindred live together in unity"	Psalm 133
"Come, bless the LORD, all you servants of the LORD"	Psalm 134
"Praise the LORD, for the LORD is good; sing to his name, for he is gracious"	Psalm 135
"For his steadfast love endures forever"	Psalm 136
"By the rivers of Babylon—there we sat down and there we wept"	Psalm 137
"I give you thanks, O LORD, with my whole heart"	Psalm 138
"O LORD, you have searched me and known me"	Psalm 139
"Deliver me, O LORD, from evildoers; protect me from those who are violent"	Psalm 140
"Let the wicked fall into their own nets, while I alone escape"	Psalm 141
"With my voice I cry to the LORD; with my voice I make supplication to the LORD"	Psalm 142
"Save me, O LORD, from my enemies; I have fled to you for refuge"	Psalm 143
"Blessed be the LORD, my rock, who trains my hands for war"	Psalm 144
"I will extol you, my God and King, and bless your name forever and ever"	Psalm 145
"Happy are those whose help is the God of Jacob"	Psalm 146
"The LORD builds up Jerusalem; he gathers the outcasts of Israel"	Psalm 147
"Praise the LORD from the earth, you sea monsters and all deeps"	Psalm 148
"Sing to the LORD a new song, his praise in the assembly of the faithful"	Psalm 149
"Praise God in his sanctuary; praise him in his mighty firmament"	Psalm 150

People

David—73 psalms associated with him
Asaphites—12 psalms associated with them
Korahites—11 psalms associated with them
Jeduthun—3 psalms associated with him
Solomon—2 psalms associated with him
Heman the Ezrahite—1 psalm associated with him
Ethan the Ezrahite—1 psalm associated with him
Moses—1 psalm associated with him

Places

Zion/Jerusalem—capital of Israel

Key Concepts

Zion—city of Jerusalem; often praised in the psalms
Praise—psalms that celebrate and honor God, Zion, or the king
Lament—psalms written from the perspective of an individual or community in mourning
Thanksgiving—psalms written from the perspective of an individual or community that give thanks
Blessings—psalms that call for the people to bless God
Complaint—psalms that offer objections to God
Wisdom—psalms associated with wisdom themes
Petitions—psalms that make requests of God
Royal—psalms that depict the king as God's earthly representative
Trust—psalms that encourage people to trust in God
Liturgy—psalms used in worship
Poetry—literary form in which all psalms are written

PROVERBS

The Hebrew book title is *Mishlei*, which means "proverbs."

Synopsis

The book of Proverbs begins with words about wisdom and knowledge. The instructions, given in a parental and educational fashion, detail the value and benefit of seeking wisdom. The reader is admonished to walk in the way of wisdom and not on the foolish path. Wisdom is personified as a woman who was present at the creation of the world.

The book transitions to long sections of wisdom sayings or sentences constructed in brief two-line verses.

Content Outline

The beginning of wisdom; enticement of fools; Wisdom cries in the streets	Proverbs 1
The benefits of wisdom	Proverbs 2
Trust God; wisdom is better than gold; wisdom keeps you secure	Proverbs 3
A father's instructions about wisdom; walk in the path of wisdom	Proverbs 4
Warnings about a strange woman; be faithful to your wife	Proverbs 5
Financial instructions; more instructions about another man's wife	Proverbs 6
Warnings about a strange woman	Proverbs 7
Wisdom calls; Wisdom at creation	Proverbs 8
Wisdom sets the table; the foolish woman also invites people	Proverbs 9
Wise sayings of Solomon	Proverbs 10–22
Words of the wise	Proverbs 22–24
More wise sayings of Solomon	Proverbs 25–29
Words of Agur	Proverbs 30
King Lemuel's words, which his mother taught him	Proverbs 31
A capable woman	Proverbs 31

People

Solomon—son of David, king of Israel
Woman Wisdom—personification of wisdom as a woman

Agur—son of Jakeh
King Lemuel—unknown king
King Lemuel's mother

Key Concepts

Wisdom—Proverbs is a book of sayings about wise behavior and character
Woman Wisdom—Wisdom is personified in Proverbs as a woman
Capable woman—Proverbs concludes with praise of this woman
Foolish—characters who are not wise in Proverbs
Creation—Wisdom was present at creation of the world
Poetry—literary form in which Proverbs is written

Important Quotations

"The fear of the LORD is the beginning of knowledge; fools despise wisdom and instruction." (Prov 1:7)

"Trust in the LORD with all your heart, and do not rely on your own insight. In all your ways acknowledge him, and he will make straight your paths." (Prov 3:5–6)

"Get wisdom; get insight; do not forget, nor turn away from the words of my mouth." (Prov 4:5)

"Does not wisdom call, and does not understanding raise her voice?" (Prov 8:1)

"Take my instruction instead of silver, and knowledge rather than choice gold; for wisdom is better than jewels, and all that you may desire cannot compare with her." (Prov 8:10–11)

"The LORD created me at the beginning of his work, the first of his acts of long ago." (Prov 8:22)

"A soft answer turns away wrath, but a harsh word stirs up anger." (Prov 15:1)

"Better is a little with righteousness than large income with injustice." (Prov 16:8)

"Pride goes before destruction, and a haughty spirit before a fall." (Prov 16:18)

"A good name is to be chosen rather than great riches, and favor is better than silver or gold." (Prov 22:1)

"Train children in the right way, and when old, they will not stray." (Prov 22:6)

"If your enemies are hungry, give them bread to eat; and if they are thirsty, give them water to drink; for you will heap coals of fire on their heads, and the LORD will reward you." (Prov 25:21–22)

"Do not boast about tomorrow, for you do not know what a day may bring." (Prov 27:1)

"A capable wife who can find? She is far more precious than jewels." (Prov 31:10)

ECCLESIASTES

The Hebrew title for this book is *Qohelet*, which means "the gatherer" or "the teacher." The English title, Ecclesiastes, comes from the Greek translation of the Hebrew title.

Synopsis

Ecclesiastes does not contain a well-defined plot or structure. The book begins with the well-known adage that "all is vanity." Nothing seems to change, and seeking wisdom is only vanity. Taking pleasure does not result in any gain. There is a season for everything, but only God can determine it. People should fulfill their vows to God, and enjoy life and work.

The book contains proverbs about wisdom and riddles about righteousness. The reader is told to obey the king and keep the commandments. Nothing can be known of the future because the world is uncertain.

Content Outline

There is nothing new under the sun; wisdom is vanity	Ecclesiastes 1
Pleasure is pointless and vexing; wisdom and folly both end in death	Ecclesiastes 2
There is a time for everything; enjoy your work because all will die	Ecclesiastes 3
Oppression exists; envy brings toil; two are better than one	Ecclesiastes 4
Fulfill vows to God; oppression by the rich; enjoy life and work	Ecclesiastes 5

The rich do not enjoy their riches; greed does not go unanswered	Ecclesiastes 6
Proverbs about wisdom and sorrow; riddles about righteousness and wisdom	Ecclesiastes 7
Obey the king; all will die; the wicked and the righteous; enjoy life	Ecclesiastes 8
Everything comes to the same fate; enjoy life; wisdom is better than might	Ecclesiastes 9
Wisdom and folly sayings; guard your thoughts and speech about the king	Ecclesiastes 10
The world is uncertain; you do not know what will happen; old age and youth	Ecclesiastes 11
Remember the creator before your old age; all is vanity; fear God, and keep the commandments	Ecclesiastes 12

People

The Teacher—sometimes translated "Preacher"; son of David

Key Concepts

Vanity—everything is transitory and fleeting
Folly—opposite of wisdom
Fear of God—reverence for God
Wisdom—Ecclesiastes contains wisdom literature; wisdom is also portrayed as superior to folly
Enjoyment—people are encouraged to enjoy life

Important Quotations

"Vanity of vanities, says the Teacher, vanity of vanities! All is vanity." (Eccl 1:2)

"What has been is what will be, and what has been done is what will be done; there is nothing new under the sun." (Eccl 1:9)

"For in much wisdom is much vexation, and those who increase knowledge increase sorrow." (Eccl 1:18)

"There is nothing better for mortals than to eat and drink, and find enjoyment in their toil." (Eccl 2:24)

"For everything there is a season, and a time for every matter under heaven: a time to be born, and a time to die; a time to plant, and a time to pluck up what is planted; a time to kill, and a time to heal; a time to break down, and a time to build up; a time to weep, and a time to laugh; a time to mourn, and a time to dance; a time to throw away stones, and a time to gather stones together; a time to embrace, and a time to refrain from embracing; a time to seek, and a time to lose; a time to keep, and a time to throw away; a time to tear, and a time to sew; a time to keep silence, and a time to speak; a time to love, and a time to hate; a time for war, and a time for peace." (Eccl 3:1–8)

"Two are better than one, because they have a good reward for their toil." (Eccl 4:9)

"As they came from their mother's womb, so they shall go again, naked as they came; they shall take nothing for their toil, which they may carry away with their hands." (Eccl 5:15)

"A good name is better than precious ointment, and the day of death, than the day of birth." (Eccl 7:1)

"The quiet words of the wise are more to be heeded than the shouting of a ruler among fools." (Eccl 9:17)

"Dead flies make the perfumer's ointment give off a foul odor; so a little folly outweighs wisdom and honor." (Eccl 10:1)

"Of making many books there is no end, and much study is a weariness of the flesh." (Eccl 12:12)

SONG OF SONGS

The English title of this book can also be "Song of Solomon" or "Canticle of Canticles." The Hebrew title is literally translated "Song of Songs" but can be understood as a superlative—that is, "the best song."

Synopsis

This book of love poetry contains two principal characters: the female lover and the male lover. Through dialogue and monologue, they convey their passion and desire for each other.

Content Outline

The woman's desire for her lover and a dialogue between lovers	Song of Songs 1
The woman speaks of her lover	Song of Songs 2
The woman seeks her lover; sees lover coming with a procession	Song of Songs 3
The man praises his lover's body	Song of Songs 4
The woman praises her lover's body	Song of Songs 5
The man speaks about his lover's beauty	Song of Songs 6
The man praises his lover's body; she responds	Song of Songs 7
Dialogue between the man and the woman	Song of Songs 8

People

Unnamed female lover
Unnamed male lover
Solomon—king of Israel
Daughters of Jerusalem

Key Concepts

Beloved—term of endearment used by the two lovers for each other
Desire—the lovers express their longing for one another
Love—erotic love between two people is celebrated
Body—both lovers compare the other's body parts to objects in nature such as plants and animals
Beauty—physical beauty is celebrated by the lovers
Poetry—literary form in which Song of Songs is written

Important Quotations

"Let him kiss me with the kisses of his mouth! For your love is better than wine." (Song 1:2)

"I am black and beautiful, O daughters of Jerusalem, like the tents of Kedar, like the curtains of Solomon." (Song 1:5)

"I am a rose of Sharon, a lily of the valleys." (Song 2:1)

"Eat, friends, drink, and be drunk with love." (Song 5:1b)

"I adjure you, O daughters of Jerusalem, do not stir up or awaken love until it is ready." (Song 8:4)

"Set me as a seal upon your heart, as a seal upon your arm; for love is strong as death, passion fierce as the grave. Its flashes are flashes of fire, a raging flame." (Song 8:6)

4

The Prophetic Books

Each of the Prophetic Books—Isaiah, Jeremiah, Lamentations, Ezekiel, Daniel, Hosea, Joel, Amos, Obadiah, Jonah, Micah, Nahum, Habakkuk, Zephaniah, Haggai, Zechariah, and Malachi—is connected to a prophetic figure, and all but one share their book name with that prophet. These books contain both stories about prophets and the words of prophets.

In the Christian canon, the books are grouped into the Major Prophets and the Minor Prophets based on their length. The Major Prophets are Isaiah, Jeremiah, Ezekiel, and Daniel. The Minor Prophets are Hosea, Joel, Amos, Obadiah, Jonah, Micah, Nahum, Habakkuk, Zephaniah, Haggai, Zechariah, and Malachi. In the Hebrew canon, the books of Lamentations and Daniel are not found in the Prophets, but in the Writings.

These prophets can be sorted into rough time periods:

Eighth Century BCE
Amos
Hosea
Isaiah
Micah

Seventh Century BCE
Zephaniah
Nahum
Habakkuk

Sixth Century BCE
Jeremiah
Ezekiel
Obadiah

Haggai
Zechariah

Fifth Century BCE or Later
Joel
Malachi
Jonah

ISAIAH

The Hebrew title of this prophetic book is the prophet's name, just as in English. The book stands at the front of the section probably because it is the longest of the Prophetic Books.

Synopsis

The opening chapters of the book of Isaiah pronounce judgment and doom for the southern kingdom of Judah and its capital city, Jerusalem. Judah was a sinful nation, but not without hope.

Isaiah 6–12 contains biographical information about the prophet Isaiah and his ministry during the reigns of King Ahaz and possibly King Hezekiah. Isaiah had a vision of God anointing him to announce judgment. Isaiah consulted with King Ahaz about the Assyrian invasion and reassured him through signs. The prophet delivered more oracles of judgment and hope to the people.

Isaiah 13–23 contains judgment oracles against other nations, such as Babylon, Egypt, and Assyria. This type of oracle is also found in other prophetic books, such as Jeremiah, Ezekiel, and Amos.

Isaiah 24–27 contains oracles about future destruction and early apocalyptic themes such as the resurrection of the dead and the swallowing up of death forever. Isaiah 28–35 contains more judgment oracles concerning both Israel and Jerusalem, but also oracles of hope in God's promise to Zion. Isaiah 36–39 is narrative material of Isaiah's interactions with King Hezekiah during the siege of Jerusalem by King Sennacherib of Assyria. Hezekiah consulted with Isaiah and prayed to God for salvation. Isaiah prophesied that Jerusalem would be delivered; however, Hezekiah became sick, and Isaiah had to pray for him. After Hezekiah's recovery, he allowed a Babylonian delegation to see his treasure house. Isaiah condemned this course of action.

Isaiah 40–66 contains oracles of hope and restoration. These prophecies speak of God's intention to comfort and restore Israel. They describe a servant figure who is identified in one passage as the nation Israel but is characterized in another passage as having a mission to Israel. This section also mentions Cyrus, the Persian ruler, who was anointed by God to subdue the nations. Several passages focus on idolatry and proper worship. Zion was also an important topic for this section of Isaiah, as Jerusalem was rebuilt after the exile.

Content Outline

Prophecies of Judgment against Judah

Prophetic judgment against Judah because of its wickedness	Isaiah 1
Vision of a future Jerusalem; judgment against Israel	Isaiah 2
Judgment against Judah; judgment against daughters of Zion	Isaiah 3
Vision of a future Jerusalem	Isaiah 4
Song of the vineyard; six laments concerning justice	Isaiah 5

Stories about Isaiah

Isaiah's vision of God and God's calling of Isaiah	Isaiah 6
Isaiah gives assurance and a sign to King Ahaz	Isaiah 7
Isaiah's son becomes a sign of judgment	Isaiah 8
A new king; judgment and destruction against Israel	Isaiah 9
Judgment against Assyria; remnant of Israel	Isaiah 10
An ideal king will judge wisely and bring peace	Isaiah 11
Thanksgiving psalm	Isaiah 12

Mostly Oracles concerning Other Nations

Oracle against Babylon	Isaiah 13
Taunt against the king of Babylon; oracle against Assyria; oracle against Philistia	Isaiah 14
Oracle against Moab	Isaiah 15–16
Oracle against Damascus	Isaiah 17
Oracle against Ethiopia (ancient Nubia)	Isaiah 18
Oracle against Egypt	Isaiah 19

Isaiah walks around naked to symbolize the defeat of Egypt and Ethiopia by Assyria	Isaiah 20
Oracles against the wilderness of the sea, Dumah, and the desert plain	Isaiah 21
Oracle against Judah; oracle against Shebna	Isaiah 22
Oracle against Tyre	Isaiah 23

Apocalyptic Materials

Vision of judgment against the earth	Isaiah 24
Praise to God for salvation	Isaiah 25
Song in Judah concerning victory	Isaiah 26
Future of Israel	Isaiah 27

Oracles of Judgment

Oracles against the unethical rulers in Israel	Isaiah 28
Oracle condemning Jerusalem	Isaiah 29
Oracle against the rebellious people of Judah	Isaiah 30
Oracle against an alliance with Egypt	Isaiah 31
An ideal king will reign rightly	Isaiah 32
Oracle against the destroyer (Assyria)	Isaiah 33
Oracle of judgment against nations, including Edom	Isaiah 34
Oracle of promise concerning a way back to Zion	Isaiah 35

Stories about King Hezekiah and Isaiah

King Sennacherib of Assyria seeks to destroy Jerusalem	Isaiah 36
Hezekiah seeks Isaiah's advice; Hezekiah prays; Sennacherib is defeated	Isaiah 37
Hezekiah is sick; Hezekiah writes a hymn	Isaiah 38
Hezekiah allows envoys from Babylon to see his treasures	Isaiah 39

Mostly Oracles of Salvation and Restoration

Comfort for God's people; to whom should we compare God?	Isaiah 40
Judgment against nations; Israel as God's servant; idols are useless	Isaiah 41
God's servant will establish justice; God goes forth like a warrior	Isaiah 42
God will protect and redeem Israel	Isaiah 43
God will bless and help Israel; idols are nothing	Isaiah 44
God will use Cyrus, God's anointed, to subdue nations	Isaiah 45
Idols and other gods do not compare to God	Isaiah 46
Daughter Babylon will be defeated	Isaiah 47
Oracle of judgment against Israel	Isaiah 48
God's servant speaks to the nations; God will restore Zion	Isaiah 49
God's servant speaks to Israel	Isaiah 50
Oracle of restoration concerning Jerusalem	Isaiah 51
Oracle of restoration concerning Jerusalem; God's servant will prosper	Isaiah 52
God's servant suffered	Isaiah 53
Oracle of restoration concerning Zion	Isaiah 54
God will make an everlasting covenant	Isaiah 55

Oracles to the Postexilic Community

Covenant given to foreigners and eunuchs	Isaiah 56
Judgment against Israel's idolatry	Isaiah 57
True worship is not fasting and fighting; justice is needed	Isaiah 58
Judgment against Israel for its injustice	Isaiah 59
Salvation has come to Jerusalem	Isaiah 60
Good news has come to Israel	Isaiah 61
Vindication comes to Jerusalem; Zion will be saved	Isaiah 62

Oracle of judgment against Edom	Isaiah 63
Prayer to God to come down and not punish	Isaiah 64
God will judge the rebellious people; God will create new heavens and a new earth	Isaiah 65
Oracle about proper worship; God will restore Jerusalem	Isaiah 66

People

Isaiah—prophet; son of Amoz
Uzziah—king of Judah
Ahaz—king of Judah
Rezin—king of Aram
Pekah—king of Israel
Shearjashub—son of Isaiah; name means "a remnant shall return"
Unnamed young woman—will bear a son named Immanuel
Prophetess—Isaiah's wife
Maher-shalal-hash-baz—Isaiah and the prophetess's son
Hezekiah—king of Judah
Sennacherib—king of Assyria
The Rabshakeh—Assyrian official; name means "chief cupbearer"
Merodach-baladan—king of Babylon
Cyrus—king of Persia

Places

Jerusalem/Zion—capital of Judah
Judah—southern kingdom
Assyria—empire that destroyed kingdom of Israel and made kingdom of Judah its vassal
Israel/Ephraim—northern kingdom
Samaria—capital of northern kingdom
Babylon—capital of Babylonia; place of exile for Israel
Edom—Judah's neighbor and enemy
Philistia—area on the Mediterranean coast
Moab—neighboring nation east of the Dead Sea
Damascus—city in the Assyrian Empire
Egypt—country southwest of Israel
Ethiopia—ancient Nubia
Tyre—city in Phoenicia

Key Concepts

Judgment—prophetic sayings that condemn particular bad behaviors, such as social injustice

Promise—prophetic sayings that assure a better future

Servant—figure chosen to bring justice to the nations

Jerusalem/Zion—capital of Judah; destroyed by the Babylonians

Holiness—God's nature as one who is set apart; God is named as the Holy One of Israel

Oracles against the nations—prophetic sayings against Israel's neighbors

Important Quotations

"Come now, let us argue it out, says the LORD: though your sins are like scarlet, they shall be like snow; though they are red like crimson, they shall become like wool." (Isa 1:18)

"He shall judge between the nations, and shall arbitrate for many peoples; they shall beat their swords into plowshares, and their spears into pruning hooks; nation shall not lift up sword against nation, neither shall they learn war any more." (Isa 2:4)

"Ah, you who join house to house, who add field to field, until there is room for no one but you, and you are left to live alone in the midst of the land!" (Isa 5:8)

"Holy, holy, holy is the LORD of hosts; the whole earth is full of his glory." (Isa 6:3)

"Therefore the Lord himself will give you a sign. Look, the young woman is with child and shall bear a son, and shall name him Immanuel." (Isa 7:14)

"For a child has been born for us, a son given to us; authority rests upon his shoulders; and he is named Wonderful Counselor, Mighty God, Everlasting Father, Prince of Peace." (Isa 9:6)

"A shoot shall come out from the stump of Jesse, and a branch shall grow out of his roots. The spirit of the LORD shall rest on him, the spirit of wisdom and understanding, the spirit of counsel and might, the spirit of knowledge and the fear of the LORD." (Isa 11:1–2)

"He will shallow up death forever. Then the Lord GOD will wipe away the tears from all faces, and the disgrace of his people he will take away from all the earth, for the LORD has spoken." (Isa 25:8)

"Comfort, O comfort my people, says your God. Speak tenderly to Jerusalem, and cry to her that she has served her term, that her penalty is paid, that she has received from the LORD's hand double for all her sins." (Isa 40:1–2)

"Here is my servant, whom I uphold, my chosen, in whom my soul delights; I have put my spirit upon him; he will bring forth justice to the nations." (Isa 42:1)

"Thus says the LORD to his anointed, to Cyrus, whose right hand I have grasped to subdue nations before him and strip kings of their robes, to open doors before him—and the gates shall not be closed." (Isa 45:1)

"For my thoughts are not your thoughts, nor are your ways my ways, says the LORD. For as the heavens are higher than the earth, so are my ways higher than your ways and my thoughts than your thoughts." (Isa 55:8–9)

"For you shall go out in joy, and be led back in peace; the mountains and the hills before you shall burst into song, and all the trees of the field shall clap their hands." (Isa 55:12)

"Arise, shine; for your light has come, and the glory of the LORD has risen upon you." (Isa 60:1)

"The spirit of the Lord GOD is upon me, because the LORD has anointed me; he has sent me to bring good news to the oppressed, to bind up the broken-hearted, to proclaim liberty to the captives, and release to the prisoners." (Isa 61:1)

"O that you would tear open the heavens and come down, so that the mountains would quake at your presence." (Isa 64:1)

JEREMIAH

The Hebrew title of this book is the prophet's name, just as in English.

Synopsis

The book opens with Jeremiah's call to prophesy to the nations. The prophet pronounced judgment on Israel and called it to repent from its unfaithfulness. Jeremiah spoke of a coming invasion from the north. The prophet stood at the gates of the Temple and called the people to amend their ways. He admonished them not to trust in the Temple for their security. He warned of the coming judgment because of the breaking of the covenant.

Jeremiah complained to God about his own suffering and his unfulfilled prophecies. He engaged in symbolic actions to reinforce his prophetic message. He bought and wore a loincloth, hid it in the rocks, and later returned to dig it up. Just as the loincloth was ruined, the people would be ruined. Jeremiah's life became symbolic: God told him not to marry and not to mourn for those already dead. Jeremiah contended with and denounced other prophets who did not announce judgment.

Jeremiah envisioned God as a potter who was shaping evil against the people. The people finally sought to bring charges against Jeremiah because of his message of judgment. Jeremiah complained again and cursed the day of his birth.

Jeremiah advised the king to submit to the Babylonians instead of hoping for God's help. The prophet claimed that God was fighting against Israel. During these oracles of judgment, God promised to gather a remnant after the destruction and to raise up a righteous Branch to reign as king. Jeremiah prophesied of a seventy-year exile and suggested that the exiles were like a basket of good figs which God would return to the land.

Jeremiah prophesied doom against the Temple and was almost put to death by the officials and the people. The prophet made a wooden yoke to put around his neck to represent Israel's submission to Babylon. Another prophet, Hananiah, opposed Jeremiah by taking away the wooden yoke. Jeremiah responded by talking about an iron yoke God would put on the nations so they would submit to the Babylonians. Hananiah's death was a sign that he had been a false prophet. Jeremiah sent a letter to the exiles saying that their exile would last for seventy years and so they should settle in Babylon, establish businesses, and build homes. One of the exiles, Shemaiah, wrote back and called Jeremiah a madman for his prophecy.

Jeremiah prophesied promise for Israel and Judah. The exiles would return to the land, and God would make a new covenant with them. Jeremiah bought land in Israel during the Babylonian siege—a rather foolish action, but one that showed God's commitment to bringing the people back after exile. The prophet spoke of a righteous Branch that would restore the Davidic monarchy. Jeremiah also stated that King Zedekiah of Judah would die in captivity because of his inability to listen and to obey the laws concerning the release of slaves.

Baruch wrote Jeremiah's words from God and read them to the people. When King Jehoiakim heard these words, he burned the scroll and tried to arrest Jeremiah and Baruch. They hid while Baruch wrote Jeremiah's words on another scroll.

Jeremiah was captured twice and brought before King Zedekiah. The king hoped to receive a favorable prophecy. Jeremiah informed him that Israel would be handed over to Babylon. Jerusalem was taken by the Babylonians, and Jeremiah was released. He decided to stay in the land with Gedaliah, the new governor, instead of going into exile. Gedaliah was murdered by Ishmael, and the people were thrown into chaos. Although Jeremiah advised the people to stay in the land, Johanan, one of the community leaders, forced all the people, including Jeremiah, to go to Egypt. Jeremiah prophesied judgment against the people because of idolatry. He offered words of comfort to Baruch.

The final chapters of Jeremiah consist of oracles against nations such as Egypt, Babylon, Philistia, Moab, Ammon, and Edom.

The last chapter reviews the Babylonians' besiegement and destruction of Jerusalem. Jehoiachin was taken captive and then freed. The book ends with Jehoiachin dining regularly at the table of the king of Babylon.

Content Outline

Poetry of Judgment

Jeremiah's prophetic call and two visions	Jeremiah 1
God uses marital imagery to accuse Jerusalem and Israel of betrayal	Jeremiah 2
God calls faithless Israel to return	Jeremiah 3
Oracle of judgment concerning evil from the north	Jeremiah 4
Israel and Judah will be destroyed because of their unfaithfulness	Jeremiah 5
Attack is coming soon	Jeremiah 6
Jeremiah's proclaims judgment in the Temple	Jeremiah 7
The people claim to be wise, but they are foolish	Jeremiah 8
The people mourn because of the impending judgment	Jeremiah 9
Warning against idolatry; daughter Zion to prepare for exile	Jeremiah 10
Curse for breaking the covenant; Jeremiah's life is endangered	Jeremiah 11
Jeremiah complains; God replies	Jeremiah 12
Two symbolic actions: wine jars and burying a loincloth	Jeremiah 13
Jeremiah prophesies about a drought; lying prophets	Jeremiah 14

Narratives of Hope

Oracle of hope about future rebuilding; righteous Branch	Jeremiah 33
Oracle about the future death of King Zedekiah in exile	Jeremiah 34
The Rechabites are faithful and therefore blessed	Jeremiah 35
Baruch writes Jeremiah's words; Jehoiakim burns the scroll; Jeremiah creates another	Jeremiah 36
Jeremiah is imprisoned	Jeremiah 37
Jeremiah is captured, put in a cistern, and rescued; Jeremiah and Zedekiah meet	Jeremiah 38
Jerusalem falls to the Babylonians	Jeremiah 39
Nebuzaradan asks Jeremiah if he wants to go into exile or stay; Jeremiah stays	Jeremiah 40
Gedaliah is murdered by Ishmael; chaos in the land	Jeremiah 41
Jeremiah tells the people to stay in the land and not escape to Egypt	Jeremiah 42
Johanan forces all the people, including Jeremiah, to go to Egypt	Jeremiah 43
Jeremiah prophesies judgment against the people because of idolatry	Jeremiah 44
Jeremiah's words of comfort to Baruch	Jeremiah 45

Oracles against the Nations

Oracles of judgment against Egypt and Babylon; salvation for Israel	Jeremiah 46
Oracle against the Philistines	Jeremiah 47
Oracle against Moab	Jeremiah 48
Oracles against Ammonites, Edomites, Damascus, Kedar and Hazor, and Elam	Jeremiah 49
Oracle against Babylon	Jeremiah 50
Oracle against Babylon; Seraiah to take the scroll to Babylon	Jeremiah 51

Conclusion

Babylonians besiege Jerusalem, then destroy it;
Jehoiachin taken captive   Jeremiah 52

People

Jeremiah—prophet; son of Hilkiah
Pashhur—son of Immer
Zedekiah—king of Judah
Nebuchadrezzar—king of Babylon
Shallum (aka Jehoahaz)—son of Josiah; king of Judah
Jeconiah—son of Jehoiakim; king of Judah
Hananiah—prophet; opposes Jeremiah
Shemaiah—exile who writes to the high priest about Jeremiah
Baruch—scribe
Jehoiakim—son of Josiah; king of Judah
Ebed-melech—Ethiopian eunuch
Gedaliah—governor
Nebuzaradan—captain of the guard

Places

Jerusalem—capital of Judah
Judah—southern kingdom
Anathoth—Jeremiah's hometown
Egypt—country southwest of Israel
Shiloh—central Israelite shrine
Babylon—place of exile for Israel

Key Concepts

Exile—forced removal of the people out of Jerusalem and Judah to live with
  their captors in Babylon
Land—promised to Israel through God's covenant with Abraham and his
  descendants; lost to the people because of their disobedience to God's
  commands
False prophets—deceitful and dishonest prophets
True prophets—Jeremiah is an example because he speaks the truth
Complaints—Jeremiah laments to God
Oracles against the nations—prophetic sayings against Israel's neighbors

Important Quotations

"Now the word of the LORD came to me saying, 'Before I formed you in the womb I knew you, and before you were born I consecrated you; I appointed you a prophet to the nations.'" (Jer 1:4–5)

"See, today I appoint you over nations and over kingdoms, to pluck up and to pull down, to destroy and to overthrow, to build and to plant." (Jer 1:10)

"Thus says the LORD of hosts, the God of Israel: Amend your ways and your doings, and let me dwell with you in this place. Do not trust in these deceptive words: 'This is the temple of the LORD, the temple of the LORD, the temple of the LORD.'" (Jer 7:3–4)

"But I was like a gentle lamb led to the slaughter. And I did not know it was against me that they devised schemes, saying, 'Let us destroy the tree with its fruit, let us cut him off from the land of the living, so that his name will no longer be remembered!'" (Jer 11:19)

"You shall not take a wife, nor shall you have sons or daughters in this place." (Jer 16:2)

"O LORD, you have enticed me, and I was enticed; you have overpowered me, and you have prevailed. I have become a laughingstock all day long; everyone mocks me." (Jer 20:7)

"The days are surely coming, says the LORD, when I will raise up for David a righteous Branch, and he shall reign as king and deal wisely, and shall execute justice and righteousness in the land." (Jer 23:5)

"For surely I know the plans I have for you, says the LORD, plans for your welfare and not for harm, to give you a future with hope. Then when you call upon me and come and pray to me, I will hear you. When you search for me, you will find me; if you seek me with all your heart, I will let you find me, says the LORD, and I will restore your fortunes and gather you from all the nations and the places where I have driven you, says the LORD, and I will bring you back to the place from which I sent you into exile." (Jer 29:11–14)

"For the days are surely coming, says the LORD, when I will restore the fortunes of my people, Israel and Judah, says the LORD, and I will bring them back to the land that I gave to their ancestors and they shall take possession of it." (Jer 30:3)

"Thus says the LORD: A voice is heard in Ramah, lamentation and bitter weeping. Rachel is weeping for her children; she refuses to be comforted for her children, because they are no more." (Jer 31:15)

"The days are surely coming, says the LORD, when I will make a new covenant with the house of Israel and the house of Judah. . . . But this is the covenant that I will make with the house of Israel after those days, says the LORD: I will put my law within them, and I will write it on their hearts; and I will be their God, and they shall be my people." (Jer 31:31, 33)

"The days are surely coming, says the LORD, when I will fulfill the promise I made to the house of Israel and the house of Judah. In those days and at that time I will cause a righteous Branch to spring up for David; and he shall execute justice and righteousness in the land. In those days Judah will be saved and Jerusalem will live in safety. And this is the name by which it will be called: 'The LORD is our righteousness.'" (Jer 33:14–16)

LAMENTATIONS

The Hebrew title of this book is its first Hebrew word, which means "How?" In the Christian Old Testament, the book of Lamentations is located immediately after the book of Jeremiah because of the traditional notion that the prophet Jeremiah wrote the book. In the Jewish canon, Lamentations is in the third and final section, Writings.

Synopsis

The book of Lamentations is a series of five laments. The city of Jerusalem was lamented because of the conquest as an empty city with little hope. The personified city then lamented her own condition as one rejected by God. The second lament pertained to the destruction of Jerusalem. In the third lament, the people complained about their suffering yet still maintained their belief in the goodness and love of God. The fourth lament continued the theme of suffering among the people because of sinful leaders. The final lament was communal and included an admittance of sinfulness and a plea for renewal.

Content Outline

Jerusalem is lamented because of its conquest;
Jerusalem laments   Lamentations 1

God has destroyed daughter Zion	Lamentations 2
Long lament about the people's suffering and God's faithfulness	Lamentations 3
Lament over the children of Zion	Lamentations 4
Communal lament and plea for restoration	Lamentations 5

People

Daughter Zion—personification of Jerusalem
Daughter Edom—personification of Edom

Places

Jerusalem—capital of Judah

Key Concepts

Lament—grief over the loss of the city of Jerusalem
Destruction—Jerusalem and its temple are destroyed by the Babylonians
Hope—belief in (or anticipation of) God's goodness and actions
Punishment—destruction of the city and exile of the people for Jerusalem's sins

Important Quotations

"How lonely sits the city that once was full of people! How like a widow she has become, she that was great among the nations! She that was a princess among the provinces has become a vassal." (Lam 1:1)

"Is it nothing to you, all you who pass by? Look and see if there is any sorrow like my sorrow, which was brought upon me, which the LORD inflicted on the day of his fierce anger." (Lam 1:12)

"The steadfast love of the LORD never ceases, his mercies never come to an end; they are new every morning; great is your faithfulness." (Lam 3:22–23)

"But you, O LORD, reign forever; your throne endures to all generations. Why have you forgotten us completely? Why have you forsaken us these many days? Restore us to yourself, O LORD, that we may be restored; renew our days as of old—unless you have utterly rejected us, and are angry with us beyond measure." (Lam 5:19–22)

EZEKIEL

The Hebrew title of this book is the prophet's name, just as in English.

Synopsis

The book of Ezekiel opens with the prophet's dramatic image of living creatures, wheels, and fire. These images together constituted a vision of the appearance of the likeness of the glory of God. Ezekiel ate a scroll full of words of woe. He was taken to a place among the Babylonian exiles and made a sentinel for Israel. The prophet engaged in some symbolic actions by first creating a clay model of Jerusalem besieged by the enemy. He shaved and burned his hair to demonstrate Jerusalem's coming fate. Ezekiel delivered words of judgment to Israel because of their idolatry.

In another vision, Ezekiel saw all the wrongdoing in the Temple and watched as God's glory left the Temple and Jerusalem. Prophetic judgments came upon the wicked officials and false prophets. The prophet compared Jerusalem to a vine given to the fire for fuel, and he depicted the city as an unfaithful wife. Ezekiel announced that people would not be judged based on the actions of their parents but on their own. Additional judgment oracles renounced the leaders of Israel and the city of Jerusalem.

Ezekiel 25–32 contains oracles against the nations. Two groups were singled out for attention: Tyre and Egypt. Babylon was not mentioned in this section. After these oracles, the tone of the book changes with the news of the fall of Jerusalem. The prophet delivered oracles of promise and restoration to the people. He prophesied about a valley of dry bones reanimated to new life.

Ezekiel's final vision pertained to a new Temple. The prophet envisioned a new building with new gates and courts and the glory of God residing within the Temple. Upon God's return, the priests' activities and offerings would begin again. The city of Jerusalem was given the name "The LORD is There."

Content Outline

Ezekiel's Prophetic Call

Ezekiel's inaugural vision of cloud, fire, creatures, wheels	Ezekiel 1
Ezekiel is sent to the rebellious people of Israel	Ezekiel 2
Ezekiel eats a scroll; the spirit of God takes Ezekiel to exile, and he is speechless	Ezekiel 3

Judgment against Jerusalem and Israel

Ezekiel creates siege works with bricks, lies on his sides, and bakes over dung	Ezekiel 4
Ezekiel cuts his hair with a sword to represent the sword against Jerusalem	Ezekiel 5
Ezekiel prophesies against the mountains of Israel for idolatry	Ezekiel 6
Doom is coming to the land of Israel	Ezekiel 7

Ezekiel's Vision

Ezekiel's vision of Jerusalem and abominations	Ezekiel 8
Ezekiel's vision of the executions of idolaters	Ezekiel 9
Ezekiel's vision of the glory of God leaving the Temple	Ezekiel 10
Ezekiel's vision about wicked leaders and the departure of God from the city	Ezekiel 11

More Judgment against Jerusalem and Israel

Ezekiel packs his baggage for exile	Ezekiel 12
Oracle concerning false prophets	Ezekiel 13
Oracle concerning elders' idols and judgment against Jerusalem	Ezekiel 14
Jerusalem is a vine given to the fire for fuel	Ezekiel 15
Jerusalem as an unfaithful bride	Ezekiel 16
The riddle of two eagles and a vine; Jerusalem's king's rebellion	Ezekiel 17
Oracle concerning individual responsibility	Ezekiel 18
Lament for the princes of Israel	Ezekiel 19
God's history with, and promise for, Israel	Ezekiel 20
God's sword against Jerusalem	Ezekiel 21
The city that sheds blood and makes idols	Ezekiel 22
Oholah and Oholibah's unfaithfulness	Ezekiel 23
Allegory of the boiling pot; the death of Ezekiel's wife	Ezekiel 24

People

Ezekiel—prophet; son of Buzi
Oholah and Oholibah—personifications of Samaria and Jerusalem
Ezekiel's wife—death becomes a sign for Israel
Pharaoh—Egyptian leader
Prince—book's name for the envisioned new leader

Places

The river Chebar—a canal in Babylon where Ezekiel has his first vision
Jerusalem—capital of Judah
Tyre—city against which the book contains several oracles
Egypt—country against which the book contains several oracles

Key Concepts

Son of man/mortal—book of Ezekiel's title for the prophet
God's glory—the glory of God leaves Jerusalem before it is destroyed
Visions—Ezekiel's prophetic images given in a trance or a dreamlike state
Valley of dry bones—Ezekiel's vision and prophecy about Israel coming back to life after becoming dry bones
Temple—place of worship and sacrifice where God's presence dwells; Ezekiel envisions a new temple after the destruction of the First Temple
Oracles against the nations—prophetic sayings against Israel's neighbors

Important Quotations

"In the thirtieth year, in the fourth month, on the fifth day of the month, as I was among the exiles by the river Chebar, the heavens were opened, and I saw visions of God." (Ezek 1:1)

"So I spoke to the people in the morning, and at evening my wife died. And on the next morning I did as I was commanded." (Ezek 24:18)

"In the twelfth year of our exile, in the tenth month, on the fifth day of the month, someone who had escaped from Jerusalem came to me and said, 'The city has fallen.'" (Ezek 33:21)

"The hand of the LORD came upon me, and he brought me out by the spirit of the LORD and set me down in the middle of a valley; it was full of bones." (Ezek 37:1)

"I will put my spirit within you, and you shall live, and I will place you on your own soil; then you shall know that I, the LORD, have spoken and will act, says the LORD." (Ezek 37:14)

DANIEL

The Hebrew title of this prophetic book is the prophet's name, just as in English. In the Christian Old Testament, the book of Daniel is located in the Prophets section. In the Jewish canon, Daniel is in the third and final section, Writings.

Synopsis

The book begins with multiple stories about Daniel and his three Hebrew companions at the court of the Babylonian king. They were taken to Babylon when King Nebuchadnezzar besieged Jerusalem during King Jehoiakim's reign. Daniel was given a special diet to eat and wine to drink, but he refused to defile himself with royal rations. He and his friends asked to be allowed to eat only vegetables and to drink only water. After some time, the four men were found to be superior to others and placed at the king's court. Daniel had the ability to interpret dreams and visions.

King Nebuchadnezzar began having troubling dreams, and Daniel was able to interpret the dreams for him. The king promoted Daniel and his friends. King Nebuchadnezzar created a large gold statue and commanded everyone worship it. Daniel's friends Shadrach, Meshach, and Abednego refused to bow. In anger, Nebuchadnezzar had them thrown into a furnace, but they were not burned as they walked in the flames. When the king looked into the furnace, he saw four men instead of three. The fourth had the appearance of a god. Seeing all of this, the king had the three men removed from the furnace. The king blessed their God and promoted them in his kingdom.

King Nebuchadnezzar had another dream, and again, only Daniel was able to interpret it. The grim interpretation was that the king would be driven from human society and forced to dwell with wild animals. These events did indeed occur.

In chapter 5, at a feast given by King Belshazzar, Nebuchadnezzar's son, a hand appeared and wrote on the wall of the palace. Daniel interpreted the handwriting as a sign of Babylon's imminent downfall at the hand of Persia. Belshazzar died that night, and Darius became king. Darius issued a decree that no one was to pray to anyone except the king for thirty days. Daniel disobeyed this command and was thrown into the lions' den. He survived in the den of lions because of God's help. Daniel prospered during Darius's reign.

Daniel had a dream of four great beasts, and an angel interpreted it for him. The beasts represented kingdoms, and the beasts' horns represented kings. Daniel had a vision involving a ram and a goat, and again, Gabriel gave the interpretation. The ram with two horns related to Media and Persia, while the goat was the king of Greece.

Daniel understood Jeremiah's prophecy of the seventy years of exile and prayed a long prayer, confessing the people's sins. Gabriel interpreted Jeremiah's prophecy about the seventy years. David received one more vision about heavenly and earthly battles, as well as the end of time when the angel Michael would appear and the dead would be resurrected.

Content Outline

Court Tales of Daniel

Daniel and his three friends at Nebuchadnezzar's court	Daniel 1
Nebuchadnezzar dreams; Daniel interprets the dream; Daniel is promoted	Daniel 2
Nebuchadnezzar's golden statue; the fiery furnace	Daniel 3
Nebuchadnezzar dreams again; Daniel interprets; Nebuchadnezzar's madness	Daniel 4
A hand writes on Belshazzar's wall; Daniel interprets	Daniel 5
Daniel and the lions' den	Daniel 6

Four Apocalyptic Visions

Visions of four great beasts and interpretations of the visions	Daniel 7
Vision of the ram and the goat and Gabriel's interpretation	Daniel 8

People

Nebuchadnezzar—king of Babylon
Ashpenaz—Nebuchadnezzar's palace master
Daniel (aka Belteshazzar)—prophet
Hananiah (aka Shadrach)—Daniel's friend
Mishael (aka Meshach)—Daniel's friend
Azariah (aka Abednego)—Daniel's friend
Belshazzar—son of Nebuchadnezzar; king of Babylon
Darius—Persian king
Cyrus—Persian king
Gabriel—angel
Michael—angel

Places

Babylon—country of exile for Israel

Key Concepts

Dreams—thoughts and images that come to one mind's during sleep; Daniel
    interprets the king's dreams
Visions—images given in a trance or a dreamlike state; the major content in
    the second half of the book; Daniel has a series of visions
Fiery furnace—large structure designed to hold extremely hot materials;
    Nebuchadnezzar tries to kill three Jews (Shadrach, Meshach, Abednego)
    by having them thrown into the furnace, but they survive
Lions' den—dwelling place for large predatory animals; Darius throws Dan-
    iel into the den, but Daniel survives
Resurrection—the dead will rise to everlasting life or everlasting contempt

Important Quotations

"Shadrach, Meshach, and Abednego answered the king, 'O Nebuchadnezzar,
    we have no need to present a defense to you in this matter. If our God

whom we serve is able to deliver us from the furnace of blazing fire and out of your hand, O king, let him deliver us. But if not, be it known to you, O king, that we will not serve your gods and we will not worship the golden statue that you have set up.'" (Dan 3:16–18)

"Then King Nebuchadnezzar was astonished and rose up quickly. He said to his counselors, 'Was it not three men that we threw bound into the fire?' They answered the king, 'True, O king.' He replied, 'But I see four men unbound, walking in the middle of the fire, and they are not hurt; and the fourth has the appearance of a god.'" (Dan 3:24–25)

"Therefore I make a decree: Any people, nation, or language that utters blasphemy against the God of Shadrach, Meshach, and Abednego shall be torn limb from limb, and their houses laid in ruins; for there is no other god who is able to deliver in this way." (Dan 3:29)

"Therefore, O king, may my counsel be acceptable to you: atone for your sins with righteousness, and your iniquities with mercy to the oppressed, so that your prosperity may be prolonged." (Dan 4:27)

"And this is the writing that was inscribed: MENE, MENE, TEKEL, and PARSIN. This is the interpretation of the matter: MENE, God has numbered the days of your kingdom and brought it to an end; TEKEL, you have been weighed on the scales and found wanting; PERES, your kingdom is divided and given to the Medes and Persians." (Dan 5:25–28)

"Then, at break of day, the king got up and hurried to the den of lions. When he came near the den where Daniel was, he cried out anxiously to Daniel, 'O Daniel, servant of the living God, has your God whom you faithfully serve been able to deliver you from the lions?' Daniel then said to the king, 'O king, live forever! My God sent his angel and shut the lions' mouths so that they would not hurt me, because I was found blameless before him; and also before you, O king, I have done no wrong.' Then the king was exceedingly glad and commanded that Daniel be taken up out of the den. So Daniel was taken up out of the den, and no kind of harm was found on him, because he trusted in his God." (Dan 6:19–23)

"As I watched, thrones were set in place, and an Ancient One took his throne, his clothing was white as snow, and the hair of his head like pure wool; his throne was fiery flames, and its wheels were burning fire." (Dan 7:9)

"As I watched in the night visions, I saw one like a human being coming with the clouds of heaven. And he came to the Ancient One and was presented before him. To him was given dominion and glory and kingship, that all peoples, nations, and languages should serve him. His dominion is an ever-lasting dominion that shall not pass away, and his kingship is one that shall never be destroyed." (Dan 7:13–14)

HOSEA

The Hebrew title of this book is the prophet's name, just as in English. In the Christian canon, Hosea stands as the first of the twelve Minor Prophets, which are labeled "Minor" because of their length, not their importance. In the Jewish canon, these books together constitute the Book of the Twelve.

Synopsis

Hosea was a prophet during the reigns of Kings Uzziah, Jotham, Ahaz, Heze-kiah, and Jeroboam. God instructed Hosea to marry Gomer, "a wife of whore-dom." Hosea and Gomer had a son. God told Hosea to name the child Jezreel as a sign of the coming judgment on Israel. Hosea and Gomer had a daughter. God told Hosea to name this child Lo-ruhamah as a sign God would not forgive Israel but would have pity and save Judah. Hosea and Gomer had a third child, another son. God told Hosea to name the child Lo-ammi as a sign God would no longer claim Israel as God's own. Hosea prophesied that God would one day restore Israel. This marriage and children represented the unfaithfulness of Israel and God's punishment. These themes of infidelity and punishment continue into the prophetic oracles of Hosea that constitute the remainder of the book. Hosea accused his wife of being unfaithful and threatened to punish her; the speech represents an allegory of the relationship between God and the people of Israel.

Other oracles in the book indict Israel for the sin of idolatry. They announce judgment on Israel and call the people to return to God. The ora-cles announce that Israel has broken the covenant and played the whore. One of the oracles switches the metaphor from one of marriage to one of par-enthood. God was the parent and Israel was the child. Even though Israel disobeyed and God wanted to punish, God decided to withhold wrath. The book ends with a call for return to God and a promise of God's forgiveness and righteousness.

Content Outline

Hosea and Gomer marry and have three children	Hosea 1

Hosea accuses Gomer of being unfaithful and threatens her	Hosea 2
God instructs Hosea to buy her back and love her	Hosea 3
God indicts Israel for its sin and idolatry	Hosea 4
Judgment on Israel and Judah for their unfaithfulness	Hosea 5
Call to return to God	Hosea 6
Corruption of Ephraim	Hosea 7
Israel has broken the covenant	Hosea 8
Israel has played the whore and will be punished	Hosea 9
Israel will be put to shame	Hosea 10
God as parent and Israel as child	Hosea 11
Israel's past	Hosea 12
Judgment on Israel	Hosea 13
Call to return to God	Hosea 14

People

Hosea—prophet
Gomer—daughter of Diblaim; wife of Hosea
Jezreel—son of Hosea and Gomer
Lo-ruhamah—daughter of Hosea and Gomer
Lo-ammi—son of Hosea and Gomer

Places

Israel/Ephraim—northern kingdom
Samaria—capital of Israel

Key Concepts

Idolatry—worship of other gods; Hosea's primary concern
Whoredom—God's description of Israel's disobedience of God's commands and their worship of idols; God commands Hosea to marry a wife of whoredom and have children of whoredom
Ephraim—another name for the northern kingdom of Israel

Important Quotations

"When the LORD first spoke through Hosea, the LORD said to Hosea, 'Go, take for yourself a wife of whoredom and have children of whoredom, for the land commits great whoredom by forsaking the LORD.' So he went and took Gomer daughter of Diblaim, and she conceived and bore him a son." (Hos 1:2–3)

"Plead with your mother, plead—for she is not my wife, and I am not her husband—that she put away her whoring from her face, and her adultery from between her breasts, or I will strip her naked and expose her as in the day she was born, and make her like a wilderness, and turn her into a parched land, and kill her with thirst." (Hos 2:2–3)

"For I desire steadfast love and not sacrifice, the knowledge of God rather than burnt offerings." (Hos 6:6)

"Sow for yourselves righteousness; reap steadfast love; break up your fallow ground; for it is time to seek the LORD, that he may come and rain righteousness upon you." (Hos 10:12)

"When Israel was a child, I loved him, and out of Egypt I called my son." (Hos 11:1)

"Shall I ransom them from the power of Sheol? Shall I redeem them from Death? O Death, where are your plagues? O Sheol, where is your destruction? Compassion is hidden from my eyes." (Hos 13:14)

JOEL

The Hebrew title of this book is the prophet's name, just as in English.

Synopsis

The book of Joel begins by describing and lamenting a devastating locust attack on the country, a disaster that ruined the crops and vines. This event led to a call for repentance. According to the prophet, the day of the LORD was coming, and it would be a dark and unbearable day. The people were admonished to return to their God with fasting and mourning.

The book then turns to God's response to such repentant actions. Joel said God would restore the crops and pour out God's spirit upon the people. They would be restored, but the nations would be judged.

Content Outline

The land is devastated by locusts; Joel calls for repentance and fasting	Joel 1
The day of the Lord is coming; God will be present and will provide	Joel 2
Israel will be restored; the nations are judged	Joel 3

People

Joel—prophet; son of Pethuel

Places

Zion—Jerusalem
Valley of Jehoshaphat—place of judgment

Key Concepts

Lament—grief over the devastation of the country
Locust—large grasshopper; a plague of them ruins the land
Repentance—changing one's behavior and turning to God

Important Quotations

"Blow the trumpet in Zion; sound the alarm on my holy mountain! Let all the inhabitants of the land tremble, for the day of the LORD is coming, it is near." (Joel 2:1)

"Yet even now, says the LORD, return to me with all your heart, with fasting, with weeping, and with mourning; rend your hearts and not your clothing. Return to the LORD, your God, for he is gracious and merciful, slow to anger, and abounding in steadfast love, and relents from punishing." (Joel 2:12–13)

"You shall eat in plenty and be satisfied, and praise the name of the LORD your God, who has dealt wondrously with you. And my people shall never again be put to shame." (Joel 2:26)

"Then afterward I will pour out my spirit on all flesh; your sons and your daughters shall prophesy, your old men shall dream dreams, and your young men shall see visions. Even on the male and female slaves, in those days, I will pour out my spirit." (Joel 2:28–29)

"The LORD roars from Zion, and utters his voice from Jerusalem, and the heavens and the earth shake. But the LORD is a refuge for his people, a stronghold for the people of Israel." (Joel 3:16)

AMOS

The Hebrew title of this book is the prophet's name, just as in English.

Synopsis

The book of Amos begins with a series of prophetic judgment oracles against the foreign nations of Damascus, Gaza, Tyre, Edom, Ammon, and Moab. The prophet turned his judgment briefly to Judah for rejecting the teachings of God and ultimately to Israel for trampling the poor. The remainder of the book addresses the northern kingdom of Israel. Israel would be judged and punished for its sins and the sins of its wealthy leaders. Israel did not return to God, so the prophet spoke a lament over Israel and warned of the darkness of the day of the LORD. Israel would be destroyed. Amos's judgment was so harsh that a priest at Bethel relayed his prophecies to King Jeroboam of Israel. The priest wanted Amos to leave Israel and return to Judah. Amos said he was not a prophet but a herdsman called by God to prophesy over Israel. Amos continued to prophesy judgment and an end to Israel. The last verses of the book speak of restoration of a Davidic king as a sign of hope in the future.

Content Outline

Prophetic judgment against Damascus, Gaza, Tyre, Edom, and Ammon	Amos 1
Prophetic judgment against Moab, Judah, and Israel	Amos 2
Israel will be punished for its iniquities	Amos 3
God judges Samaria's wealthy; Israel did not return to God after affliction	Amos 4
Lamentation and call to repentance; the day of the Lord is darkness	Amos 5
Israel is not better than other neighbors and will go into exile first	Amos 6

Locusts, a shower of fire, a plumb line; confrontation between Amos and Amaziah	Amos 7
Basket of summer fruit and the end of Israel	Amos 8
Israel will be destroyed; God will restore Israel	Amos 9

People

Amos—prophet; shepherd from Tekoa
Uzziah—king of Judah
Jeroboam—king of Israel
Amaziah—priest of Bethel

Places

Tekoa—Amos's hometown
Zion—Jerusalem
Damascus—city in the Assyrian Empire
Gaza—Philistine city
Tyre—city in Phoenicia
Edom—Judah's neighbor and enemy
Ammon—neighboring nation east of the Jordan River
Moab—neighboring nation east of the Dead Sea
Judah—southern kingdom; rarely mentioned in Amos
Israel—northern kingdom and Amos's primary audience
Samaria—capital city of Israel

Key Concepts

Judgment—prophetic sayings that condemn particular bad behaviors, such as social injustice
Day of the Lord—future event that is described as darkness
Oracles against the nations—prophetic sayings against Israel's neighbors

Important Quotations

"And he said: The LORD roars from Zion, and utters his voice from Jerusalem; the pastures of the shepherds wither, and the top of Carmel dries up." (Amos 1:2)

"Come to Bethel—and transgress; to Gilgal—and multiply transgression; bring your sacrifices every morning, your tithes every three days." (Amos 4:4)

"Alas for you who desire the day of the LORD! Why do you want the day of the LORD? It is darkness, not light." (Amos 5:18)

"I hate, I despise your festivals, and I take no delight in your solemn assemblies." (Amos 5:21)

"But let justice roll down like waters, and righteousness like an ever-flowing stream." (Amos 5:24)

"Then Amos answered Amaziah, 'I am no prophet, nor a prophet's son; but I am a herdsman, a dresser of sycamore trees, and the LORD took me from following the flock, and the LORD said to me, "Go, prophesy to my people Israel."'" (Amos 7:14–15)

OBADIAH

The Hebrew title of this book is the prophet's name, just as in English.

Synopsis

The book of Obadiah is a prophecy against Edom. God promised to destroy the Edomites because they stood by and gloated as Jerusalem and Judah were destroyed. God promised that Mount Zion and the house of Jacob would survive and retaliate against the Edomites. Ultimately, the Edomites would not survive.

Content Outline

God's judgment against Edom and promise for Israel	Obadiah

People

Obadiah—prophet
Esau—ancestor of the Edomites
Jacob—ancestor of the Judahites
Teman—another name for Edom

Places

Edom—Judah's neighbor and enemy

Key Concepts

Judgment—prophetic sayings that condemn particular bad behaviors

Revenge—Israel desires vengeance for Edom's betrayal at the time of the destruction of Jerusalem

Sibling rivalry—Edom and Israel in association with Esau and Jacob

Day of the Lord—a future event that is described as near and against all nations

Important Quotations

"Your proud heart has deceived you, you that live in the clefts of the rock, whose dwelling is in the heights. You say in your heart, 'Who will bring me down to the ground?'" (Obad 3)

"For the slaughter and violence done to your brother, Jacob, shame shall cover you, and you shall be cut off forever." (Obad 10)

"But you should not have gloated over your brother on the day of his misfortune; you should not have rejoiced over the people of Judah on the day of their ruin; you should not have boasted on the day of distress." (Obad 12)

"But on Mount Zion there shall be those that escape, and it shall be holy; and the house of Jacob shall take possession of those who dispossessed them." (Obad 17)

JONAH

The Hebrew title of this book is the prophet's name, just as in English.

Synopsis

God instructed Jonah to go to Nineveh to condemn the wickedness of the Ninevites. Jonah instead boarded a ship headed to Tarshish. God caused a great storm to come upon the sea. The frightened sailors began to pray, but Jonah remained asleep. The ship captain woke Jonah and called upon him to pray. The sailors cast lots to determine who was at fault, and the lots fell on Jonah. The sailors asked him to tell them about himself and to explain why he might be the cause of God's wrath. Jonah admitted that he was a Hebrew and worshiped the Lord, the God of heaven. When they asked what they should do with him, he suggested they throw him overboard. Instead, the men rowed harder. Finally, after praying again, the sailors threw Jonah into the sea. The sea immediately calmed down.

Jonah was swallowed by a big fish. While in the fish, Jonah prayed to God regarding his situation and distress. After three days and three nights, God caused the fish to spew Jonah onto the land.

God repeated his instruction for Jonah to go to Nineveh, and Jonah obeyed. He walked into the city declaring the prophecy that Nineveh would soon be overthrown. In response, the people, including the king, repented and fasted. Because of their repentance, God's mind was changed and Nineveh was not destroyed.

Jonah responded with anger to God's change of heart and said that that was why he fled to Tarshish in the first place; Jonah knew that God was forgiving. Jonah asked to die. He walked outside the city and made a booth to sit under where he could watch what would happen to Nineveh. God caused a bush to grow as shade for Jonah, but then God provided a worm to attack the bush, causing it to wither and die. God caused a hot wind to blow and the sun to beat down on Jonah. Jonah again asked to die. God asked why if Jonah was concerned about the withering of the bush, which he did not grow, then should not God likewise be concerned about Nineveh, the great city of many people and many animals.

Content Outline

God tells Jonah to go to Nineveh, but he sails elsewhere; Jonah is swallowed by a big fish	Jonah 1
Jonah prays to God from the belly of the fish	Jonah 2
God tells Jonah to go to Nineveh, and he does; Nineveh repents	Jonah 3
Jonah becomes angry; Jonah and the bush; God's response to Jonah's anger	Jonah 4

People

Jonah—prophet
Mariners—sailors on the ship with Jonah
King of Nineveh—hears Jonah's prophecy and repents

Places

Nineveh—capital of Assyria
Tarshish—city far away
Joppa—seaport city

Key Concepts

Repentance—changing one's behavior and turning to God; Jonah's message to Nineveh as commanded by God
Mercy of God—God's compassion and decision not to punish; an action that causes Jonah to become angry
Reluctant prophet—Jonah's initial hesitancy to listen to the call of God

Important Quotations

"'I am a Hebrew,' he replied. 'I worship the LORD, the God of heaven, who made the sea and the dry land.'" (Jonah 1:9)

"But the LORD provided a large fish to swallow up Jonah; and Jonah was in the belly of the fish three days and three nights." (Jonah 1:17)

"Jonah began to go into the city, going a day's walk. And he cried out, 'Forty days more, and Nineveh shall be overthrown!'" (Jonah 3:4)

"When God saw what they did, how they turned from their evil ways, God changed his mind about the calamity that he had said he would bring upon them; and he did not do it." (Jonah 3:10)

"He prayed to the LORD and said, 'O LORD! Is not this what I said while I was still in my own country? That is why I fled to Tarshish at the beginning; for I knew that you are a gracious God and merciful, slow to anger, and abounding in steadfast love, and ready to relent from punishing." (Jonah 4:2)

MICAH

The Hebrew title of this book is the prophet's name, just as in English.

Synopsis

The book of Micah begins with prophecies of doom: God's destruction of Israel because of the wickedness of Samaria and destruction of Judah's cities because of the sins of economic injustice and idolatry. The leaders and prophets of Samaria and Judah's cities were corrupt and did not pursue justice. God would destroy Jerusalem.

The book of Micah also contains prophecies of promise. God would bring peace and restoration to Zion in the future, God would bring forth a ruler to feed God's flock, and the remnant of Jacob would be as powerful as a lion.

Micah concludes by mixing judgment and promise. God required justice and kindness, not excessive offerings. Micah could not find anyone who was faithful, so he implored the people to trust in God with the hope that God would show faithfulness and restore Israel.

Content Outline

God will appear and destroy Israel because of its evil; Judah also faces doom	Micah 1
Sins of oppressive economics	Micah 2
Evil leaders and prophets are the cause of the coming destruction	Micah 3
Peace and restoration promised for Zion in the future	Micah 4
A shepherd-king will come forth; the remnant of Israel will be like a lion	Micah 5
God contends with Israel; God requires justice, kindness, and wisdom	Micah 6
Faithful people have disappeared; God will restore Israel	Micah 7

People

Micah—prophet from Moresheth in Judah
Jotham—king of Judah
Ahaz—king of Judah
Hezekiah—king of Judah
Daughter Zion—personification of Jerusalem

Places

Israel—northern kingdom
Judah—southern kingdom

Samaria—capital of Israel
Jerusalem—capital of Judah
Bethlehem—city in Judah

Key Concepts

Economic injustice—economic sins such as exploitation
Idolatry—worship of other gods; major theme of Micah's preaching
Wicked leaders—prophets who are corrupt and receive money for their messages
Restoration—reestablishment of Zion after the exile
Remnant of Jacob—portion of Judah who survives exile

Important Quotations

"Then they will cry to the Lord, but he will not answer them; he will hide his face from them at that time, because they have acted wickedly." (Mic 3:4)

"Therefore because of you Zion shall be plowed as a field; Jerusalem shall become a heap of ruins, and the mountain of the house a wooded height." (Mic 3:12)

"He shall judge between many peoples, and shall arbitrate between strong nations far away; they shall beat their swords into plowshares, and their spears into pruning hooks; nation shall not lift up sword against nation, neither shall they learn war any more; but they shall all sit under their own vines and under their own fig trees, and no one shall make them afraid; for the mouth of the Lord of hosts has spoken." (Mic 4:3–4)

"But you, O Bethlehem of Ephrathah, who are one of the little clans of Judah, from you shall come forth for me one who is to rule in Israel, whose origin is from of old, from ancient days." (Mic 5:2)

"He has told you, O mortal, what is good; and what does the Lord require of you but to do justice, and to love kindness, and to walk humbly with your God?" (Mic 6:8)

NAHUM

The Hebrew title of this book is the prophet's name, just as in English.

Synopsis

The book of Nahum is a prophecy against Nineveh, the capital city of Assyria. The opening chapter describes a wrathful and good God who protected God's people and punished their enemies. The defeat, plunder, destruction, and scattering of Nineveh is detailed and followed by an oracle of woe.

Content Outline

God's wrath upon enemies; God will not afflict Israel again	Nahum 1
God's destruction of the city of Nineveh	Nahum 2
Woe oracle against Nineveh	Nahum 3

People

Nahum—prophet from Elkosh

Places

Nineveh—capital of Assyria

Key Concepts

Wrath of God—expression of God's vengeance
Woe—oracle of calamity against Nineveh
Destruction—fate of Nineveh because of its wickedness
Oracle against the nations—prophetic sayings against Israel's neighbors

Important Quotations

"A jealous and avenging God is the LORD, the LORD is avenging and wrathful; the LORD takes vengeance on his adversaries and rages against his enemies. The LORD is slow to anger but great in power, and the LORD will by no means clear the guilty." (Nah 1:2–3)

"The LORD is good, a stronghold in a day of trouble; he protects those who take refuge in him." (Nah 1:7)

"I am against you, says the LORD of hosts, and will lift up your skirts over your face; and I will let nations look on your nakedness and kingdoms on your shame." (Nah 3:5)

HABAKKUK

The Hebrew title of this book is the prophet's name, just as in English.

Synopsis

The book of Habakkuk opens with a dialogue between the prophet and God. The prophet complained about the wicked and their violence, crying out to God about the destruction around him. Habakkuk asked if God would help. God replied by pointing to the nations, especially the Chaldeans, who committed violence. Habakkuk was not satisfied with God's response and wondered why the God of all creation would not act. God responded by noting that the proud would not endure but the righteous would live. The proud and oppressive people would be punished.

The book concludes with a prayer by the prophet. He praised God for God's power and concluded that he would rejoice in God even in times of difficulty.

Content Outline

Habakkuk and God's Dialogue

Prophet's complaint; God's response; prophet's complaint	Habakkuk 1
God's reply	Habakkuk 2

Habakkuk's Prayer

Prophet's prayer about God's power and victory over enemies	Habakkuk 3

Key Concepts

Injustice—suffering without reason and violence in the land; major theme of the prophecies

Lament—the prophet complains to God about violence

Violence—major topic for the prophet, who is concerned about violence against his people

Important Quotations

"O LORD, how long shall I cry for help, and you will not listen? Or cry to you 'Violence!' and you will not save?" (Hab 1:2)

"I will stand at my watchpost, and station myself on the rampart; I will keep watch to see what he will say to me, and what he will answer concerning my complaint." (Hab 2:1)

"Look at the proud! Their spirit is not right in them, but the righteous live by their faith." (Hab 2:4)

"But the LORD is in his holy temple; let all the earth keep silence before him!" (Hab 2:20)

"Though the fig tree does not blossom, and no fruit is on the vines; though the produce of the olive fails, and the fields yield no food; though the flock is cut off from the fold, and there is no herd in the stalls, yet I will rejoice in the LORD; I will exult in the God of my salvation." (Hab 3:17–18)

"God, the Lord, is my strength; he makes my feet like the feet of a deer, and makes me tread upon the heights." (Hab 3:19)

ZEPHANIAH

The Hebrew title of this book is the prophet's name, just as in English.

Synopsis

During King Josiah's reign, Zephaniah announced harsh judgment on Judah and Jerusalem through a series of judgment oracles: God would sweep away everything on the day of the Lord; God's judgment was for both Judah and enemy nations, including the Moabites, Ammonites, and Cushites; and God would focus on Jerusalem's defilement and profanity, thereby condemning its officials, judges, prophets, and priests. The book concludes with a hymn commanding Israel to praise God because of God's salvation of Jerusalem.

Content Outline

God will sweep away Judah; the day of the Lord is near	Zephaniah 1
The humble of the land should seek God; judgment against the nations	Zephaniah 2
Judgment against Jerusalem; judgment against nations; restoration for Israel	Zephaniah 3

People

Zephaniah—prophet; son of Cushi
Josiah—son of Amon; king of Judah
Daughter Zion—personification of Jerusalem

Places

Judah—southern kingdom
Jerusalem—capital of Judah

Key Concepts

Day of the Lord—future event that is described as near and as a day of wrath
Judgment—prophetic sayings that condemn particular bad behaviors of Judah and other nations

Important Quotations

"I will utterly sweep away everything from the face of the earth, says the LORD." (Zeph 1:2)

"Seek the LORD, all you humble of the land, who do his commands; seek righteousness, seek humility; perhaps you may be hidden on the day of the LORD's wrath." (Zeph 2:3)

"At that time I will change the speech of the peoples to a pure speech, that all of them may call on the name of the LORD and serve him with one accord." (Zeph 3:9)

"The LORD, your God, is in your midst, a warrior who gives victory; he will rejoice over you with gladness, and he will renew you in his love; he will exult over you with loud singing." (Zeph 3:17)

HAGGAI

The Hebrew title of this book is the prophet's name, just as in English.

Synopsis

Haggai focuses on the rebuilding of the Temple after the Babylonian exile. God commanded Zerubbabel and Joshua to begin work on the destroyed structure. God also promised that the new Temple would be even more glorious than the one before. God reprimanded the people for working more on their own houses than on the Temple. God promised that Zerubbabel would play a part in the restoration of the Davidic monarchy.

Content Outline

God's command to rebuild the Temple	Haggai 1
New Temple will be splendorous; Zerubbabel as a signet ring	Haggai 2

People

Darius—king of Persia
Haggai—prophet
Zerubbabel—son of Shealtiel; governor of Judah
Joshua—son of Jehozadak; high priest

Places

Judah—southern kingdom

Key Concepts

Temple—place of worship and sacrifice where God's presence dwells; Haggai calls the people to rebuild the temple in Jerusalem
Signet ring—God's reference to Zerubbabel as his chosen one

Important Quotations

"Is it a time for you yourselves to live in your paneled houses, while this house lies in ruins?" (Hag 1:4)

"The silver is mine, and the gold is mine, says the LORD of hosts." (Hag 2:8)

"The latter splendor of this house shall be greater than the former, says the LORD of hosts; and in this place I will give prosperity, says the LORD of hosts." (Hag 2:9)

"On that day, says the LORD of hosts, I will take you, O Zerubbabel my servant, son of Shealtiel, says the LORD, and make you like a signet ring; for I have chosen you, says the LORD of hosts." (Hag 2:23)

ZECHARIAH

The Hebrew title of this book is the prophet's name, just as in English.

Synopsis

The book of Zechariah begins with a call to return to God, followed by a series of eight visions. The prophet was given a vision of certain objects, followed by a dialogue with an angel and God about the explanation of the objects. The first vision concerned a man and several horses patrolling the earth—God's message of compassion and restoration to Jerusalem. The brief, second vision concerned four horns and four blacksmiths—the horns representing Babylon who destroyed Judah, and the four blacksmiths representing Persia who destroyed the Babylonians. The third vision portrayed a man measuring the length and width of Jerusalem to rebuild it. The fourth vision included Joshua, the high priest, and his instatement as high priest. The fifth vision featured a lampstand and two olive trees representing God's presence and the leadership of the governor and high priest, respectively. The sixth vision contained a flying scroll going out across the land. The seventh vision featured a woman sitting in a basket, representing wickedness. The eighth vision consisted of four chariots.

People came from Bethel to Jerusalem to ask about fasting. Zechariah condemned their fasting and admonished them to show kindness and mercy. In addition, the prophet delivered a message of hope and promise to Zion and spoke about fasting with joy.

The book of Zechariah concludes with messages from three oracles. The first spoke judgment against Israel's enemies and the coming salvation through a new king. The second spoke of restoration for Judah and Israel. The final oracle spoke of the future victory of Jerusalem, the end of false prophets, and worship of God in Jerusalem.

Content Outline

Eight Visions

First vision, of a man with horses; second vision, of four horns and four blacksmiths	Zechariah 1
Third vision, of a man with a measuring line	Zechariah 2
Fourth vision, of the high priest Joshua and Satan	Zechariah 3

Fifth vision, of a lampstand and two olive trees	Zechariah 4
Sixth vision, of a flying scroll; seventh vision, of a woman sitting in a basket	Zechariah 5
Eighth vision, of four chariots; Joshua, the high priest, is crowned	Zechariah 6

Fasting

| People of Bethel inquire about fasting; God calls for kindness and mercy | Zechariah 7 |
| God promises to return to Jerusalem; fasts of joy and gladness | Zechariah 8 |

Hopeful

Judgment against the enemies of Israel; the coming king	Zechariah 9
Restoration of Judah and Ephraim (Israel)	Zechariah 10
Two shepherds	Zechariah 11
Victory to Jerusalem	Zechariah 12
Cut off the idols; strike the shepherd	Zechariah 13
Final day of destruction	Zechariah 14

People

Zechariah—prophet; son of Berechiah
Darius—king of Persia
Joshua—high priest

Places

Jerusalem—capital of Judah
Bethel—town in Israel

Key Concepts

Visions—images given in a trance or a dreamlike state; comprise the first half of the book of Zechariah

Fasting—abstinence from food and drink; the book condemns the people's hypocritical fasting

False prophets—people who make deceitful or untruthful claims; God will remove false prophecy from the land

Branch—name given to the high priest

High priest—Joshua, the first high priest after the Babylonian exile, is given a crown

Important Quotations

"Take the silver and gold and make a crown, and set it on the head of the high priest Joshua son of Jehozadak; say to him: Thus says the LORD of hosts: Here is a man whose name is Branch: for he shall branch out in his place, and he shall build the temple of the LORD." (Zech 6:11–12)

"Rejoice greatly, O daughter Zion! Shout aloud, O daughter Jerusalem! Lo, your king comes to you; triumphant and victorious is he, humble and riding on a donkey, on a colt, the foal of a donkey." (Zech 9:9)

"I will strengthen the house of Judah, and I will save the house of Joseph. I will bring them back because I have compassion on them, and they shall be as though I had not rejected them; for I am the LORD their God and I will answer them." (Zech 10:6)

MALACHI

The Hebrew title of this book is the prophet's name, just as in English. In Christian Bibles, it is the last book in the Prophets section and in the Old Testament canon. In Jewish Bibles, Malachi is followed by the Writings section.

Synopsis

The book of Malachi contains prophetic oracles concerning multiple topics. It opens with clarification of Israel's relationship to Edom. Judgment was declared against Edom, against Israel's priesthood for improper sacrifices, and against Israel for committing the abomination of marrying foreign women. God would send a messenger to purify the priesthood. Malachi accused the people of robbing God by not bringing the full tithe into the storehouse. The book ends by speaking of a coming day of judgment.

Content Outline

God loved Jacob and hated Esau; priests offer wrong sacrifices	Malachi 1
Covenant with Levi; Judah profaned the sanctuary and married foreign women	Malachi 2
A messenger is coming; bring tithes to God	Malachi 3
Day of judgment is coming; remember the teaching of Moses; Elijah will come	Malachi 4

People

Malachi—prophet; name means "my messenger"
Levi—priest from an earlier time in Israel's history
Messenger—someone coming to purify the priesthood
Moses—prophet from an earlier time in Israel's history
Elijah—prophet from an earlier time in Israel's history

Places

Edom—Judah's neighbor and enemy

Key Concepts

Edom—Esau's land; desolated by God
Priesthood—body of worship leaders who say prayers and make sacrifices on behalf of the people; God condemns the priests who offer polluted food
Improper sacrifices—polluted food offered by priests
Covenant with Levi—covenant between the priests and God; corrupted by the priests' improper sacrifices
Tithing—one-tenth of the harvest and the produce brought to the Temple as offerings to God; God commands the people to bring their full tithe to the Temple's storehouses
Messenger—person whom God promises to send to help restore the priesthood
Day of the Lord—future event that is described as burning

Important Quotations

"I have loved you, says the LORD. But you say, 'How have you loved us?' Is not Esau Jacob's brother? says the LORD. Yet I have loved Jacob but I have hated Esau; I have made his hill country a desolation and his heritage a desert for jackals." (Mal 1:2–3)

"Have we not all one father? Has not one God created us? Why then are we faithless to one another, profaning the covenant of our ancestors? Judah has been faithless, and abomination has been committed in Israel and in Jerusalem; for Judah has profaned the sanctuary of the LORD, which he loves, and has married the daughter of a foreign god." (Mal 2:10–11)

"See, I am sending my messenger to prepare the way before me, and the Lord whom you seek will suddenly come to his temple. The messenger of the covenant in whom you delight—indeed, he is coming, says the LORD of hosts." (Mal 3:1)

"Bring the full tithe into the storehouse, so that there may be food in my house, and thus put me to the test, says the LORD of hosts; see if I will not open the windows of heaven for you and pour down for you an overflowing blessing." (Mal 3:10)

"Remember the teaching of my servant Moses, the statutes and ordinances that I commanded him at Horeb for all Israel." (Mal 4:4)

"Lo, I will send you the prophet Elijah before the great and terrible day of the LORD comes. He will turn the hearts of parents to their children and the hearts of children to their parents, so that I will not come and strike the land with a curse." (Mal 4:5)

5

The Gospels and the Acts of the Apostles

The first four books of the New Testament narrate the life of Jesus and are named after their traditional authors: Matthew, Mark, Luke, and John. Some of them speak of Jesus' birth, but the focus of all four is his adult life as a teacher and healer. Each of these Gospels also tells the story of Jesus' final week of life in Jerusalem: his arrival in the city, conflict with the religious and political leaders, arrest, crucifixion, death, and burial. Some of the Gospels also recount his resurrection appearances to people. Gospels are a form of ancient biography.

These four Gospels are not the only Gospels of early Christianity. They are the four that were included in the New Testament. Extracanonical Gospels include the Gospel of Thomas, the Gospel of Peter, and the Gospel of Mary.

The Gospels contain all types of literary materials—for example, birth narratives, miracle stories, parables, teachings, healing stories, genealogies. Most of the stories in the Gospel of Mark are also in the Gospel of Matthew, and much of the Gospel of Mark is also in the Gospel of Luke. Because these three Gospels share so much material, they are often called the Synoptic ("seeing together") Gospels. The Gospel of John presents its own unique version of the story of Jesus that is different from the other canonical Gospels.

The fifth book in the New Testament, the Acts of the Apostles, is a sequel to the Gospel of Luke and narrates the story of the early Christian community. Both the apostle Peter and the apostle Paul figure prominently. Together, Acts and the four Gospels constitute most of the narrative material in the New Testament.

Map 6. Palestine in the First Century CE

(Originally published in M. Eugene Boring, *An Introduction to the New Testament* [Louisville, KY: Westminster John Knox Press, 2012], end plate.)

MATTHEW

The Gospel of Matthew, the first Gospel in the New Testament, is named for Jesus' early disciple. This disciple is mentioned twice in the book. Matthew contains some material that is not found in any other Gospel.

Synopsis

The Gospel of Matthew begins with a genealogy of Jesus: from Abraham, through King David and the Babylonian exile, to Joseph, the husband of Mary. This unique genealogy also includes some women among Jesus' ancestors. Mary was betrothed to Joseph but was found to be pregnant from the Holy Spirit. Joseph wanted to dismiss her; however, an angel appeared to him and told him to take Mary as his wife and to name the baby boy Jesus. Joseph did exactly as the angel instructed him. After the birth of Jesus, wise men from the East followed a star to find him and offered him gifts. An angel appeared to Joseph warning him of King Herod's plan to kill Jesus, so he fled to Egypt with Mary and the baby. They did not return to Israel until after King Herod's death.

John the Baptist preached a message of repentance in the wilderness and baptized people in the Jordan River. Jesus came to be baptized, and the Spirit of God descended upon him as a dove. The Spirit then led Jesus into the wilderness for forty days to be tempted by Satan. After his temptation, Jesus returned to Galilee and lived in Capernaum. He called his first four disciples—Simon Peter, Andrew, James, and John—and began his ministry of teaching and healing.

Jesus delivered a long sermon, typically called the Sermon on the Mount, which included blessings, interpretations of older biblical passages, and other admonishments. Jesus performed many miraculous deeds. He cleansed a leper, healed the servant of a Roman centurion, relieved the fever of Peter's mother-in-law, stilled a storm on the sea, healed a demoniac from the country of the Gadarenes and a paralyzed man, brought a girl back to life, healed a bleeding woman, returned sight to two blind men, and cast a demon from a mute person. During the period of these miracles, he called Matthew to follow him.

Jesus selected and assembled the twelve apostles and delivered another teaching about their mission. He explained the role of John the Baptist and identified him as Elijah. He reproached the neighboring cities for their lack of repentance and gave thanks to God. Jesus healed on the Sabbath, which caused the Pharisees to conspire against him. He healed a demoniac and was accused by the Pharisees of casting out demons by Beelzebul. When the scribes and

Pharisees asked for a sign, Jesus reminded them of the sign of Jonah, who was in the belly of the big fish for three days and three nights, and said that the Son of Man would likewise be in the earth for three days and three nights.

Jesus told many parables, including the parable of the Sower, the parable of the Weeds, and the parable of the Mustard Seed. He taught in his hometown of Nazareth but did not perform miraculous deeds there because the people took offense at his wisdom and power. After hearing of the beheading of John the Baptist, Jesus desired to be alone, so he departed Nazareth by boat. Jesus' ministry continued as he fed five thousand, calmed the sea, and walked on water. He visited Tyre and Sidon for a brief period. In Galilee he healed many people and fed four thousand. Jesus warned his disciples about the Pharisees and Sadducees. Peter declared Jesus as the Christ, the Son of the living God. Jesus predicted his death and resurrection.

Jesus took Peter, James, and John to a mountain and was transfigured before them. God's voice was heard from a cloud declaring Jesus as God's son. When they came down from the mountain, Jesus rebuked and cast a demon out of a boy. Jesus' ministry of teaching resumed, including lessons about the greatest in the kingdom and stumbling blocks, and the parables of the Lost Sheep and the Unforgiving Servant. The Pharisees asked Jesus about divorce and how to gain eternal life. He told the parable of the Laborers in the Vineyard and predicted his death for a third time.

Jesus entered Jerusalem riding on a borrowed donkey and colt while a large crowd shouted, "Hosanna to the Son of David!" Jesus entered the Temple and drove out the money changers. The next day, Jesus cursed a fruitless fig tree. He told the Jewish leaders the parables of the Two Sons, the Wicked Tenants, and the Wedding Banquet. He answered questions about paying taxes, the resurrection, the greatest commandment, and the Messiah. Jesus cursed some of the Jewish leaders and delivered teachings about the end of the age, including the need to be watchful, and he told the parables of the Ten Bridesmaids and the Talents.

The Jewish leaders conspired to arrest Jesus and kill him. Jesus was anointed by a woman at Bethany and celebrated Passover with his disciples, thus instituting the Lord's Supper. He predicted Peter's denial and prayed in Gethsemane, where he was betrayed by Judas and arrested. Jesus was taken before the high priest, Caiaphas. As predicted, Peter denied Jesus three times. Jesus was brought before Pilate for questioning. Judas committed suicide. Pilate handed Jesus over to be crucified. The soldiers mocked and crucified him. Jesus died and was buried, and the guards secured the tomb. The following day, Mary Magdalene and the other Mary went to the tomb, where an angel told them Jesus had risen. As the women left, Jesus appeared to them.

Jesus later appeared to the disciples in Galilee and commanded them to go and make disciples of all nations.

Content Outline

Jesus' Birth and Early Years

Genealogy of Jesus from Abraham to Joseph; birth of Jesus	Matthew 1
Wise men visit; Jesus' family flees to Egypt; Herod kills infants; Jesus' family returns from Egypt	Matthew 2

Preparation for Ministry

John the Baptist preaches; John baptizes Jesus	Matthew 3
Jesus is tempted by Satan; Jesus calls four disciples; Jesus teaches and cures	Matthew 4

Sermon on the Mount

Beatitudes; salt and light; murder, adultery, divorce, swearing falsely, and love	Matthew 5
Giving alms; the Lord's Prayer; fasting; treasures in heaven; two masters; do not worry	Matthew 6
Do not judge; the Golden Rule; a good tree bears good fruit; do the will of the Father	Matthew 7

Jesus' Deeds and Teaching around Galilee

Jesus makes a leper clean and heals a servant; Peter's mother-in-law; demoniacs	Matthew 8
Jesus heals a paralytic, calls Matthew, heals a woman and restores a girl, and heals two blind men	Matthew 9
Jesus calls and sends out twelve apostles; be wise as serpents; Jesus has come to bring a sword, not peace	Matthew 10
Jesus talks about John the Baptist; he reproaches the cities and thanks the Father	Matthew 11
Jesus heals on the Sabbath; Beelzebul; the sign of Jonah; true mothers and brothers	Matthew 12

Seven parables: Sower, Weeds, Mustard Seed, Yeast, Treasure, Pearls, Net	Matthew 13
John the Baptist dies; Jesus feeds five thousand and walks on water	Matthew 14
What defiles; daughter of a Canaanite woman healed; Jesus feeds the four thousand	Matthew 15
Sign from heaven; Peter says, "You are the Messiah"; Jesus predicts his death	Matthew 16
Jesus' transfiguration; Jesus cures an epileptic; temple tax	Matthew 17
Greatness in humility; parable of the Lost Sheep; parable of the Unforgiving Slave	Matthew 18

Jesus Travels from Galilee to Jerusalem

Jesus teaches about divorce; Jesus says, "Let the little children come to me"; rich young man	Matthew 19
Householder parable; Jesus predicts his death and heals two blind men	Matthew 20

Jesus in Jerusalem

Jesus' entry into Jerusalem; Jesus cleanses the Temple and curses a fig tree; parable of the Two Sons	Matthew 21
Parable of the Wedding Banquet; conflict stories; greatest commandment	Matthew 22
Jesus curses some Jewish leaders	Matthew 23
Signs of the end of the age; desolating sacrilege; sign of the Son of Man	Matthew 24
Parables of the Ten Bridesmaids and the Talents; the Son of Man will come to judge	Matthew 25
Woman anoints Jesus; Passover; Peter's denial; Gethsemane; Jesus' arrest	Matthew 26
Jesus before Pilate; Judas kills himself; Barabbas; Jesus' crucifixion, death, and burial	Matthew 27
Resurrection of Jesus; guards report events; Jesus commissions disciples	Matthew 28

People

Jesus—the Messiah; "son of Abraham"; "son of David"
Mary—Jesus' mother
Joseph—husband of Mary; Jesus' earthly father
King Herod—king of Judea who attempts to kill Jesus
Wise men from the East—travelers who bring gifts to the baby Jesus
John the Baptist—prophet who baptizes Jesus
Pharisees—Jewish leaders
Sadducees—Jewish leaders
The devil/the tempter/Satan—figure who tempts Jesus in the wilderness
Simon Peter (aka Peter)—one of Jesus' first disciples
Andrew—one of Jesus' first disciples
James—one of Jesus' first disciples; son of Zebedee
John—one of Jesus' first disciples; son of Zebedee
Matthew—one of Jesus' disciples; tax collector
Philip—one of Jesus' disciples
Bartholomew—one of Jesus' disciples
Thomas—one of Jesus' disciples
James—one of Jesus' disciples; son of Alphaeus
Thaddaeus—one of Jesus' disciples
Simon—one of Jesus' disciples
Judas Iscariot—one of Jesus' disciples; betrays Jesus
Beelzebul—ruler of the demons
Herod (aka Herod Antipas)—Roman ruler/tetrarch of Galilee; son of King Herod (the Great)
Simon—leper; Jesus stays at his house
Caiaphas—high priest
Pilate—governor
Jesus Barabbas—prisoner
Simon—from Cyrene; carries Jesus' cross
Mary Magdalene—witness at the crucifixion and resurrection
Mary—witness at the crucifixion and resurrection
Joseph—from Arimathea; wraps Jesus' body and lays it in the tomb

Places

Bethlehem of Judea—place of Jesus' birth
Jordan River—place of Jesus' baptism
Galilee—area where Jesus ministers
Nazareth—town in Galilee

Capernaum—town in Galilee by the sea
Tyre and Sidon—cities Jesus visits
Caesarea Philippi—city Jesus visits
Judea beyond the Jordan—area Jesus visits on his way to Jerusalem
Bethphage—town on the Mount of Olives
Bethany—place where a woman anoints Jesus
Jerusalem—place of Jesus' death and burial
Gethsemane—place where Jesus prays

Key Concepts

Beatitudes—series of blessings from Matthew 5
Kingdom of heaven—Matthew's preferred term; Mark and Luke use "kingdom of God"
Law/Scriptures—Jesus reinterprets the law; Jesus as the new Moses who offers new legal teachings
Fulfillment of prophecy—Jesus and his teachings are a realization of Old Testament prophecy
Apocalyptic dualism—conflict between good and evil

Material Unique to Matthew

Matt 1–2: Genealogy; focus on Joseph in Jesus' birth story; visit of the wise men; Jesus' family flees to Egypt
Matt 5:17–20: Jesus has come not to abolish but to fulfill the law
Matt 5:21, 27, 31, 33, 38, 43: "You have heard it said . . . , but I say to you . . ."
Matt 13:24–30, 36–52: Parables of the Weeds, Treasure, Pearls, and Net
Matt 14:28–31; 16:17–19; 17:24–27; 18:21–22: Stories involving Peter
Matt 18:23–35: Parable of the Unforgiving Slave
Matt 20:1–16: Parable of the Vineyard Laborers
Matt 25:1–13: Parable of the Ten Bridesmaids
Matt 25:31–46: Son of Man will come to judge the nations
Matt 27:3–10: Judas kills himself
Matt 27:62–66; 28:11–15: Stories about the guard at the tomb
Matt 28:16–20: Jesus commissions his disciples

Matthew's Five Teaching Sections

Sermon on the Mount	Matt 5–7
Mission teaching	Matt 10

Seven parables	Matt 13
Church teaching	Matt 18
Teaching on the end of the age	Matt 24–25

Important Quotations

"An account of the genealogy of Jesus the Messiah, the son of David, the son of Abraham." (Matt 1:1)

"But just when he had resolved to do this, an angel of the Lord appeared to him in a dream and said, 'Joseph, son of David, do not be afraid to take Mary as your wife, for the child conceived in her is from the Holy Spirit. She will bear a son, and you are to name him Jesus, for he will save his people from their sins.'" (Matt 1:20–21)

"I baptize you with water for repentance, but one who is more powerful than I is coming after me; I am not worthy to carry his sandals. He will baptize you with the Holy Spirit and fire." (Matt 3:11)

"And when Jesus had been baptized, just as he came up from the water, suddenly the heavens were opened to him and he saw the Spirit of God descending like a dove and alighting on him. And a voice from heaven said, 'This is my Son, the Beloved, with whom I am well pleased.'" (Matt 3:16–17)

"Blessed are the poor in spirit, for theirs is the kingdom of heaven." (Matt 5:3)

"You are the salt of the earth. . . . You are the light of the world." (Matt 5:13a; 14a)

"Do not think that I have come to abolish the law or the prophets; I have come not to abolish but to fulfill." (Matt 5:17)

"You have heard that it was said, 'You shall love your neighbor and hate your enemy.' But I say to you, Love your enemies and pray for those who persecute you." (Matt 5:43)

"Pray then in this way: Our Father in heaven, hallowed be your name. Your kingdom come. Your will be done, on earth as it is in heaven. Give us this day our daily bread. And forgive us our debts, as we also have forgiven our debtors. And do not bring us to the time of trial, but rescue us from the evil one." (Matt 6:9–13)

"Do not judge, so that you may not be judged." (Matt 7:1)

"Ask, and it will be given you; search, and you will find; knock, and the door will be opened for you." (Matt 7:7)

"In everything do to others as you would have them do to you; for this is the law and the prophets." (Matt 7:12)

"Come to me, all you that are weary and are carrying heavy burdens, and I will give you rest. Take my yoke upon you, and learn from me; for I am gentle and humble in heart, and you will find rest for your souls. For my yoke is easy, and my burden is light." (Matt 11:28–30)

"So the last will be first, and the first will be last." (Matt 20:16)

"And Jesus came and said to them, 'All authority in heaven and on earth has been given to me. Go therefore and make disciples of all nations, baptizing them in the name of the Father and of the Son and of the Holy Spirit, and teaching them to obey everything that I have commanded you. And remember, I am with you always, to the end of the age.'" (Matt 28:18–20)

MARK

Mark is the second book and the second Gospel in the New Testament. It is named after the book's traditional author. Mark is the briefest Gospel but contains a detailed narrative of Jesus' suffering and death. Most of the stories in Mark can also be found in Matthew or Luke or both. However, Mark does contain a few stories that are unique.

Synopsis

Mark begins with John the Baptist proclaiming repentance in the wilderness and moves directly to the baptism of Jesus in the Jordan River. Immediately after his baptism, Jesus was led into the wilderness to be tempted by Satan for forty days and forty nights. Jesus arrived in Galilee, where he proclaimed the good news and called his first disciples. He exorcised an unclean spirit from a man and healed many, including Simon's mother-in-law, a leper, and a paralytic. Jesus called another disciple, Levi, and engaged the scribes and Pharisees in controversial matters related to sharing meals with sinners, fasting, and the Sabbath.

Jesus appointed twelve apostles to proclaim his message and responded to some who thought he was out of his mind. He told several parables: the Sower, the Seed, and the Mustard Seed. While sleeping on a boat as he and the disciples crossed the sea, Jesus was awakened to calm a storm and rebuked his disciples for their lack of faith. He healed a demoniac, a bleeding woman, and Jairus's daughter.

Jesus was rejected in his hometown of Nazareth. He sent out the Twelve, two by two, to heal the suffering and proclaim repentance. King Herod beheaded John the Baptist at his daughter's request. Jesus fed five thousand people and later walked on water to reach the boat carrying his disciples. The Jewish leaders questioned Jesus about his disciples and their nonobservance of the tradition of the elders. In Tyre, Jesus cast the demon out of the daughter of a Syrophoenician woman; in Sidon, he cured a deaf man; at the Sea of Galilee, he fed four thousand people and warned the disciples about the yeast of the Pharisees.

In Bethsaida, Jesus healed a blind man and predicted the Son of Man's death and resurrection. Peter declared Jesus as the Messiah. Jesus took Peter, James, and John to a high mountain and was transfigured in front of them. Jesus healed a boy with a demonic spirit and predicted his death for the second time. Jesus taught about divorce and blessed the little children. He told a story about a rich man who wished to inherit eternal life, and he predicted his death and resurrection a third time. James and John responded to the story by requesting to sit at the right and left hand of Jesus in his glory.

Jesus entered Jerusalem on a colt with the people shouting, "Hosanna!" He cursed a fruitless fig tree before entering the Temple to drive out the money changers. Jesus told the parable of the Wicked Tenants and answered the Jewish leaders' questions about the resurrection, paying taxes, and the first commandment. Jesus predicted that the Temple would fall and that his followers would endure harassment. He spoke of the desolating sacrilege and the Son of Man coming in clouds.

The Jewish leaders began to look for a way to arrest Jesus. Jesus was anointed by a woman at Bethany with an expensive ointment. Judas Iscariot looked for an opportunity to betray Jesus and conspired with the chief priests. Jesus celebrated Passover with his disciples and instituted the Lord's Supper. He predicted Peter's denial and prayed in Gethsemane, where he was betrayed by Judas and arrested. Jesus was taken before the Jewish council and then to Pilate for questioning. As predicted, Peter denied Jesus three times. Pilate handed Jesus over to soldiers, who mocked and crucified him. Jesus died and was buried on the day before the Sabbath. After the Sabbath ended, Mary Magdalene, Mary, and Salome went to the tomb to anoint him but found an empty tomb and fled in fear.

Content Outline

Jesus in Galilee

John the Baptist baptizes Jesus; Jesus is tempted, calls his first disciples, and heals	Mark 1
Jesus heals a paralyzed man, calls Levi, and talks about fasting and the Sabbath	Mark 2
Jesus heals on the Sabbath and appoints the twelve apostles; scribes think that Jesus is possessed by Beelzebul	Mark 3
Parables of the Sower and the Mustard Seed; Jesus calms the sea	Mark 4
Jesus heals a demoniac, a hemorrhaging woman, and Jairus's daughter	Mark 5
Jesus is rejected in his hometown; Jesus sends out his disciples; death of John; Jesus feeds the five thousand	Mark 6
Jesus and Pharisees discuss the role of tradition; Jesus heals the Syrophoenician woman's daughter and a deaf man	Mark 7
Jesus feeds the four thousand; Pharisees test Jesus; Jesus heals a blind man; Peter's proclamation	Mark 8

Jesus on the Way to and in Jerusalem

Jesus' transfiguration; Jesus heals a boy; disciples argue; Jesus speaks of stumbling blocks	Mark 9
Jesus teaches about divorce and blesses little children; rich man's encounter with Jesus; Jesus heals blind Bartimaeus	Mark 10
Jesus' entry into Jerusalem; Jesus curses a fig tree and enters the Temple	Mark 11
Parable of the Wicked Tenants; Jesus answers a question about paying taxes; first commandment; beware of scribes	Mark 12
Jesus predicts the fall of the Temple and the persecution of his followers; desolating sacrilege	Mark 13

Jesus' Passion

Woman anoints Jesus; Passover; Jesus predicts Peter's denial; Gethsemane; Jesus' arrest; Peter denies Jesus	Mark 14
Pilate hands over Jesus to be crucified; crucifixion, death, and burial of Jesus	Mark 15
Empty tomb	Mark 16
Shorter, later ending to the Gospel of Mark	End of Mark 16
Longer, later ending to the Gospel of Mark	Mark 16:9–20

People

Jesus—son of God

John the Baptist—religious leader who preaches a baptism of repentance for the forgiveness of sins

Simon—one of Jesus' first disciples; brother of Andrew

Andrew—one of Jesus' first disciples; brother of Simon

James—one of Jesus' first disciples; brother of John; son of Zebedee

John—one of Jesus' first disciples; brother of James; son of Zebedee

Levi—one of Jesus' disciples; son of Alphaeus

Pharisees—Jewish leaders

Philip—one of Jesus' disciples

Bartholomew—one of Jesus' disciples

Matthew—one of Jesus' disciples

Thomas—one of Jesus' disciples

James—one of Jesus' disciples; son of Alphaeus

Thaddaeus—one of Jesus' disciples

Simon the Cananaean—one of Jesus' disciples

Judas Iscariot—one of Jesus' disciples; betrays Jesus

Mary—Jesus' mother

James—Jesus' brother

Joses—Jesus' brother

Judas—Jesus' brother

Simon—Jesus' brother

Herod—tetrarch of Galilee; called "King"

Places

Nazareth—Jesus' hometown

Galilee—area where Jesus ministers

Capernaum—town on the northern shore of the Sea of Galilee
Decapolis—ten cities east of the Jordan River; a Gentile area
Tyre—Gentile city
Bethsaida—town along the Sea of Galilee
Caesarea Philippi—area north of Galilee

Key Concepts

Kingdom of God—Mark's alternative to the Roman Empire
Immediately—word used over forty times in Mark to create a sense of urgency
Messianic secret—Jesus tells his followers to remain silent about his actions
Conflict stories—encounters between Jesus and his antagonists
Disciple—follower of Jesus

Material Unique to Mark

Mark 3:20–21: Jesus' family members worry about him
Mark 4:26–29: Parable of the Growing Seed
Mark 7:31–37: Jesus cures a deaf man
Mark 8:22–26: Jesus cures the blind man of Bethsaida
Mark 14:51–52: Young man following Jesus runs away naked

Important Quotations

"The beginning of the good news of Jesus Christ, the Son of God." (Mark 1:1)

"Then he said to them, 'The sabbath was made for humankind, and not humankind for the sabbath; so the Son of Man is lord even of the sabbath.'" (Mark 2:27–28)

"He also said, 'The kingdom of God is as if someone would scatter seed on the ground, and would sleep and rise night and day, and the seed would sprout and grow, he does not know how. The earth produces of itself, first the stalk, then the head, then the full grain in the head. But when the grain is ripe, at once he goes in with his sickle, because the harvest has come.'" (Mark 4:26–29)

"Then Jesus said to them, 'Prophets are not without honor, except in their hometown, and among their own kin, and in their own house.' And he could do no deed of power there, except that he laid his hands on a few sick people and cured them. And he was amazed at their unbelief." (Mark 6:4–6)

"Then Jesus laid his hands on his eyes again; and he looked intently and his sight was restored, and he saw everything clearly." (Mark 8:25)

"A certain young man was following him, wearing nothing but a linen cloth. They caught hold of him, but he left the linen cloth and ran off naked." (Mark 14:51–52)

LUKE

Luke, named after its traditional author, is the third book and third Gospel in the New Testament. This Gospel is connected to the Acts of the Apostles as a single-authored, two-volume work. Luke contains some material that is not found in the other Gospels.

Synopsis

Luke begins with a prologue that mentions the Gospel's addressee, Theophilus. The birth of John the Baptist was foretold by an angel. Zechariah was told that his wife Elizabeth would have a son. The birth of Jesus was foretold by an angel who informed Mary she would also have a son. Mary visited Elizabeth and praised God in song. John the Baptist was born, and his father Zechariah prophesied.

Jesus was born in Bethlehem, where Mary and Joseph had journeyed to register for the census, as ordered by Emperor Augustus. An angel appeared to shepherds announcing the birth, and they traveled to Bethlehem to see the child. After eight days, Jesus was named and circumcised. When he was presented in the Temple, the righteous man Simeon and the prophet Anna praised God. Mary, Joseph, and Jesus returned to Nazareth. When Jesus was twelve years old, he was accidently left in Jerusalem after a trip to celebrate the Passover. His parents found him talking to the teachers in the Temple.

John the Baptist proclaimed a baptism of repentance for the forgiveness of sins, and Jesus was baptized by John. (Luke interjects the genealogy of Jesus here, tracing his ancestry to Adam.) After the baptism of Jesus by John the Baptist, he was led into the wilderness to be tempted by the devil.

As Jesus began his ministry in Galilee, he was rejected in his hometown of Nazareth. He went to Capernaum, drove a demon out of a man, and healed many people, including Simon's mother-in-law. Jesus called his first disciples, cleansed a leper, and healed a paralytic man. He called Levi, a tax collector, to follow him, and answered the Pharisees' questions about fasting and the Sabbath. To the dismay of the scribes and Pharisees, Jesus healed a man with a withered hand on the Sabbath. He chose twelve disciples to be apostles and taught about blessings and woes, loving one's enemies, judging others, and forgiving.

In Capernaum, Jesus healed a centurion's slave and raised the son of a widow in Nain. He forgave the sins of a woman who washed his feet with her tears and anointed him with ointment. He told the parable of the Sower, calmed a storm, and healed a naked Gerasene demoniac who called himself Legion. He brought a girl back to life and healed a woman who had bled for twelve years. Jesus sent the twelve apostles to heal as they proclaimed the kingdom of God. On a hillside near Bethsaida, he fed five thousand people with five loaves and two fish. Jesus took Peter, James, and John to a mountain and was transfigured before them. God's voice was heard from a cloud declaring Jesus as God's son. When they came down from the mountain, Jesus rebuked a demon and cast it out of a boy. Jesus predicted his death for a second time. After being rejected in a Samaritan village, Jesus appointed seventy more people to preach and heal who later returned joyously proclaiming the success of their mission. Jesus told the parable of the Good Samaritan and visited with Martha and Mary. At the request of one of them, Jesus taught his disciples to pray.

Jesus was questioned about his authority to drive out demons and denounced the Pharisees and lawyers. He taught about hypocrisy and greed through the parable of the Rich Fool; he instructed his disciples not to worry; he told the parable of the Fig Tree and healed a crippled woman. The lessons continued with the parable of the Mustard Seed and the parable of the Yeast. Jesus lamented about Jerusalem and visited the house of a Pharisee, where he healed a man with dropsy. At the meal in the home of the Pharisee, Jesus told the parable of the Great Banquet. As Jesus traveled, he told the parables of the Lost Sheep, the Lost Coin, the Prodigal Son, and the Dishonest Manager. He told the story of the Rich Man and Lazarus, cleansed ten lepers, and spoke about the kingdom of God already being among them. Jesus told the parable of the Widow and the Judge and the parable of the Pharisee and the Tax Collector. He blessed the little children and answered the rich ruler's question about inheriting eternal life. Jesus predicted his death for a third time. In Jericho, he healed a blind man and met the chief tax collector, Zacchaeus. At the home of Zacchaeus, Jesus told the parable of the Ten Pounds.

Jesus entered Jerusalem riding on a borrowed colt, and crowds rejoiced and shouted; however, Jesus wept over the city. He went into the Temple and drove out the money changers. He told the people the parable of the Wicked Tenants and answered questions about paying taxes, the resurrection, and the Messiah. He predicted the fall of Jerusalem and spoke about the signs of the coming of the Son of Man.

The Jewish leaders conspired to kill Jesus, and Judas offered to betray him for money. Jesus celebrated Passover with his disciples and instituted the Lord's Supper. During the meal, Jesus predicted Peter's denial and then went to pray on the Mount of Olives. As foretold, Jesus was arrested after being betrayed by Judas, and Peter denied Jesus three times. He was taken before the assembly of the elders and then brought before Pilate for questioning and then before Herod. Pilate handed Jesus over to soldiers to be crucified. Jesus died and was buried in a new tomb by Joseph of Arimathea. On the first day of the week, the women who went to see the tomb found it empty. They were confused, but two men in white told them Jesus had risen. They ran to tell the apostles, but only Peter went to the tomb to confirm their story. Later that day, Jesus appeared to two of them on their way to Emmaus, but they did not recognize him until they shared a meal together. Jesus appeared to the eleven apostles, who thought he was a ghost until he asked for food to eat. He blessed them at Bethany before he ascended to heaven.

Content Outline

Jesus in Galilee

Prologue; John's and Jesus' births announced; Mary's song; Zechariah's prophecy	Luke 1
Birth of Jesus; shepherds and angels; boy Jesus in the Temple	Luke 2
John the Baptist preaching; Jesus' baptism; Jesus' genealogy	Luke 3
Temptation of Jesus in the wilderness; sermon and rejection of Jesus in Nazareth	Luke 4
Jesus calls disciples, cleanses a leper, and heals a paralyzed man; Jesus talks about fasting	Luke 5
Choosing the Twelve; Sermon on the Plain	Luke 6
Jesus heals a centurion's slave and forgives the sins of a woman	Luke 7
Parable of the Sower; Jesus speaks about a lamp on a lampstand; Jesus calms a storm and heals a demoniac	Luke 8
Jesus sends the Twelve; Jesus feeds five thousand; Transfiguration	Luke 9

Journey to Jerusalem

Jesus sends the seventy disciples; the seventy return; parable of the Good Samaritan	Luke 10
Lord's Prayer; Jesus and Beelzebul; sign of Jonah; woe to the Pharisees	Luke 11
Teachings on possessions: parable of the Rich Fool; finding treasure in heaven	Luke 12
Parables: Fig Tree, Mustard Seed, Yeast, Narrow Door; healing of a crippled woman	Luke 13
Humble yourselves; parable of the Great Banquet	Luke 14
Parables of the Lost Sheep, the Lost Coin, and the Prodigal Son	Luke 15
Parable of the Unjust Steward; parable of the Rich Man and Lazarus	Luke 16
Jesus cleanses lepers; Jesus says, "The kingdom of God is among you"	Luke 17
Parable of the Widow and the Judge; parable of the Pharisee and the Tax Collector	Luke 18
Story of Zacchaeus; Jesus' entry into Jerusalem; Jesus cleanses the Temple	Luke 19

Jesus in Jerusalem

Parable of the Wicked Tenants; Jesus answers questions about taxes and resurrection	Luke 20
Teachings about the end times	Luke 21
The Last Supper; Gethsemane; betrayal and arrest of Jesus; Peter's denial; Jesus' captors mock him	Luke 22
Crucifixion, death, and burial of Jesus	Luke 23
Resurrection; Jesus' appearances on the Emmaus Road and to the eleven apostles; Jesus' ascension	Luke 24

People

Jesus—Messiah and prophet
Theophilus—addressee of this Gospel
Herod—king of Judea at the birth of Jesus
Zechariah—priest in the line of Abijah; husband to Elizabeth; father of John the Baptist
Elizabeth—descendent of Aaron; wife of Zechariah; mother of John the Baptist
Gabriel—angel
Joseph—engaged to Mary
Mary—virgin engaged to Joseph; mother of Jesus
John the Baptist—Zechariah and Elizabeth's son
Emperor Augustus—first emperor of the Roman Empire
Quirinius—governor of Syria
Simeon—righteous man
Anna—prophet; daughter of Phanuel; from the tribe of Asher
Emperor Tiberius—second emperor of the Roman Empire
Pontius Pilate—governor of Judea
Herod (aka Herod Antipas)—ruler/tetrarch of Galilee; son of King Herod
Annas and Caiaphas—high priests
Simon (aka Simon Peter)—one of Jesus' first disciples
James—one of Jesus' first disciples; son of Zebedee
John—one of Jesus' first disciples; son of Zebedee
Levi—one of Jesus' first disciples; tax collector
Andrew—one of Jesus' first disciples; Simon Peter's brother
Philip—one of Jesus' disciples
Bartholomew—one of Jesus' disciples
Matthew—one of Jesus' disciples
Thomas—one of Jesus' disciples
James—one of Jesus' disciples; son of Alphaeus
Simon the Zealot—one of Jesus' disciples
Judas—one of Jesus' disciples; son of James
Judas Iscariot—one of Jesus' disciples; betrays Jesus
Mary Magdalene—traveler with Jesus
Joanna—wife of Herod's steward Chuza; traveler with Jesus
Susanna—traveler with Jesus
Martha—hosts Jesus with her sister, Mary
Mary—hosts Jesus with her sister, Martha

Places

Nazareth—town in Galilee; Joseph's hometown; Jesus' childhood home
Jerusalem—place of Jesus' death and burial
Judea—Roman province
Capernaum—city in Galilee
Bethlehem—city in Judea; place of Jesus' birth

Key Concepts

Kingdom of God—content of Jesus' proclamation of the good news
Meals—Jesus eats three meals at the homes of Pharisees
Reversals—society is turned upside down by Jesus' ministry
Good news to the poor—Jesus speaks about possessions frequently
Women—Luke mentions women more than other Gospels, and they play a
significant role in the narrative

Material Unique to Luke

Luke 1:26–38: Gabriel's announcement of Jesus' birth to Mary
Luke 1:57–80: Birth of John the Baptist
Luke 2:1–20: Newborn Jesus is laid in a manger and visited by shepherds
Luke 2:22–38: Baby Jesus is presented at the Temple
Luke 2:41–52: Jesus, at age twelve, visits the Temple and asks questions
Luke 5:1–11: Jesus catches fish with his first disciples
Luke 7:11–17: Jesus raises up a widow's dead son at Nain
Luke 10:29–37: Parable of the Good Samaritan
Luke 12:13–21: Parable of the Rich Fool
Luke 15:8–10: Parable of the Lost Coin
Luke 15:11–32: Parable of the Prodigal Son
Luke 16:19–31: Parable of the Rich Man and Lazarus
Luke 17:11–19: Cleansing of ten lepers
Luke 18:1–8: Parable of the Widow and the Judge
Luke 18:9–14: Parable of the Pharisee and the Tax Collector
Luke 19:1–10: Zacchaeus
Luke 19:41–44: Jesus weeps over Jerusalem
Luke 23:6–12: Jesus before Herod
Luke 23:13–16: Pilate says Jesus is innocent
Luke 24:13–35: Jesus appears to two people on the road to Emmaus
Luke 24:50–53: Jesus' ascension to heaven

Important Quotations

"I too decided, after investigating everything carefully from the very first, to write an orderly account for you, most excellent Theophilus, so that you may know the truth concerning the things about which you have been instructed." (Luke 1:3–4)

"And Mary said, 'My soul magnifies the Lord, and my spirit rejoices in God my Savior.'" (Luke 1:46–47)

"And she gave birth to her firstborn son and wrapped him in bands of cloth, and laid him in a manger, because there was no place for them in the inn." (Luke 2:7)

"As he came near and saw the city, he wept over it, saying, 'If you, even you, had only recognized on this day the things that make for peace! But now they are hidden from your eyes.'" (Luke 19:41–42)

"Then beginning with Moses and all the prophets, he interpreted to them the things about himself in all the scriptures." (Luke 24:27)

"While he was blessing them, he withdrew from them and was carried up into heaven." (Luke 24:51)

JOHN

John, named after the traditional author, is the fourth book and the fourth Gospel in the New Testament. This Gospel fundamentally presents the story of Jesus differently from the other three Gospels.

Synopsis

The Gospel of John begins by declaring that the Word was with God at the beginning of time. It then introduces John the Baptist—a man who came to testify to the light—proclaiming that the Word became flesh and lived as a human. John testified that he was not the Messiah because he baptized with water only, and he declared that Jesus was the Lamb of God who would take away the sins of the world. After this, Jesus gathered his first disciples and attended a wedding at Cana, where he performed one of his first miraculous signs by turning water into wine. Before the Passover, Jesus went to Jerusalem and cleansed the Temple by driving out the money changers.

The Pharisee Nicodemus visited Jesus at night and talked to him about being born again. John the Baptist talked about purification and the one who came from heaven. Jesus encountered a Samaritan woman at Jacob's well and told her about living water. Jesus returned to Galilee and healed the son of a royal official as another sign. In Jerusalem, after Jesus healed a sick man on the Sabbath, the Jews began persecuting him. Jesus explained his relationship with God and his authority as God's son. On a hillside near the Sea of Galilee, Jesus fed five thousand people with a boy's lunch of five loaves and two fish. Later that same evening, Jesus walked on the water to reach the boat carrying his disciples across the sea to Capernaum. Jesus identified himself as "the bread of life."

Jesus returned to Jerusalem for the Festival of Booths and began teaching in the Temple. The Jews were astonished and tried to have Jesus arrested. Jesus was tested by the Jewish leaders regarding a woman caught in adultery. He told the people he was the light of the world and predicted his own death. Jesus and the Jews argued about their relationship with God, Abraham, and the prophets until the Jews became so angry they threw stones at Jesus, causing him to leave the Temple. Jesus restored the sight of a man who had been blind since birth, and the Pharisees interrogated the man about the healing. Jesus intervened and told them that he was the good shepherd who would lay down his life for his sheep. Again, the Jews tried to stone him and then to arrest him, but he slipped away. Jesus called himself the resurrection and the life and raised Lazarus from the dead. The plot to kill Jesus became so serious that he could no longer walk around openly, so he remained in Ephraim with his disciples. Mary anointed Jesus' feet with a costly perfume and wiped them with her hair. Jesus entered Jerusalem on a young donkey as the crowd shouted, "Hosanna!"

During a final meal with his disciples, Jesus washed their feet as an example. He predicted his betrayal by Judas Iscariot. He gave the disciples a new commandment that they love one another, and he predicted Peter's denial before delivering his final instructions and promises to his disciples. He told them he was going to the Father to prepare a place for them but would send the Holy Spirit to be with them. He called himself "the true vine" and instructed them to bear fruit in his name. He warned them of the hatred they would experience from the world and then prayed for them.

Jesus and his disciples went to a garden, where Jesus was betrayed by Judas, arrested, and taken before the high priest. Peter denied Jesus as predicted while the high priest questioned Jesus about his teaching. Peter denied Jesus two more times. Jesus was taken before Pilate, who sentenced him to death. Jesus was crucified and died. His legs were not broken as was the custom, but his side was pierced by the soldiers. He was taken down from the cross and buried by Joseph of Arimathea and Nicodemus. On the first day of the week, Mary Magdalene went to the tomb and found the stone rolled away from the entrance. She told Peter and the disciple whom Jesus loved, who ran to the tomb to confirm her story. Jesus appeared to Mary Magdalene outside the tomb and to the disciples later that evening. A week later, Jesus appeared again to the disciples and chided Thomas for his unbelief. Jesus appeared to seven disciples by the Sea of Tiberias and had a breakfast of fish and bread with them. Jesus told Peter to feed his sheep.

The book concludes by noting that "the disciple whom Jesus loved" is the one testifying to all of these things by writing them in this book.

Content Outline

Jesus' Public Ministry

Prologue; testimony of John the Baptist; Jesus calls his first disciples	John 1
Jesus turns water into wine and cleanses the Temple	John 2
Jesus' dialogue with Nicodemus	John 3
Jesus and the Samaritan woman at the well	John 4
Jesus heals on the Sabbath and creates controversy	John 5
Jesus feeds five thousand and walks on water; Jesus as the bread of life	John 6
Jesus teaches in the Temple during the Festival of Booths	John 7
Woman caught in adultery; Jesus as the light of the world; conflict with Jews	John 8
Healing of the man born blind	John 9
Jesus the good shepherd; Jesus is questioned by Jewish leaders	John 10
Raising of Lazarus; Jesus is the resurrection and the life; leaders plan to arrest Jesus	John 11
Mary anoints Jesus; Jesus enters Jerusalem	John 12

Jesus' Private Teaching to His Disciples on the Eve of His Death

Jesus washes his disciples' feet, then gives them a new commandment to love each other	John 13

Jesus goes to prepare a place; the promise of the Holy Spirit	John 14
Jesus the true vine; the world hates Jesus' own	John 15
Expulsion from the synagogues; the Spirit as Advocate	John 16
Jesus' farewell prayer	John 17

Jesus' Arrest, Trial before Pilate, and Crucifixion

Jesus is betrayed and arrested; Jesus appears before the high priest; Peter denies Jesus; Jesus appears before Pilate	John 18
Jesus is flogged and crucified; Jesus dies, and his side is pierced; Jesus is buried	John 19

Jesus' Resurrection Appearances

Empty tomb and appearance to Mary Magdalene; doubting Thomas	John 20
More resurrection appearances: miraculous catch of fish; encounter with Peter	John 21

People

Jesus—the Word; "I am"
John—the beloved disciple
Andrew—one of Jesus' first disciples; Simon Peter's brother
Simon—one of Jesus' first disciples; Andrew's brother
Philip—one of Jesus' first disciples
Nathanael—one of Jesus' first disciples
Nicodemus—Pharisee and leader of the Jews
Pharisees—Jewish leaders
Lazarus—brother of Mary and Martha
Mary—sister of Lazarus and Martha
Martha—sister of Lazarus and Mary
Judas Iscariot—one of Jesus' first disciples
Pilate—governor of Judea
Joseph of Arimathea—disciple of Jesus; buries Jesus
Mary—wife of Clopas; present at the crucifixion
Mary Magdalene—present at the crucifixion; Jesus appears to her after his resurrection

Places

Bethany—place across the Jordan River; site of John's baptizing
Galilee—region in the north of ancient Palestine
Bethsaida—Philip's hometown
Nazareth—Jesus' hometown
Cana—town in Galilee
Judea—southern region of ancient Palestine
Samaria—area between Judea and Galilee
Jerusalem—place of Jesus' death and burial
Tiberias—city in Galilee
Capernaum—town along the Sea of Galilee

Key Concepts

Signs—seven miracles demonstrating Jesus' glory
Eternal life—alternative image to the kingdom of God, which is rarely mentioned
Paraclete—role of the Spirit
Jesus as light—the world is full of darkness, and Jesus is the light
The Jews—term used frequently for Jesus' opponents; refers to Jewish leaders

Material Unique to John

John 2:1–12: Jesus turns water into wine at a wedding in Cana
John 3:1–21: Jesus and Nicodemus, a Pharisee
John 4:7–26: Jesus and the Samaritan Woman
John 5:1–18: Jesus heals a man at the pool called Bethzatha
John 7:53–8:11: Woman caught in adultery
John 9: Jesus heals a man born blind
John 11:1–44: Raising of Lazarus
John 17: Jesus prays at his final meal with the disciples
John 20:24–29: Jesus and Thomas

Seven "I Am" Statements

I am the bread of life (John 6:35)
I am the light of the world (John 8:12)
I am the gate (John 10:7)
I am the good shepherd (John 10:11)
I am the resurrection and the life (John 11:25)

I am the way, and the truth, and the life (John 14:6)

I am the vine (John 15:1)

Important Quotations

"In the beginning was the Word, and the Word was with God, and the Word was God." (John 1:1)

"And the Word became flesh and lived among us, and we have seen his glory, the glory as of a father's only son, full of grace and truth." (John 1:14)

"For God so loved the world that he gave his only Son, so that everyone who believes in him may not perish but may have eternal life." (John 3:16)

"Jesus answered, 'Neither this man nor his parents sinned; he was born blind so that God's works might be revealed in him.'" (John 9:3)

"Jesus said to him, 'I am the way, and the truth, and the life. No one comes to the Father except through me.'" (John 14:6)

"This is my commandment, that you love one another as I have loved you. No one has greater love than this, to lay down one's life for one's friends." (John 15:12–13)

"When Jesus had received the wine, he said, 'It is finished.' Then he bowed his head and gave up his spirit." (John 19:30)

ACTS OF THE APOSTLES

The Acts of the Apostles, the fifth book in the New Testament, is Luke's second book and a sequel to the Gospel of Luke. It begins with Jesus' ascension to heaven and ends with Paul's imprisonment in Rome. The early chapters focus on Peter and the ministry of the apostles in Jerusalem and then in Judea and Samaria. The middle and concluding chapters follow the apostle Paul on his three missionary journeys. The word *apostle* comes from the Greek and means "one sent away."

Synopsis

The book of Acts begins where the Gospel of Luke ends—with the ascension of Jesus into heaven—and is again addressed to Theophilus. After the ascension, Matthias was chosen to replace Judas Iscariot as the twelfth apostle by the casting of lots. On the day of Pentecost, Jesus' followers were filled

with the Holy Spirit and spoke in other languages so that the crowd was able
to understand them, each in their own language. Peter spoke to the crowd,
quoting the prophet Joel and preaching about Jesus. About three thousand
people responded and were baptized. Peter healed a lame man at the gate of
the Temple and preached in Solomon's Portico about Jesus, which resulted
in the arrest of both Peter and John. The Jewish leaders ordered them not to
speak of Jesus again and released them. All the believers shared possessions
with one another except Ananias and Sapphira, who kept a portion of the
profit from the sale of property for themselves. Their deception caused them
both to fall dead to the ground. The apostles continued to preach and heal in
Jesus' name and were again imprisoned, but an angel came in the night and
set them free. The twelve apostles appointed seven more men to help with
the distribution of food to the widows. Stephen, one of the new disciples,
was arrested and gave a long speech to the Jewish council. After he spoke,
he was stoned to death, while Saul watched with approval. Saul increased his
persecution of the Christians. Philip went to Samaria to preach, and Simon
the magician was converted. Philip also converted an Ethiopian eunuch on
the road from Jerusalem to Gaza.

Saul was converted while on his way to Damascus when he was blinded
by a bright light and heard the voice of Jesus. In Damascus, Ananias (not the
same one who had acted deceptively) helped Saul regain his sight and prayed
for him to be filled with the Holy Spirit. Saul immediately began to preach
in Damascus, but the Jews wanted to kill him, so his followers helped him
escape. He went from there to Jerusalem, where the disciples were initially
afraid of Saul. With the help of Barnabas, however, he was accepted. He was
then sent to Tarsus. Peter healed Aeneas in Lydda and raised Tabitha from
the dead in Joppa. Cornelius had a vision of an angel in Caesarea who told
him to send for Peter, who was still in Joppa. Peter went to Caesarea, and
many Gentiles were baptized. Barnabas traveled to Antioch and brought Saul
there as well; they remained there for a year.

King Herod killed James, the brother of John, and imprisoned Peter.
Although heavily guarded, Peter escaped from prison with the help of an
angel. Herod was killed by an angel of God. Barnabas and Saul (also known
as and heretofore called Paul) were commissioned and preached in Cyprus,
Antioch of Pisidia, Iconium, Lystra, Derbe, and Antioch in Syria.

The leaders of the church gathered in Jerusalem to discuss the question of
whether Gentiles needed to be circumcised to be saved. They decided that this
was not necessary but that they must follow certain laws particularly related
to food. Paul and Barnabas parted ways after a dispute over whether to take
John Mark with them. Paul and Silas began to travel together and took Timothy with them as they journeyed through Asia Minor and into Greece. Paul

preached in Thessalonica, Athens, and Corinth before returning to Antioch. He also went to Ephesus, where he found disciples who had not yet received the Holy Spirit. While in Ephesus, the silversmith Demetrius created a disturbance because the many conversions there were taking away his livelihood as a maker of idols. Paul visited Macedonia, Greece, Troas, and Miletus.

Paul arrived back in Jerusalem and gave a full report of the conversions to James. Paul went to the Temple, where he was arrested. Paul defended himself in Hebrew and told of his conversion and mission to the Gentiles. When his accusers realized he was a Roman citizen, they brought him before the Jewish leaders, who decided to kill him. The Roman tribune sent Paul to Felix, the governor in Caesarea, who heard Paul's defense but still sentenced him to two years in prison. Paul came before Festus, the new governor, and made his appeal. Festus asked King Agrippa for advice, and Agrippa asked to hear directly from Paul. Paul defended himself before Agrippa and was declared innocent. However, since Paul had first appealed to Festus, Agrippa could not set him free. Paul was put on a boat bound for Rome, but the boat was shipwrecked on the island of Malta during a storm. Paul finally reached Rome and was placed under house arrest. Still, he continued to preach to the Jewish leaders there. The book concludes by noting that Paul lived in Rome for two years and preached about Jesus.

Content Outline

In Jerusalem

Ascension of Jesus; Matthias added to the group of apostles	Acts 1
Pentecost; Peter's speech	Acts 2
Healing at the Beautiful Gate and Peter's speech about division in Israel	Acts 3
Peter and John before the Jewish leaders	Acts 4
Ananias and Sapphira's deception; apostles imprisoned and freed	Acts 5
Seven chosen to serve; Stephen arrested	Acts 6
Stephen's speech and martyrdom	Acts 7
Saul's involvement in the persecution of the church; Philip and an Ethiopian eunuch	Acts 8

Paul's Early Ministry and First Journey

Conversion of Saul/Paul; Aeneas healed; Tabitha brought back to life	Acts 9
Conversion of Cornelius	Acts 10
Peter gives a report to Jerusalem Christians about Gentile conversion	Acts 11
Martyrdom of James; Peter's miraculous deliverance from prison; Herod's death	Acts 12
Barnabas and Paul travel to Cyprus and Antioch of Pisidia	Acts 13
Barnabas and Paul travel to Iconium, Lystra, Derbe, and Antioch in Syria	Acts 14

Back in Jerusalem

Council at Jerusalem	Acts 15

Paul's Second and Third Journeys

Paul and Silas are joined by Timothy; Lydia converts; Paul and Silas in prison	Acts 16
Paul preaches in Thessalonica and Athens	Acts 17
Paul preaches in Corinth, then returns to Antioch and Jerusalem; Apollos encounters Priscilla and Aquila	Acts 18
Disturbance in Ephesus arises because conversions are interfering with sales of idols	Acts 19
Paul visits Macedonia, Greece, Troas, and Miletus	Acts 20

Paul in Jerusalem

Paul arrested in Jerusalem at the Temple	Acts 21
Paul speaks of his conversion	Acts 22
Jews plot to kill Paul	Acts 23

End of Paul's Ministry

Paul is sent to Felix in Caesarea	Acts 24

Paul appeals to the emperor	Acts 25
Before King Agrippa, Paul speaks of his conversion	Acts 26
Paul sails for Rome and is shipwrecked	Acts 27
Jews visit Paul while he is under house arrest; he preaches to them	Acts 28

People

Theophilus—addressee of this book
Peter—apostle
John—apostle
James—apostle
Andrew—apostle
Philip—apostle
Thomas—apostle
Bartholomew—apostle
Matthew—apostle
James—apostle; son of Alphaeus
Simon—apostle
Judas—apostle; son of James
Mary—mother of Jesus
Joseph called Barsabbas—candidate to replace Judas as apostle
Matthias—replaced Judas as apostle
Annas—high priest
Barnabas—Levite from Cyprus; also known as Joseph
Ananias—husband of Sapphira; sold a piece of property and kept some of the profit; collapsed dead
Sapphira—wife of Ananias; sold a piece of property and kept some of the profit; collapsed dead
Stephen—chosen to be a new leader by the Twelve; first martyr
Philip—chosen to be a new leader by the Twelve
Paul (aka Saul)—apostle and main character in Acts
Ethiopian eunuch—converted and baptized by Philip
Aeneas—healed by Peter after being bedridden for eight years
Tabitha—raised from death by Peter; also known as Dorcas
Cornelius—centurion of the Italian Cohort
King Herod (aka Herod Agrippa)—grandson of King Herod the Great
Mary—mother of John Mark
Rhoda—maid of Mary

John Mark—companion of Paul and Barnabas on their first journey
Silas—chosen by Paul to go with him after he separates from Barnabas
Timothy—disciple from Lystra; accompanies Paul on his travels
Lydia—from Thyatira; baptized by Paul
Apollos—Jew from Alexandria
Demetrius—silversmith in Ephesus
Eutychus—young man who falls asleep while Paul is talking
Felix—governor
Porcius Festus—governor after Felix
King Agrippa (aka Herod Agrippa II)—Herodian king; Paul presents his case before him
Drusilla—wife of Felix; brother of King Agrippa

Places

Jerusalem—city in Judea
Judea—southern region of ancient Palestine
Samaria—city in the north of ancient Palestine
Caesarea—seaport in the north built by Herod the Great
Damascus—city where Paul is headed when he is converted
Tarsus—Paul's hometown
Lydda—city between Jerusalem and the Mediterranean coast
Joppa—seaport
Antioch—Roman city in ancient Syria; place where disciples are first called "Christians"
Cyprus—island in the Mediterranean Sea; Barnabas's hometown
Antioch of Pisidia—Roman colony
Iconium—capital of Lycaonia
Lystra—Roman colony
Thessalonica—provincial capital city
Athens—large Greek city
Corinth—port city in Greece
Rome—capital of the Roman Empire
Malta—island where Paul is shipwrecked

Key Concepts

Holy Spirit—spirit of God; promised to and received by some Jews and some Gentiles
Pentecost—Jewish festival that commemorates the fiftieth day after Passover; the day in which Jesus' followers are filled with the Holy Spirit

Salvation—forgiveness for Jews and Gentiles
Gentile mission—preaching of the gospel to the Gentiles
Jerusalem—site of origin for the postresurrection Jesus movement; location of primary leadership; Paul returns to the city several times

Important Quotations

"In the first book, Theophilus, I wrote about all that Jesus did and taught from the beginning until the day when he was taken up to heaven, after giving instructions through the Holy Spirit to the apostles whom he had chosen." (Acts 1:1–2)

"But you will receive power when the Holy Spirit has come upon you; and you will be my witnesses in Jerusalem, in all Judea and Samaria, and to the ends of the earth." (Acts 1:8)

"All of them were filled with the Holy Spirit and began to speak in other languages, as the Spirit gave them ability." (Acts 2:4)

"But Peter said, 'I have no silver or gold, but what I have I give you; in the name of Jesus Christ of Nazareth, stand up and walk.'" (Acts 3:6)

"When they heard these things, they became enraged and ground their teeth at Stephen. But filled with the Holy Spirit, he gazed into heaven and saw the glory of God and Jesus standing at the right hand of God. 'Look,' he said, 'I see the heavens opened and the Son of Man standing at the right hand of God!'" (Acts 7:54–56)

"The voice said to him again, a second time, 'What God has made clean, you must not call profane.'" (Acts 10:15)

6

Pauline Epistles

Thirteen letters in the New Testament are attributed to the apostle Paul. They are arranged from the longest (Romans) to the shortest (Philemon). The letters were written to churches or individuals in order to address specific situations.

All of these letters follow a basic, five-part structure of an ancient letter:

1. Salutation—opening that identifies the letter's sender and addressee and offers a greeting
2. Thanksgiving—prayer of gratitude delineating major themes of the letter

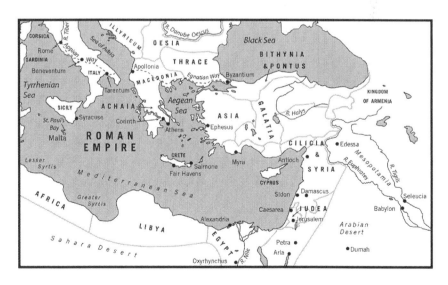

Map 7. The Mediterranean Region in the First Century CE
(Originally published in M. Eugene Boring, *An Introduction to the New Testament* [Louisville, KY: Westminster John Knox Press, 2012], front plate.)

3. Body—main argument and substance of the letter
4. Commands/instructions—final exhortations for living
5. Conclusion—greetings and a benediction

ROMANS

The sixth book in the New Testament is Paul's letter to the Romans. The letter is a carefully argued presentation of the essence of Paul's gospel to a church that he did not found but whose favor and support he sought.

Synopsis

The letter begins with a salutation identifying Paul as the sender and God's beloved in Rome as the recipients. Paul thanked God for them and expressed a desire to visit them. He spoke of the gospel as the power of God for salvation to Jews and to Greeks. He explained humanity's wickedness and declared that God has been made plain to the Gentiles but that they were unwilling to see it. They judged others while doing the same things themselves. Paul said God did not show partiality but provided sorrow for someone who did evil and honor for someone who did good. He then indicted the Jews for boasting about their relationship to God yet not keeping the law. Real circumcision was not physical but a matter of the heart.

After asking "Then what advantage has the Jew?" Paul answered his own question by saying the Jews had been entrusted with God's oracles. Both Jews and Greeks were under the power of sin, but the death of Jesus brought the gift of justification for all. Paul used Abraham as an example; he was justified through faith and not through works.

Believers could have peace with God because they were justified by faith. Paul used the examples of Adam and Christ to explain sin and righteousness; sin came into the world through one man, Adam, and the gift of righteousness came through one man, Christ. Justification by faith was not to be used as an excuse to continue sinning; rather, the readers should be slaves of righteousness. Paul developed a marriage analogy to discuss the relationship between sin and the Jewish law. He called the law holy and good in its capacity to draw an awareness of sin, but the Spirit of God dwelling in them would give the ability to avoid living according to the flesh. Paul noted that he did not understand his actions because nothing good dwelt within him. He did the very thing he hated to do.

Paul addressed Israel and the fact that not all Jews were receiving Christ. Paul argued that not all Israelites in the past truly belonged to Israel, for God elected some to be children of the promise. All who call on the name of God would be saved; salvation was open to all. Israel's disbelief opened the way of salvation to the Gentiles, yet Israel would eventually become jealous and repent because of the salvation of the Gentiles. Paul gave the assurance that God had not rejected Israel; Israel would be saved.

Paul appealed to his readers to present themselves as a living sacrifice to God and not to be conformed to the world. He listed virtues congruent with Christian living and admonished the readers to subject themselves to the governing authorities and to love one another. Believers were instructed not to judge each other based on the festivals they might observe or what they might eat or drink. They were to welcome one another as Christ had welcomed them, for the glory of God.

Paul wrote of his plan to visit his readers in Rome before concluding with greetings and a doxology.

Content Outline

The gospel as the power of God for salvation; indictment (of Gentiles) for idolatry	Romans 1
Those who judge others but do the same; Jews are also in need of God's grace	Romans 2
All have sinned; God has acted through the faith of Jesus to save all	Romans 3
Faith of Abraham	Romans 4
Peace with God; Adam's sin and Christ's obedience	Romans 5
Being baptized into Christ's death and raised to newness of life	Romans 6
The problem with the law; the dilemma of weakness of the will	Romans 7
Life according to the Spirit; nothing can separate us from God's love	Romans 8
History of the Jews shows that God has always exercised a principle of election	Romans 9
Jews' zeal is unenlightened; the Torah intended Christ from the beginning	Romans 10
God has not rejected Israel; salvation has come to the Gentiles	Romans 11
Call to readers to present their bodies as a living sacrifice and for the transformation of their minds	Romans 12
Instruction to obey authorities and love one another	Romans 13

Achieving communal harmony in the face of differences	Romans 14
Instruction to please others, not selves; the gospel is for Jews and Gentiles alike	Romans 15
Greetings; final instruction; doxology	Romans 16

People

Paul—apostle
Phoebe—deacon of the church of Cenchreae
Aquila and Prisca—couple with a church in their house

Places

Rome—capital of the empire

Key Concepts

Justification—being made righteous before God; comes through faith in Jesus
Salvation—deliverance from sin for all, including Israel and the Gentiles
Living sacrifice—life that is acceptable to God in one's spiritual worship, relationship with others, and personal character; proper response to the gospel
Faith in/of Christ—could mean "faith of Christ" (i.e., Christ's faith), or "the faith one has in Christ" (Rom 3)
Sin—deficit common to all people

Important Quotations

"For I am not ashamed of the gospel; it is the power of God for salvation to everyone who has faith, to the Jew first and also to the Greek." (Rom 1:16)

"For God shows no partiality." (Rom 2:11)

"All have sinned and fall short of the glory of God." (Rom 3:23)

"Therefore, since we are justified by faith, we have peace with God through our Lord Jesus Christ, through whom we have obtained access to this grace in which we stand; and we boast in our hope of sharing the glory of God." (Rom 5:1–2)

"But God proves his love for us in that while we still were sinners Christ died for us." (Rom 5:8)

"For the wages of sin is death, but the free gift of God is eternal life in Christ Jesus our Lord." (Rom 6:23)

"I do not understand my own actions. For I do not do what I want, but I do the very thing I hate." (Rom 7:15)

"There is therefore now no condemnation for those who are in Christ Jesus." (Rom 8:1)

"We know that the whole creation has been groaning in labor pains until now; and not only the creation, but we ourselves, who have the first fruits of the Spirit, groan inwardly while we wait for adoption, the redemption of our bodies." (Rom 8:22–23)

"We know that all things work together for good for those who love God, who are called according to his purpose." (Rom 8:28)

"No, in all these things we are more than conquerors through him who loved us. For I am convinced that neither death, nor life, nor angels, nor rulers, nor things present, nor things to come, nor powers, nor height, nor depth, nor anything else in all creation, will be able to separate us from the love of God in Christ Jesus our Lord." (Rom 8:37–39)

"I ask, then, has God rejected his people? By no means! I myself am an Israelite, a descendant of Abraham, a member of the tribe of Benjamin." (Rom 11:1)

"I appeal to you therefore, brothers and sisters, by the mercies of God, to present your bodies as a living sacrifice, holy and acceptable to God, which is your spiritual worship. Do not be conformed to this world, but be transformed by the renewing of your minds, so that you may discern what is the will of God—what is good and acceptable and perfect." (Rom 12:1–2)

"Let every person be subject to the governing authorities; for there is no authority except from God, and those authorities that exist have been instituted by God." (Rom 13:1)

"I commend to you our sister Phoebe, a deacon of the church at Cenchreae, so that you may welcome her in the Lord as is fitting for the saints, and help her in whatever she may require from you, for she has been a benefactor of many and of myself as well." (Rom 16:1–2)

"Now to God who is able to strengthen you according to my gospel and the proclamation of Jesus Christ, according to the revelation of the mystery that was kept secret for long ages but is now disclosed, and through the prophetic writings is made known to all the Gentiles, according to the command of the eternal God, to bring about the obedience of faith—to the only wise God, through Jesus Christ, to whom be the glory forever! Amen." (Rom 16:25–27)

1 CORINTHIANS

The seventh book in the New Testament is the first letter of Paul to the Corinthians. The letter responds to reports Paul received regarding various conflicts and problems among the Corinthian believers. Paul's overarching strategy was to admonish those who are socially strong to forgo their privilege wherever doing so would assist those who were weaker in their faith.

Synopsis

First Corinthians opens with a salutation identifying the sender as Paul and the recipient as the church in Corinth. Paul offered thanks to God for God's grace to the Corinthians and for giving them spiritual gifts. He appealed to them to be united without divisions after hearing of quarrels and disunity. He called Christ the power and wisdom of God. Paul said he came to them preaching Christ crucified, which might seem as foolishness to the world but was better than any human wisdom.

Paul declared that the Corinthians were not ready for solid food because they were still of the flesh, as demonstrated by their quarrelling. He presented Jesus Christ as the only foundation. Others, such as Apollos, may have taught them, but Apollos was a servant of God the same as himself. He then admonished them to imitate him.

Paul addressed sexual immorality within the congregation and instructed the Corinthian church not to associate with people guilty of it but to allow God to judge them. Among other things, he spoke against bringing lawsuits against one another, fornication, idolatry, and adultery. He then addressed marital issues such as sex within marriage, remarriage for widows, and divorce. He also noted that circumcision was not important and gave advice to the unmarried.

After addressing the issue of eating food offered to idols, Paul offered himself as an example or model of a free person with rights but one who had decided to give up those rights. He presented the example of Israel at the time of the exodus to teach the community not to desire evil or become idolaters.

Paul presented a hierarchy: God is the head of Christ, Christ is the head of every man, and the husband is the head of the wife. He taught that women should wear head coverings but men should not. He addressed abuses and instructions regarding the partaking of the Lord's Supper.

Writing about spiritual gifts, Paul used the analogy of the body to demonstrate that believers were one body with many different members. There were a variety of spiritual gifts but one Lord and Spirit. He provided an exposition on love and concluded that among faith, hope, and love, it is the greatest. He returned to a discussion of spiritual gifts, particularly prophecy, and admonished the Corinthians to strive for this gift, as it could encourage and console.

Paul addressed the resurrection of Christ and the resurrection of the dead. The letter ends with Paul's travel plans, greetings, and a benediction.

Content Outline

Against divisions and overestimating wisdom	1 Corinthians 1
God's countercultural wisdom to be discerned by the spiritual	1 Corinthians 2
Divisions and boasting of leaders; Paul and Apollos work cooperatively	1 Corinthians 3
Apostles as servants and how they are viewed as last of all	1 Corinthians 4
Sexual immorality in the Corinthian congregation	1 Corinthians 5
Against taking brothers or sisters to court; visiting prostitutes	1 Corinthians 6
Defining appropriate sexual relationships within marriage	1 Corinthians 7
Food sacrificed to idols	1 Corinthians 8
Apostolic rights	1 Corinthians 9
Examples from Israel's history; do everything for the glory of God	1 Corinthians 10
Head veilings and abuses at the Lord's Supper	1 Corinthians 11
Spiritual gifts; one body, many members	1 Corinthians 12
The nature of love	1 Corinthians 13
Spiritual gifts, especially prophecy and speaking in tongues	1 Corinthians 14

The resurrection of Christ and the day of the Lord yet to come	1 Corinthians 15
Collection for the saints; Paul's travel plans; final greetings	1 Corinthians 16

People

Paul—apostle
Sosthenes—Paul's coauthor
Chloe—mentioned as reporting to Paul about quarrels
Apollos—Paul's coworker
Cephas—also known as Peter
Crispus—man Paul mentions baptizing
Gaius—man Paul mentions baptizing
Stephanas—man whose household Paul mentions baptizing
Aquila and Prisca—couple with a church in their house
Timothy—Paul's coworker

Places

Corinth—Roman colony in Greece
Macedonia—Roman province

Key Concepts

Divisions—factions among the Corinthian believers
Idolatry—sacrifices of food offered to idols
Sexual immorality—major topic for Paul; covers any number of sexual behaviors
Relinquishing of privilege in order to serve others—Paul encourages this action
The Lord's Supper/Eucharist—Paul teaches about the proper way to perform this ritual
Spiritual gifts—abilities empowered by the Holy Spirit for the work of the body of Christ, including wisdom, knowledge, faith, gifts of healing, miracle working, prophecy, and tongues

Important Quotations

"Now I appeal to you, brothers and sisters, by the name of our Lord Jesus Christ, that all of you be in agreement and that there be no divisions among you, but that you be united in the same mind and the same purpose." (1 Cor 1:10)

"Has Christ been divided? Was Paul crucified for you? Or were you baptized in the name of Paul?" (1 Cor 1:13)

"For the message about the cross is foolishness to those who are perishing, but to us who are being saved it is the power of God." (1 Cor 1:18)

"We are fools for the sake of Christ, but you are wise in Christ. We are weak, but you are strong. You are held in honor, but we in disrepute." (1 Cor 4:10)

"For though I am free with respect to all, I have made myself a slave to all, so that I might win more of them. To the Jews I became as a Jew, in order to win Jews. To those under the law I become as one under the law (though I myself am not under the law) so that I might win those under the law. To those outside the law I became as one outside the law (though I am not free from God's law but am under Christ's law) so that I might win those outside the law." (1 Cor 9:19–21)

"But I want you to understand that Christ is the head of every man, and the husband is the head of his wife, and God is the head of Christ." (1 Cor 11:3)

"For I received from the Lord what I also handed on to you, that the Lord Jesus on the night when he was betrayed took a loaf of bread, and when he had given thanks, he broke it and said, 'This is my body that is for you. Do this in remembrance of me.' In the same way he took the cup also, after supper, saying, 'This cup is the new covenant in my blood. Do this, as often as you drink it, in remembrance of me.' For as often as you eat this bread and drink the cup, you proclaim the Lord's death until he comes." (1 Cor 11:23–26)

"Now there are varieties of gifts, but the same Spirit; and there are varieties of services, but the same Lord; and there are varieties of activities, but it is the same God who activates all of them in everyone." (1 Cor 12:4–6)

"For just as the body is one and has many members, and all the members of the body, though many, are one body, so it is with Christ. For in the one Spirit we were all baptized into one body—Jews or Greeks, slaves or free—and we were all made to drink of one Spirit." (1 Cor 12:12–13)

"And now faith, hope, and love abide, these three; and the greatest of these is love." (1 Cor 13:13)

"For I handed on to you as of first importance what I in turn had received: that Christ died for our sins in accordance with the scriptures, and that he was buried, and that he was raised on the third day in accordance with the scriptures, and that he appeared to Cephas, then to the twelve. Then he appeared to more than five hundred brothers and sisters at one time, most of whom are still alive, though some have died. Then he appeared to James, then to all the apostles. Last of all, as to one untimely born, he appeared also to me." (1 Cor 15:3–8)

"If there is no resurrection of the dead, then Christ has not been raised; and if Christ has not been raised, then our proclamation has been in vain and your faith has been in vain." (1 Cor 15:13–14)

2 CORINTHIANS

The eighth book in the New Testament is the second letter of Paul to the Corinthians. This letter was written after Paul became estranged from the Corinthians and appealed for mutual reconciliation even as he condemned competitors, whom he labeled the "super-apostles."

Synopsis

The letter, from Paul and Timothy, opens with a salutation to the church in Corinth. Paul offered thanksgiving for consolation during affliction and noted that his intended visit to Corinth had been postponed. He spoke of his time in Troas.

Paul reflected on a new covenant through Christ and compared it to Moses' reception of the law. He wrote about ministry and stated that the treasure of the gospel was contained in the fragile clay jars of believers. He noted that though these believers were afflicted, they were not to lose heart. Their permanent home in heaven was not made by hands like their earthly tents.

God gave them a ministry of reconciliation as ambassadors for Christ, and the world was reconciled to God in Christ. Paul appealed to the Corinthians to be reconciled to him after a period of estrangement, inasmuch as Paul's heart was open to them.

Paul discussed the report Titus brought to him regarding Corinth and then encouraged the Corinthians to be financially generous by using the generosity of the churches of Macedonia as an example. God loves a cheerful giver.

Paul defended himself against charges of contemptible speech and weak bodily presence. He called those who preach a different gospel "super-apostles." He boasted of being caught up to the third heaven but said a thorn was given to him in the flesh to keep him from being too elated. Paul shared of his plans to visit the Corinthians a third time. He concluded the letter with greetings and a benediction.

Content Outline

Paul praises the God of consolation and speaks of his own affliction	2 Corinthians 1
Paul's changing itinerary; Christ leads us in triumphal procession	2 Corinthians 2
Paul's boldness of speech as minister of the new covenant	2 Corinthians 3
Treasure in clay jars; momentary affliction prepares us for eternal glory	2 Corinthians 4
Earthly tent versus heavenly dwelling; ministry of reconciliation	2 Corinthians 5
Appeal to be reconciled to Paul; do not be mismatched with unbelievers	2 Corinthians 6
Continuation of Paul's appeal for reconciliation	2 Corinthians 7
Excel in generosity	2 Corinthians 8
Collection for the saints	2 Corinthians 9
Paul defends himself, then prepares for the ironic boasting of the next chapter	2 Corinthians 10
Paul "boasts" of his sufferings as an apostle	2 Corinthians 11
Paul's visions and revelations and his "thorn in the flesh"	2 Corinthians 12
Admonition to self-testing; greetings and benediction	2 Corinthians 13

People

Paul—apostle
Timothy—Paul's coauthor
Titus—Paul's coworker
Beliar—also known as Satan

Places

Corinth—Roman colony in Greece; capital of Achaia
Achaia—Roman province in southern Greece, with Corinth as the capital
Macedonia—Roman province north of Achaia

Key Concepts

Reconciliation—coming together across differences; God gives people a ministry of reconciliation just as Christ has reconciled the world to himself
Suffering—Paul recounts being imprisoned, beaten, and in danger
Giving generously—Paul encourages the Corinthians to contribute to a collection for the Jerusalem church

Important Quotations

"For we are the aroma of Christ to God among those who are being saved and among those who are perishing." (2 Cor 2:15)

"Not that we are competent of ourselves to claim anything as coming from us; our competence is from God, who has made us competent to be ministers of a new covenant, not of letter but of spirit; for the letter kills, but the Spirit gives life." (2 Cor 3:5–6)

"Now the Lord is the Spirit, and where the Spirit of the Lord is, there is freedom." (2 Cor 3:17)

"But we have this treasure in clay jars, so that it may be made clear that this extraordinary power belongs to God and does not come from us." (2 Cor 4:7)

"All this is from God, who reconciled us to himself through Christ, and has given us the ministry of reconciliation." (2 Cor 5:18)

"So we are ambassadors for Christ, since God is making his appeal through us; we entreat you on behalf of Christ, be reconciled to God. For our sake he made him to be sin who knew no sin, so that in him we might become the righteousness of God." (2 Cor 5:20–21)

"The point is this: the one who sows sparingly will also reap sparingly, and the one who sows bountifully will also reap bountifully. Each of you must give as you have made up your mind, not reluctantly or under compulsion, for God loves a cheerful giver." (2 Cor 9:6–7)

"But he said to me, 'My grace is sufficient for you, for power is made perfect in weakness.' So, I will boast all the more gladly of my weaknesses, so that the power of Christ may dwell in me." (2 Cor 12:9)

GALATIANS

The ninth book of the New Testament is Paul's letter to the churches of Galatia. This letter responded to those within the community who had turned to a different understanding of the gospel than the one Paul preached.

Synopsis

The letter opens with a salutation followed by Paul's reason for writing: the turning of the readers to a different gospel. There was no other gospel, but the one gospel had been perverted. Paul stated that his gospel came not from humans but through a revelation of Jesus Christ, and he told the story of his conversion. Paul had been zealous as a Jew and persecutor of the church, but he was then called to proclaim Christ to the Gentiles. He went to Jerusalem and received approval from the leaders there to do so. He rebuked Peter at Antioch for his hypocrisy in withdrawing from table fellowship with Gentiles. Paul declared that a person is justified not by works of the law but through faith in Jesus. Those who relied on works of the law would be cursed. The law was a disciplinarian until Christ came and made all one in Christ, male and female, Jew and Greek, slave and free.

Paul used an allegory of Sarah and Hagar, two women from the Old Testament, to address two covenants, one of freedom and the other of slavery. He said the Galatians did not need to be circumcised. He wrote about the works of the flesh (fornication, impurity, licentiousness, idolatry, and so forth) and the fruit of the spirit (love, joy, peace, patience, kindness, generosity, faithfulness, gentleness, and self-control). He admonished the readers to bear one another's burdens. The letter concludes with other admonitions and a benediction.

Content Outline

No gospel besides Paul's; Paul's early history in the faith	Galatians 1
Paul's agreement with the leaders in Jerusalem; Cephas's hypocrisy	Galatians 2

Abraham's faith and descendants; Christ redeemed us from the curse of the law	Galatians 3
Believers as adopted heirs of God; allegory of Mount Sinai and Jerusalem	Galatians 4
Only faith working through love counts; works of flesh versus fruit of the spirit	Galatians 5
Admonitions and benediction	Galatians 6

People

Paul—apostle
Cephas—apostle; also known as Peter
Barnabas—Paul's companion to Jerusalem
Titus—Paul's companion to Jerusalem
James—leader in Jerusalem
John—leader in Jerusalem
Abraham—patriarch from the Old Testament
Sarah—Abraham's wife from the Old Testament; mother of Isaac
Hagar—Sarah's maidservant from the Old Testament; mother of Ishmael

Places

Galatia—territory in Asia Minor
Jerusalem—where Paul visits
Antioch—where Paul confronts Peter

Key Concepts

Circumcision—removal of the foreskin on boys and men; sign of the covenant between God and the descendants of Abraham; unnecessary for Gentiles as believers of the gospel
Law—commandments, ordinances, and statutes given to Moses
Fruit of the Spirit—nine attributes of individual and communal life in Christ: love, joy, peace, patience, kindness, generosity, faithfulness, gentleness, and self-control; contrast to the works of the flesh
Justification by faith—righteousness that comes by faith; Paul's understanding of righteousness

Important Quotations

"I am astonished that you are so quickly deserting the one who called you in the grace of Christ and are turning to a different gospel—not that there is another gospel, but there are some who are confusing you and want to pervert the gospel of Christ." (Gal 1:6–7)

"Just as Abraham 'believed God, and it was reckoned to him as righteousness,' so, you see, those who believe are the descendants of Abraham." (Gal 3:6–7)

"Christ redeemed us from the curse of the law by becoming a curse for us—for it is written, 'Cursed is everyone who hangs on a tree.'" (Gal 3:13)

"Therefore the law was our disciplinarian until Christ came, so that we might be justified by faith." (Gal 3:24)

"There is no longer Jew or Greek, there is no longer slave or free, there is no longer male and female; for all of you are one in Christ Jesus." (Gal 3:28)

"But when the fullness of time had come, God sent his Son, born of a woman, born under the law, in order to redeem those who were under the law, so that we might receive adoption as children." (Gal 4:4–5)

"For freedom Christ has set us free. Stand firm, therefore, and do not submit again to a yoke of slavery." (Gal 5:1)

"For in Christ Jesus neither circumcision nor uncircumcision counts for anything; the only thing that counts is faith working through love." (Gal 5:6)

"By contrast, the fruit of the Spirit is love, joy, peace, patience, kindness, generosity, faithfulness, gentleness, and self-control. There is no law against such things." (Gal 5:22–23)

"Bear one another's burdens, and in this way you will fulfill the law of Christ." (Gal 6:2)

"Do not be deceived; God is not mocked, for you reap whatever you sow." (Gal 6:7)

EPHESIANS

The tenth book of the New Testament is the letter of Paul to the saints in Ephesus. The occasion for the letter is unclear, since it does not address any specific situation in Ephesus.

Synopsis

The letter begins with a salutation and long benediction listing many spiritual blessings found in Christ. Paul prayed for the readers, gave thanks, and asked for wisdom and revelation. The letter focused on the move from death to new life. The readers had been dead through their sins, but were made alive with Christ by grace through faith. They were Gentiles and strangers to the covenant of promise but had been brought near and reconciled as one humanity in Christ. Paul spoke of his ministry to the Gentiles and prayed that his readers might have power to comprehend the love of Christ.

The letter then turns to more practical instructions for living in unity as one body. The readers were told to love with humility and gentleness, to put away the old self and clothe themselves with the new self, to put away falsehood and speak truth, and to put away their former behaviors. Wives were told to be subject to their husbands, and husbands were commanded to love their wives. Children were to obey their parents, and slaves were to obey their masters. Paul encouraged the readers to put on the whole armor of God and to stand strong. The letter concludes with a few personal remarks and a benediction.

Content Outline

Praise of God for spiritual blessings; prayer that readers receive enlightenment	Ephesians 1
Contrast between old life and new; Gentiles brought near	Ephesians 2
Gentiles as fellow heirs with Jews; prayer for the Ephesians to be strengthened in their inner being	Ephesians 3
Unity in the body of Christ; live no longer as Gentiles but as clothed with the new self	Ephesians 4
Pagan ways; the Christian household	Ephesians 5
Children and parents; slaves and masters; the armor of God	Ephesians 6

People

Paul—apostle
Tychicus—deliverer of the letter

Places

Ephesus—Roman capital of Asia, which was a province in Asia Minor

Key Concepts

Unity in Christ—one body and one Spirit, one Lord, one faith, one baptism
Armor of God—military metaphor of what is needed to stand against the devil
Household duties/codes—list of duties for members in a household (husbands, wives, children)
Reconciliation—God's desire for Jews and Gentiles

Important Quotations

"For by grace you have been saved through faith, and this is not your own doing; it is the gift of God." (Eph 2:8)

"Now to him who by the power at work within us is able to accomplish abundantly far more than all we can ask or imagine, to him be glory in the church and in Christ Jesus to all generations, forever and ever. Amen." (Eph 3:20–21)

"There is one body and one Spirit, just as you were called to the one hope of your calling, one Lord, one faith, one baptism, one God and Father of all, who is above all and through all and in all." (Eph 4:4–6)

"Be subject to one another out of reverence for Christ." (Eph 5:21)

"Put on the whole armor of God, so that you may be able to stand against the wiles of the devil. For our struggle is not against enemies of blood and flesh, but against the rulers, against the authorities, against the cosmic powers of this present darkness, against the spiritual forces of evil in the heavenly places." (Eph 6:11–12)

PHILIPPIANS

The eleventh book in the New Testament is Paul's letter to the saints in Philippi. Paul wished to thank them for their gift and to address some of the external and internal conflicts present.

Synopsis

After the initial salutation, Paul said he prayed constantly for the recipients of this letter. He spoke of his present situation as a prisoner and his confidence that the proclamation of Christ was ongoing. He rejoiced and hoped he would not be put to shame.

Paul exhorted the saints to stand firm and together in unity, to imitate Christ and Christ's humility, and to work together in unity. He wrote of his hope to send Timothy and Epaphroditus to Philippi soon.

Paul warned the community not to boast in the flesh but in Christ Jesus. He suggested he had every reason to boast in the flesh because of his status as a Pharisee, but he contended his righteousness did not come from the law but through faith in Christ, which encouraged him to press onward to the goal.

The letter concludes with various exhortations, including a command to rejoice, followed by Paul's expression of thanks for a gift from the Philippians.

Content Outline

Paul's prayer for the Philippians and his present circumstances	Philippians 1
Have the mind of Christ; shining as lights in the world; Timothy and Epaphroditus	Philippians 2
Boasting in Christ; pressing toward the goal	Philippians 3
Exhortations; thanks for the gift; final greetings and benediction	Philippians 4

People

Paul—apostle
Timothy—Paul's coauthor; Paul's traveling companion, whom he plans to send to Philippi
Epaphroditus—Paul's coworker, whom he plans to send to Philippi
Euodia—Paul's female coworker
Syntyche—Paul's female coworker
Clement—Paul's coworker

Places

Philippi—city in Macedonia
Thessalonica—city in Macedonia

Key Concepts

Humility—state of being humble; to be like Christ, who humbled himself
Rejoice—response that Paul encourages the Philippians to make

Important Quotations

"I am confident of this, that the one who began a good work among you will bring it to completion by the day of Jesus Christ." (Phil 1:6)

"For to me, living is Christ and dying is gain." (Phil 1:21)

"Let the same mind be in you that was in Christ Jesus, who, though he was in the form of God, did not regard equality with God as something to be exploited, but emptied himself, taking the form of a slave, being born in human likeness. And being found in human form, he humbled himself and became obedient to the point of death—even death on a cross. Therefore God also highly exalted him and gave him the name that is above every name, so that at the name of Jesus every knee should bend, in heaven and on earth and under the earth, and every tongue should confess that Jesus Christ is Lord, to the glory of God the Father." (Phil 2:5–11)

"Therefore, my beloved, just as you have always obeyed me, not only in my presence, but much more now in my absence, work out your own salvation with fear and trembling; for it is God who is at work in you, enabling you both to will and to work for his good pleasure." (Phil 2:12–13)

"Yet whatever gains I had, these I have come to regard as loss because of Christ. More than that, I regard everything as loss because of the surpassing value of knowing Christ Jesus my Lord. For his sake I have suffered the loss of all things, and I regard them as rubbish, in order that I may gain Christ." (Phil 3:7–8)

"I press on toward the goal for the prize of the heavenly call of God in Christ Jesus." (Phil 3:14)

"Rejoice in the Lord always; again I will say, Rejoice." (Phil 4:4)

"Do not worry about anything, but in everything by prayer and supplication with thanksgiving let your requests be made known to God. And the peace of God, which surpasses all understanding, will guard your hearts and your minds in Christ Jesus." (Phil 4:6–7)

"I can do all things through him who strengthens me." (Phil 4:13)

COLOSSIANS

The twelfth book of the New Testament is a letter from Paul to the church in Colossae. Paul writes to warn that community about a particular philosophy that is not the gospel of Christ.

Synopsis

The epistle begins by identifying the senders as Paul and Timothy, and the recipients as the saints in Colossae. Paul thanked God for the Colossians and their faith, and noted how the gospel was bearing fruit among them.

Paul turned his attention to Christ, the image of the invisible God— Christ who was before all things and in whom all things hold together. Paul encouraged the Colossians to have the knowledge of God's mystery, which was in Christ, and not to be deceived by others. He reminded them they had undergone a spiritual circumcision and a baptism; God had forgiven them and erased all record of their sins. The Colossians were admonished to guard against being led into false practices.

Paul encouraged them to set their minds on heavenly matters and not on things of the earth, to have compassion and patience with one another, and ultimately, to love. Wives were instructed to be subject to their husbands; husbands were to love their wives. Children were to obey their parents; slaves were to obey their masters. Paul requested the Colossians' prayers and encouraged them to be bold but grace-filled.

The letter ends with greetings to several individuals.

Content Outline

Praise for the Colossians; prayer for their strengthening; high Christology	Colossians 1
Christ as God's mystery; God erased the record of sins; warning against heresy	Colossians 2
Set your minds on things above; clothe yourselves with love; household rules	Colossians 3
Exhortations and greetings	Colossians 4

People

Paul—apostle
Timothy—Paul's traveling companion
Epaphras—founder of the Colossian church
Tychicus—deliverer of the letter
Onesimus—deliverer of the letter
Nympha—church meets in her house

Places

Colossae—city in Asia Minor (modern-day Turkey)
Laodicea—city near Colossae

Key Concepts

Forgiveness of sins—God's act of setting people free from sin and absolving sin
Virtues—personal and communal behaviors of compassion, kindness, humility, meekness, and patience
Household duties/codes—list of duties for members in a household (wives, husbands, children, fathers, slaves, masters)

Important Quotations

"He is the image of the invisible God, the firstborn of all creation; for in him all things in heaven and on earth were created, things visible and invisible, whether thrones or dominions or rulers or powers—all things have been created through him and for him." (Col 1:15–16)

"Therefore do not let anyone condemn you in matters of food and drink or of observing festivals, new moons, or sabbaths. These are only a shadow of what is to come, but the substance belongs to Christ." (Col 2:16–17)

"Set your minds on things that are above, not on things that are on earth, for you have died, and your life is hidden with Christ in God." (Col 3:2–3)

"In that renewal there is no longer Greek and Jew, circumcised and uncircumcised, barbarian, Scythian, slave and free; but Christ is all and in all!" (Col 3:11)

"Above all, clothe yourselves with love, which binds everything together in perfect harmony." (Col 3:14)

"Wives, be subject to your husbands, as is fitting in the Lord. Husbands, love your wives and never treat them harshly. Children, obey your parents in everything, for this is your acceptable duty in the Lord. Fathers, do not provoke your children, or they may lose heart. Slaves, obey your earthly masters in everything, not only while being watched and in order to please them, but wholeheartedly, fearing the Lord." (Col 3:18–22)

1 THESSALONIANS

The thirteenth book of the New Testament is the first letter from Paul to the church at Thessalonica.

Synopsis

The letter opens with a salutation identifying the senders as Paul, Silvanus, and Timothy and the recipient as the church of the Thessalonians. Paul offered thanks to God for the community's faith, love, and hope. He reminded them of his earlier visit to Thessalonica and his work among them while he proclaimed the gospel. He thanked God again for their acceptance of the gospel. Although Paul had wanted to visit them again, Timothy was sent instead and brought back a positive report of the community's faith and love.

Paul exhorted them to continue in their sanctification and to love each other. He addressed the issues of the death of some within the community and the delayed return of Christ. Paul admonished them not to grieve as others who had no hope; the dead would be raised to live with Christ. He encouraged the Thessalonians to continue to live with faith even as they waited for the second coming of Christ. The letter concludes with greetings and a benediction.

Content Outline

Paul greets the Thessalonians and remembers their faith, love, and hope	1 Thessalonians 1
Paul remembers his time with them and recalls his demeanor among them	1 Thessalonians 2
Paul rejoices over Timothy's report on their steadfastness	1 Thessalonians 3

Sexual morality; brotherly/sisterly love; coming of the Lord	1 Thessalonians 4
How to behave while waiting for Jesus; closing exhortations	1 Thessalonians 5

People

Paul—apostle
Silvanus—Paul's traveling companion and coauthor
Timothy—Paul's traveling companion and coauthor

Places

Thessalonica—capital of Macedonia
Macedonia—Roman province in Greece
Achaia—Roman province in southern Greece; Corinth was the capital
Philippi—city in Macedonia

Key Concepts

Reception of Paul's ministry—Paul had visited Thessalonica and wanted to return
Sexual purity—control over one's body
Mutual love—Paul calls the Thessalonians to continue to love one another
Rapture/Parousia—Jesus' return to earth after his ascension

Important Quotations

"For the Lord himself, with a cry of command, with the archangel's call and with the sound of God's trumpet, will descend from heaven, and the dead in Christ will rise first." (1 Thess 4:16)

"For you yourselves know very well that the day of the Lord will come like a thief in the night." (1 Thess 5:2)

"See that none of you repays evil for evil, but always seek to do good to one another and to all." (1 Thess 5:15)

2 THESSALONIANS

The fourteenth book of the New Testament is the second letter from Paul to the church at Thessalonica.

Synopsis

Paul began this letter as before with a salutation and words of thanksgiving. He said God would afflict those who caused distress for the faithful and would give relief to the afflicted at the time of Christ's return. The day of the Lord had not come yet, because the lawless one had not yet been revealed. They were instructed to stand firm in their traditions and to beware of the idle and disruptive. Paul requested their continued prayers and ended the letter with greetings and a benediction.

Content Outline

Paul promises relief for the afflicted and vengeance on their afflicters	2 Thessalonians 1
The lawless one and the restrainer who holds him back	2 Thessalonians 2
Warning against the idle; final greetings	2 Thessalonians 3

People

Paul—apostle
Silvanus—Paul's traveling companion and coauthor
Timothy—Paul's traveling companion and coauthor

Places

Thessalonica—capital of Macedonia

Key Concepts

Affliction—persecutions of the Thessalonian church
Apocalyptic—of the revelation of Jesus being in heaven with angels and inflicting vengeance
Future coming of Christ—expectation that Christ will return

Important Quotations

"Let no one deceive you in any way; for that day will not come unless the rebellion comes first and the lawless one is revealed, the one destined for destruction." (2 Thess 2:3)

"For even when we were with you, we gave you this command: Anyone unwilling to work should not eat." (2 Thess 3:10)

1 TIMOTHY

The fifteenth book of the New Testament is the first letter of Paul to Timothy.

Synopsis

The letter opens with a salutation identifying Paul as the sender and the recipient as Timothy. Paul immediately warned Timothy of false teachers and repeated his story of conversion. He gave instructions on appropriate practices of prayer, particularly the proper manner for men to pray. Women were to remain silent, to dress modestly, and were not to teach or have authority over men. He also outlined the qualifications for bishops and deacons. Paul then returned to the theme of false teachers who encouraged celibacy and asceticism.

Paul gave Timothy advice on dealing with certain fellow believers such as older men, younger brothers, older and younger women, widows, elders, and slaves. Timothy was encouraged to continue in the faith and to fight the good fight. The letter concludes with a brief benediction.

Content Outline

Warning against false teachers; Paul as great sinner and recipient of mercy	1 Timothy 1
Women should dress modestly and be silent; they will be saved through childbearing	1 Timothy 2
Qualifications of bishops and deacons; on the mystery of the faith	1 Timothy 3
Avoid false asceticism; train yourself in godliness; exhortations to Timothy	1 Timothy 4

Exhortations regarding widows	1 Timothy 5
False teachings; the danger of loving money; fight the good fight of faith	1 Timothy 6

People

Paul—apostle
Timothy—Paul's "loyal child in the faith"
Hymenaeus—person Paul accuses of blaspheming
Alexander—person Paul accuses of blaspheming

Places

Macedonia—Roman province
Ephesus—Roman capital of Asia, a province in Asia Minor

Key Concepts

False teachers—people who teach about myths and genealogies; the letter warns believers to beware of them
Silence of women—women are instructed to learn by listening and without speaking
Bishops—characteristics of these leaders are listed (e.g., temperate, hospitable, good teacher)
Deacons—characteristics of these leaders are listed (e.g., serious, not greedy)
Widow—woman who needs help from the church because her husband is dead and she receives no support from her husband's family

Important Quotations

"The saying is sure and worthy of full acceptance, that Christ Jesus came into the world to save sinners—of whom I am the foremost." (1 Tim 1:15)

"Let a woman learn in silence with full submission. I permit no woman to teach or to have authority over a man; she is to keep silent." (1 Tim 2:11–12)

"Deacons likewise must be serious, not double-tongued, not indulging in much wine, not greedy for money; they must hold fast to the mystery of the faith with a clear conscience." (1 Tim 3:8–9)

"Let no one despise your youth, but set the believers an example in speech and conduct, in love, in faith, in purity." (1 Tim 4:12)

"Fight the good fight of the faith; take hold of the eternal life, to which you were called and for which you made the good confession in the presence of many witnesses." (1 Tim 6:12)

2 TIMOTHY

The sixteenth book of the New Testament is the second letter of Paul to Timothy.

Synopsis

The letter opens with a salutation identifying Paul as the sender and Timothy as the recipient. Paul gave thanks to God for Timothy's faith, which first lived in his grandmother and mother. He exhorted Timothy not to be ashamed of the gospel but to join him in suffering for the gospel. Timothy was to avoid wrangling over words and youthful passions and was reminded in the last days that people would love themselves, desire pleasure, and turn from God. Timothy was to continue in the faith by observing the example of Paul's faith and through the study of Scripture. The letter ends with greetings and a benediction.

Content Outline

Salutation; remembrance of the faith of Lois and Eunice	2 Timothy 1
Pass on the tradition even while suffering hardship	2 Timothy 2
Prediction of distressing times; hold fast to tradition	2 Timothy 3
Exhortation to be persistent and patient in teaching; time of heresy is coming	2 Timothy 4

People

Paul—apostle
Timothy—Paul's "beloved child"
Lois—Timothy's grandmother
Eunice—Timothy's mother

Hymenaeus—person whom Paul notes has "swerved from the truth"
Philetus—person whom Paul notes has "swerved from the truth"
Jannes—Pharaoh's magician from the Old Testament
Jambres—Pharaoh's magician from the Old Testament
Moses—leader from the Old Testament

Places

Asia—Roman province in Asia Minor
Rome—capital of the Roman Empire
Ephesus—capital of Asia

Key Concepts

Suffering—may be required by the gospel
False teachers—will appear in the last days to mislead people
Last days—days when false teachings appear

Important Quotations

"For this reason I remind you to rekindle the gift of God that is within you through the laying on of my hands; for God did not give us a spirit of cowardice, but rather a spirit of power and of love and of self-discipline." (2 Tim 1:6–7)

"Hold to the standard of sound teaching that you have heard from me, in the faith and love that are in Christ Jesus." (2 Tim 1:13)

"All scripture is inspired by God and is useful for teaching, for reproof, for correction, and for training in righteousness." (2 Tim 3:16)

"I have fought the good fight, I have finished the race, I have kept the faith." (2 Tim 4:7)

TITUS

The seventeenth book of the New Testament is Paul's letter to Titus.

Synopsis

The letter begins with a salutation followed by a note about Titus's purpose in Crete: to appoint elders and bishops, to silence the rebellious people, and to rebuke Cretans, who were known as liars. Titus was instructed to teach sound doctrine and behaviors to older men, older women, younger men, and slaves. He was also to exhort the people to do good deeds and to remember they had been saved by God's mercy and not because of any works of righteousness. They were to avoid controversies and divisive people. The letter ends with the customary final greetings and a benediction.

Content Outline

Instructions on elders; exhortation to avoid rebellious people and to rebuke Cretans	Titus 1
Teach behavioral standards consistent with sound doctrine	Titus 2
How we were changed and saved by God our Savior	Titus 3

People

Paul—apostle
Titus—Paul's assistant

Places

Crete—Greek island that became a Roman province

Key Concepts

Elders—characteristics of these leaders are listed (e.g., blameless, married once, not rebellious)
Bishops—characteristics of these leaders are listed (e.g., blameless, not arrogant, not violent, not greedy)
Household duties/codes—duties for members in a household (older men, older women, younger men, slaves)

Important Quotations

"I left you behind in Crete for this reason, so that you should put in order what remained to be done, and should appoint elders in every town, as I directed you." (Titus 1:5)

"But when the goodness and loving kindness of God our Savior appeared, he saved us, not because of any works of righteousness that we had done, but according to his mercy, through the water of rebirth and renewal by the Holy Spirit." (Titus 3:4–5)

PHILEMON

The eighteenth book of the New Testament is Paul's letter to Philemon.

Synopsis

Paul began with a salutation before expressing thankfulness for Philemon's love and faith. He then made a plea for Philemon to accept Onesimus back "no longer as a slave but more than a slave, a beloved brother." Paul asked Philemon to offer the same welcome to Onesimus that he would afford Paul. The letter concludes with greetings and a benediction.

Content Outline

Salutations; Philemon's faith; Paul's plea for Onesimus; final greetings	Philemon

People

Paul—apostle
Timothy—Paul's traveling companion and coauthor
Philemon—recipient of the letter
Apphia—recipient of the letter
Archippus—recipient of the letter
Onesimus—subject of the letter
Epaphras—Paul's fellow prisoner

Key Concepts

Slave—person who is owned by another person or household; Onesimus is one
Equality in Christ—Paul argues for the equality of people in this letter

Important Quotations

"I am sending him, that is, my own heart, back to you." (Phlm 12)

"Perhaps this is the reason he was separated from you for a while, so that you might have him back forever, no longer as a slave but more than a slave, a beloved brother—especially to me but how much more to you, both in the flesh and in the Lord." (Phlm 15–16)

"So if you consider me your partner, welcome him as you would welcome me." (Phlm 17)

7

General Epistles and Revelation

This section of the New Testament includes nine books: eight letters attributed to writers other than Paul and the book of Revelation. The eight letters are called the General Epistles or the Catholic Epistles because they are understood to be addressed to a general audience, unlike Paul's more specific addressees. Two of the letters are attributed to the apostle Peter (1 and 2 Peter), and three are attributed to the apostle John (1, 2, and 3 John). The book of Revelation is an apocalypse.

HEBREWS

The nineteenth book in the New Testament is the letter to the Hebrews. Although this book concludes as a letter might, it begins much differently than a typical ancient letter.

Synopsis

Hebrews opens with a declaration: although in the past God had spoken through prophets, God has now spoken through Jesus, God's Son. Old Testament quotations declare God's Son superior to the angels, and though he was made lower than the angels for a brief time, he was then exalted through death. As an apostle and high priest, Jesus is delineated as superior to Moses and earthly high priests.

The readers of the book of Hebrews were encouraged to move toward maturity in faith. The writer included the Old Testament story of King Melchizedek while pointing to Christ as another priest of the order of Melchizedek. Christ offered himself as a sacrifice once for all, leaving no need for the daily sacrifices of earthly priests. Jesus came as the mediator of a better covenant; the first covenant would soon disappear. The contrast is made between the earthly tabernacle of the Old Testament and Jesus as a high priest, who entered the Holy Place of heaven, with his own blood providing eternal redemption.

The writer of Hebrews listed examples of faith from the Old Testament, including Abel, Enoch, Noah, Abraham, Isaac, Jacob, Joseph, Moses, the people in the exodus, Rahab, and others. Readers were encouraged to look to those examples and to run the race set before them with perseverance. Trials could be endured by considering them as God's discipline of God's children. Love and hospitality were encouraged. The book concludes as a letter with a benediction and greetings.

Content Outline

God has spoken by a Son; Christ is superior to the angels	Hebrews 1
Jesus was crowned with glory and tasted death for everyone	Hebrews 2
Christ is superior to Moses; exhortation not to harden hearts	Hebrews 3
Israel failed to "enter its rest"; Christ is a high priest able to sympathize	Hebrews 4
Superiority of Jesus' high priesthood to that of earthly priests	Hebrews 5
Exhortation to continue on to perfection	Hebrews 6
More on Jesus as high priest according to the order of Melchizedek	Hebrews 7
Jesus as mediator of a better covenant	Hebrews 8
Superiority of the heavenly sanctuary to the earthly one	Hebrews 9
Christ offered a single sacrifice for sins; continue on in patient endurance	Hebrews 10
Litany of Old Testament faithful	Hebrews 11
Suffering as discipline	Hebrews 12
Final exhortations for Christian living, including remarks on love and hospitality	Hebrews 13

People

Jesus—high priest
Abraham—patriarch from the Old Testament
Moses—servant from the Old Testament
David—king from the Old Testament
Melchizedek—king of Salem from the Old Testament

Key Concepts

Priesthood—book speaks of Melchizedek's priesthood and Christ's priesthood
Sacrifice—once-for-all work of Christ
New covenant—better covenant mediated by Christ, who made the first covenant obsolete
Faith—"assurance of things hoped for, the conviction of things not seen" (Heb 11:1); belief that something is possible when there is no evidence

Important Quotations

"Long ago God spoke to our ancestors in many and various ways by the prophets, but in these last days he has spoken to us by a Son, whom he appointed heir of all things, through whom he also created the worlds." (Heb 1:1–2)

"Indeed, the word of God is living and active, sharper than any two-edged sword, piercing until it divides soul from spirit, joints from marrow; it is able to judge the thoughts and intentions of the heart." (Heb 4:12)

"Since, then, we have a great high priest who has passed through the heavens, Jesus, the Son of God, let us hold fast to our confession." (Heb 4:14)

"You are a priest forever, according to the order of Melchizedek." (Heb 5:6)

"But Jesus has now obtained a more excellent ministry, and to that degree he is the mediator of a better covenant, which has been enacted through better promises." (Heb 8:6)

"But when Christ came as a high priest of the good things that have come, then through the greater and perfect tent (not made with hands, that is, not of this creation), he entered once for all into the Holy Place, not with the blood of goats and calves, but with his own blood, thus obtaining eternal redemption." (Heb 9:11–12)

"Now faith is the assurance of things hoped for, the conviction of things not seen. Indeed, by faith our ancestors received approval." (Heb 11:1–2)

"Therefore, since we are surrounded by so great a cloud of witnesses, let us also lay aside every weight and the sin that clings so closely, and let us run with perseverance the race that is set before us." (Heb 12:1)

"Do not neglect to show hospitality to strangers, for by doing that some have entertained angels without knowing it." (Heb 13:2)

"Jesus Christ is the same yesterday and today and forever." (Heb 13:8)

JAMES

The twentieth book of the New Testament is the letter of James.

Synopsis

The letter begins with a brief salutation identifying James as the writer and the twelve tribes in the Dispersion as the recipients. In orderly fashion, an overview of the epistle's major themes follows: exhortation to endure testing and seek divine wisdom, warning against double-mindedness, counsel to avoid careless speech, admonition of the wealthy, statement on fulfilling God's perfect law. Through anecdote the church was admonished to not show favoritism, to follow the law, to love one's neighbor as oneself, and to recognize that faith without works is dead. The writer gave a lengthy warning of the dangers of speech and the difficulty of controlling the tongue. A contrast was made between gentle divine wisdom and the envy and selfish ambition of those informed by the world. The consequences of envy and ambition were murder and war. Friends of the world should submit to God and repent of their double-mindedness. The writer condemned the rich for exploiting the poor and counseled the faithful to endure trials, live in harmony, anoint the sick, and save the wandering.

Content Outline

Salutation; facing trials and seeking wisdom; temptations	James 1
Showing favoritism; law summed up as loving one's neighbor as oneself	James 2
Dangers of speech; controlling the tongue	James 3

Friendship with the world is enmity with God; do not speak evil against another	James 4
The rich have exploited the poor; endure trials; live in harmony	James 5

People

James—servant of God and of Jesus Christ

Places

Dispersion—places outside of Palestine; the Jewish diaspora

Key Concepts

Trials—temptations that produce maturity
Speech—letter speaks of the importance of controlling one's tongue
Faith and works—belief in God needs actions

Important Quotations

"My brothers and sisters, whenever you face trials of any kind, consider it nothing but joy, because you know that the testing of your faith produces endurance; and let endurance have its full effect, so that you may be mature and complete, lacking in nothing." (Jas 1:2–4)

"Every generous act of giving, with every perfect gift, is from above, coming down from the Father of lights, with whom there is no variation or shadow due to change." (Jas 1:17)

"But be doers of the word, and not merely hearers who deceive themselves." (Jas 1:22)

"Religion that is pure and undefiled before God, the Father, is this: to care for orphans and widows in their distress, and to keep oneself unstained by the world." (Jas 1:27)

"So faith by itself, if it has no works, is dead." (Jas 2:17)

"But no one can tame the tongue—a restless evil, full of deadly poison." (Jas 3:8)

"Submit yourselves therefore to God. Resist the devil, and he will flee from you." (Jas 4:7)

"Therefore confess your sins to one another, and pray for one another, so that you may be healed. The prayer of the righteous is powerful and effective." (Jas 5:16)

1 PETER

The twenty-first book of the New Testament is Peter's first letter.

Synopsis

The letter begins with a salutation from Peter to the exiles of the Dispersion, followed by a lengthy benediction regarding the living hope and inheritance offered through the resurrected Christ. It speaks of rejoicing during trials and the testing of faith. The readers were encouraged to be holy in conduct, to rid themselves of all vices such as envy and slander, and to be living stones built into a spiritual house, with the living stone of Christ as the foundation. They were called to be a holy priesthood.

Slaves were instructed to accept the authority of their masters, and wives were instructed to accept the authority of their husbands. Husbands were to show consideration for their wives. The readers were encouraged to love and serve one another, rejoicing in their shared suffering with Christ. Elders were exhorted to tend the flock of God. The book concludes with greetings and a benediction.

Content Outline

Joy in suffering; call to holiness through Christ who ransomed you	1 Peter 1
The Lord as a living stone; obey higher governing authorities; slaves obey masters	1 Peter 2
Wives, obey your husbands; husbands, consider your wives; repay evil with blessing	1 Peter 3
Exhortations to discipline and love; rejoice in sharing Christ's sufferings	1 Peter 4
Elders are to tend the flock; younger ones are to obey the elders; watch out for the prowling devil	1 Peter 5

People

Peter—apostle
Exiles of the Dispersion—recipients of the letter
Sarah—matriarch from the Old Testament
Abraham—patriarch from the Old Testament
Silvanus—bearer of the letter

Places

Pontus—province in Asia Minor
Galatia—province in Asia Minor
Cappadocia—province in Asia Minor
Asia—province in Asia Minor
Bithynia—province in Asia Minor
Babylon—reference to Rome

Key Concepts

Suffering—sharing in Christ's suffering
Household rules—the duties for members in a household
Living stone—Christ is the stone rejected by people but chosen by God
Holy priesthood—followers of Christ are to be priests

Important Quotations

"In this you rejoice, even if now for a little while you have had to suffer various trials, so that the genuineness of your faith—being more precious than gold that, though perishable, is tested by fire—may be found to result in praise and glory and honor when Jesus Christ is revealed." (1 Pet 1:6–7)

"Come to him, a living stone, though rejected by mortals yet chosen and precious in God's sight, and like living stones, let yourselves be built into a spiritual house, to be a holy priesthood, to offer spiritual sacrifices acceptable to God through Jesus Christ." (1 Pet 2:4–5)

"But you are a chosen race, a royal priesthood, a holy nation, God's own people, in order that you may proclaim the mighty acts of him who called you out of darkness into his marvelous light. Once you were not a people, but now you are God's people; once you had not received mercy, but now you have received mercy." (1 Pet 2:9–10)

"Always be ready to make your defense to anyone who demands from you an accounting for the hope that is in you." (1 Pet 3:15)

"Discipline yourselves, keep alert. Like a roaring lion your adversary the devil prowls around, looking for someone to devour." (1 Pet 5:8)

2 PETER

The twenty-second book in the New Testament is Peter's second letter.

Synopsis

The letter opens with a salutation identifying Simeon Peter as the writer, but the recipients are unidentified. Peter encouraged the readers to continue to be faithful and not stumble, then issued a warning against false prophets. He addressed the delay of the promised coming of the Lord with reassurance. He concluded with an appeal to wait patiently.

Content Outline

Keep on being faithful; eyewitnesses of Christ's majesty	2 Peter 1
Expect false prophets to arise; sins of the ungodly	2 Peter 2
In the last days scoffers will come; the Lord's slowness gives time for repentance	2 Peter 3

People

Simeon Peter—apostle

Key Concept

False prophets—letter criticizes false prophets and teachers

Important Quotations

"Thus he has given us, through these things, his precious and very great promises, so that through them you may escape from the corruption that is in the world because of lust, and may become participants of the divine nature." (2 Pet 1:4)

"Then the Lord knows how to rescue the godly from trial, and to keep the unrighteous under punishment until the day of judgment." (2 Pet 2:9)

"But do not ignore this one fact, beloved, that with the Lord one day is like a thousand years, and a thousand years are like one day." (2 Pet 3:8)

1 JOHN

The twenty-third book of the New Testament is John's first letter.

Synopsis

The letter begins with the affirmation that God is light, followed by encouragement to walk in the light so as to have fellowship with one another. The unidentified author, traditionally assumed to be the apostle John, encouraged readers not to sin but observed that if they did, Jesus was their advocate and atoning sacrifice. John encouraged people to love, writing of love as both a new and an old commandment. He warned of the presence of many antichrists. He identified the readers as children of God who were to love one another, and he commanded them to test every spirit to see if it was from God. God is love, so everyone who loves is from God and knows God. The letter concludes with exhortations to not sin and to keep away from idols.

Content Outline

God is light and not darkness	1 John 1
Jesus as our advocate; obey the Father; love one another; antichrists have come	1 John 2
Sin is lawlessness; love one another; do not be like Cain	1 John 3
On testing the spirits; God is love; perfect love casts out fear	1 John 4
Obey God's commandments; the world under the power of the evil one	1 John 5

Key Concepts

Light—God is light
Love—God is love
Antichrists—people who left the community and are against Christ; the letter warns against antichrists who have come at the last hour

Important Quotations

"This is the message we have heard from him and proclaim to you, that God is light and in him there is no darkness at all." (1 John 1:5)

"If we say that we have no sin, we deceive ourselves, and the truth is not in us. If we confess our sins, he who is faithful and just will forgive us our sins and cleanse us from all unrighteousness." (1 John 1:8–9)

"Little children, let us love, not in word or speech, but in truth and action." (1 John 3:18)

"And this is his commandment, that we should believe in the name of his Son Jesus Christ and love one another, just as he has commanded us." (1 John 3:23)

"By this you know the Spirit of God: every spirit that confesses that Jesus Christ has come in the flesh is from God, and every spirit that does not confess Jesus is not from God. And this is the spirit of the antichrist, of which you have heard that it is coming; and now it is already in the world." (1 John 4:2–3)

"Beloved, let us love one another, because love is from God; everyone who loves is born of God and knows God. Whoever does not love does not know God, for God is love." (1 John 4:7–8)

2 JOHN

The twenty-fourth book of the New Testament is John's second letter.

Synopsis

The letter opens by identifying the writer as the elder and the addressee as the elect lady and her children. The elder commanded the readers to love and to walk according to God's commandments. He warned them of deceivers who did not confess Jesus. The letter concludes with greetings.

Content Outline

Walk according to God's commandments; greetings   2 John

People

Elder—writer of the letter
Elect lady—recipient of the letter

Key Concepts

Love—commandment given to love
Deceivers—those who claim that Jesus has not come in the flesh
Antichrist—name given to the deceivers

Important Quotations

"The elder to the elect lady and her children, whom I love in the truth, and not only I but also all who know the truth." (2 John 1)

"Many deceivers have gone out into the world, those who do not confess that Jesus Christ has come in the flesh; any such person is the deceiver and the antichrist!" (2 John 7)

3 JOHN

The twenty-fifth book of the New Testament is John's third letter.

Synopsis

The letter opens with the elder commending Gaius, the recipient, for walking in the truth. The elder encouraged support for those who travel from community to community. The letter ends with a greeting.

Content Outline

Show hospitality to traveling workers who are good	3 John

People

Elder—writer of the letter
Gaius—recipient of the letter
Diotrephes—selfish person mentioned in the letter
Demetrius—person mentioned positively in the letter

Key Concept

Hospitality—Gaius is mentioned for his welcome

Important Quotations

"Beloved, do not imitate what is evil but imitate what is good. Whoever does good is from God; whoever does evil has not seen God." (3 John 11)

JUDE

The twenty-sixth book of the New Testament is the letter of Jude.

Synopsis

The letter opens with a salutation identifying the writer as Jude and the recipients as those who are called. Jude explained the purpose of the letter: to appeal to the readers to contend for the faith against the false teachers who pervert the gospel. He provided multiple examples from the Old Testament of God punishing evildoers and connected these actions to the contemporary situation. The letter concludes with exhortations to love and have mercy and includes a benediction.

Content Outline

Contend for the faith; false teachers   Jude

People

Jude—servant of Jesus Christ; brother of James
James—brother of Jude
Michael—archangel

Key Concept

False teachers—letter condemns their behavior of rejecting authority

Important Quotations

"These are blemishes on your love-feasts, while they feast with you without fear, feeding themselves. They are waterless clouds carried along by the winds; autumn trees without fruit, twice dead, uprooted; wild waves of the sea, casting up the foam of their own shame; wandering stars, for whom the deepest darkness has been reserved forever." (Jude 12–13)

"Now to him who is able to keep you from falling, and to make you stand without blemish in the presence of his glory with rejoicing, to the only God our Savior, through Jesus Christ our Lord, be glory, majesty, power, and authority, before all time and now and forever. Amen." (Jude 24–25)

REVELATION

The twenty-seventh and last book of the New Testament is the Revelation to John.

Synopsis

The book opens with a title and a blessing. The letter was written by John to the seven churches in Asia. John narrated the appearance of Christ to him while he was on the island of Patmos. Christ told him to write a book to the seven churches. Each of the seven churches was then evaluated and warned and/or encouraged.

The scene then shifted from the seven churches on earth to a vision in heaven that depicted God on a throne around which were four six-winged creatures, each praising God. In the right hand of God was a scroll sealed with seven seals. The only one who was worthy to open the scroll was the Lion of the tribe of Judah. John saw a Lamb standing with seven horns and seven eyes, and the Lamb took the scroll from God on the throne. Everyone praised the Lamb and God. Each of the seals was opened, which was accompanied by terrible calamities on the earth. From the twelve tribes of Israel, 144,000 were marked with a seal on their foreheads, and a multitude of people worshiped God. When the seventh and final seal was opened, heaven fell silent. Seven angels were given seven trumpets. Six of these trumpets were blown one after another, accompanied by more judgment. John ate a little scroll given to him by a mighty angel. The seventh trumpet was blown, and a pregnant woman and a red dragon appeared. The dragon waited to devour the woman's child, but when she gave birth, the child was taken to God. Michael and his angels fought the dragon, who was called the Devil and Satan, and he was thrown to the earth.

The vision continued as John saw two beasts, one rising from the sea and the other from the earth. The number of the beast was 666. On Mount Zion, 144,000 people gathered with the Lamb and sang a new song, followed by three angels announcing God's judgment. The Son of Man appeared seated on a white cloud and swinging his sickle over the earth to reap it. Seven angels with seven plagues were given seven golden bowls full of the wrath of God. They poured out the bowls of wrath. The last bowl announced the judgment of Babylon, depicted as a great whore sitting on a scarlet beast. This judgment led to great rejoicing in heaven.

Revelation includes seven final visions of the end: Christ returning as a rider on a white horse, a final battle depicting the beast and the false prophet thrown into the lake of fire, Satan being bound, Christ reigning on earth for a thousand years, Gog and Magog being defeated, the final judgment occurring, and a new heaven and a new earth, including a new Jerusalem. The book ends with an epilogue and a benediction.

Content Outline

John's self-introduction and the glorious Son of Man	Revelation 1
Letters to the churches of Ephesus, Smyrna, Pergamum, and Thyatira	Revelation 2
Letters to the churches of Sardis, Philadelphia, and Laodicea	Revelation 3
Heavenly scene: God on the throne and four living creatures	Revelation 4
Scroll with seven seals; Lamb slaughtered	Revelation 5
Seven seals opened by the Lamb; four horsemen	Revelation 6
144,000 plus a countless throng before the throne	Revelation 7
Blowing of the six trumpets	Revelation 8–9
Angel with a little scroll	Revelation 10
Two witnesses in Jerusalem; seventh trumpet blown	Revelation 11
Woman clothed with the sun gives birth; Michael battles the dragon	Revelation 12
Beast from the sea and beast from the earth; the number of the beast is 666	Revelation 13
144,000 redeemed; the Son of Man comes on a cloud	Revelation 14
Seven angels with seven plagues	Revelation 15

Pouring out of seven bowls, with additional plagues	Revelation 16
Whore of Babylon sitting on a beast with seven heads and ten horns	Revelation 17
Ironic laments and songs taunting Babylon	Revelation 18
Heavenly multitude praising God; white horse with a warrior; lake of fire	Revelation 19
Angel binds the devil; thousand-year reign of Christ; devil unbound and cast into the lake of fire	Revelation 20
New creation and descent of heavenly Jerusalem	Revelation 21
River of the water of life; epilogue	Revelation 22

People

John—servant of God
Michael—angel

Places

Patmos—island in the Aegean Sea
Ephesus—one of the seven churches
Smyrna—one of the seven churches
Pergamum—one of the seven churches
Thyatira—one of the seven churches
Sardis—one of the seven churches
Philadelphia—one of the seven churches
Laodicea—one of the seven churches

Key Concepts

God's judgment—God's punishment of the wicked
Suffering—those who are suffering because of their faith; addressees of the revelation
Satan's defeat—Jesus' decisive victory over Satan
End times—the end of the world; expected to happen in the foreseeable future
New heaven and earth—paradise where sin and evil do not exist; God's reign

Important Quotations

"'I am the Alpha and the Omega,' says the Lord God, who is and who was and who is to come, the Almighty." (Rev 1:8)

"So, because you are lukewarm, and neither cold nor hot, I am about to spit you out of my mouth." (Rev 3:16)

"Listen! I am standing at the door, knocking; if you hear my voice and open the door, I will come in to you and eat with you, and you with me." (Rev 3:20)

"Then one of the elders said to me, 'Do not weep. See, the Lion of the tribe of Judah, the Root of David, has conquered, so that he can open the scroll and its seven seals.'" (Rev 5:5)

"Then the seventh angel blew his trumpet, and there were loud voices in heaven, saying, 'The kingdom of the world has become the kingdom of our Lord and of his Messiah, and he will reign forever and ever.'" (Rev 11:15)

"Then I saw an angel coming down from heaven, holding in his hand the key to the bottomless pit and a great chain. He seized the dragon, that ancient serpent, who is the Devil and Satan, and bound him for a thousand years, and threw him into the pit, and locked and sealed it over him, so that he would deceive the nations no more, until the thousand years were ended. After that he must be let out for a little while." (Rev 20:1–3)

"Blessed are those who wash their robes, so that they will have the right to the tree of life and may enter the city by the gates." (Rev 22:14)

Appendix
Resources for Biblical Study

For those people who are interested in continuing in their study of the Bible, I provide the following resources from biblical scholarship.

Atlases

Aharoni, Yohanan, Michael Avi-Yonah, Anson F. Rainey, Ze'ev Safrai, R. Steven Notley, eds. *The Carta Bible Atlas.* 5th rev. and expanded ed. Jerusalem: Carta, 2011.

Curtis, Adrian, ed. *Oxford Bible Atlas.* 4th ed. New York: Oxford University Press, 2009.

Dowley, Tom. *The Student Bible Atlas.* Rev. ed. Minneapolis: Fortress Press, 2015.

Dictionaries and Encyclopedias

Coogan, Michael David, ed. *The Oxford Encyclopedia of the Books of the Bible.* 2 vols. New York: Oxford University Press, 2011.

Freedman, David Noel, ed. *Anchor Bible Dictionary.* 6 vols. New York: Doubleday, 1992.

———, ed. *Eerdmans Dictionary of the Bible.* Grand Rapids, MI: W. B. Eerdmans Publishing Co., 2000.

Hayes, John H., ed. *Dictionary of Biblical Interpretation.* 2 vols. Nashville: Abingdon Press, 1999.

Metzger, Bruce M., and Michael D. Coogan, eds. *The Oxford Guide to People and Places of the Bible.* New York: Oxford University Press, 2004.

Meyers, Carol, and Toni Craven, eds. *Women in Scripture: A Dictionary of Named and Unnamed Women in the Hebrew Bible, the Apocryphal/Deuterocanonical Books, and the New Testament.* Grand Rapids, MI: W. B. Eerdmans Publishing Co., 2001.

Powell, Mark Allan, ed. *HarperCollins Bible Dictionary*. 3rd rev. and updated ed. San Francisco: HarperOne, 2011.
Sakenfeld, Katharine Doob, ed. *The New Interpreter's Dictionary of the Bible*. 5 vols. Nashville: Abingdon Press, 2006.

Multivolume Commentary Series

Abingdon New Testament Commentaries (Abingdon Press)
Abingdon Old Testament Commentaries (Abingdon Press)
Anchor Yale Bible Commentaries (Yale University Press)
Interpretation (Westminster John Knox Press)
JPS Torah Commentary (Jewish Publication Society)
New Interpreter's Bible (Abingdon Press)
New Testament Library (Westminster John Knox Press)
Old Testament Library (Westminster John Knox Press)
Westminster Bible Companion (Westminster John Knox Press)
Wisdom Commentary (Liturgical Press)
Word Biblical Commentary (Word Publishing)

One-Volume Commentaries

Adeyemo, Tokunboh, ed. *Africa Bible Commentary*. 2nd ed. Grand Rapids, MI: Zondervan, 2010.
Barton, John, and John Muddiman, eds. *The Oxford Bible Commentary*. New York: Oxford University Press, 2001.
Farmer, William, Armando Levoratti, David L. Dungan, and Andre LaCocque, eds. *The International Bible Commentary*. Collegeville, MN: Liturgical Press, 1998.
Guest, Deryn, Robert E. Goss, Mona West, and Thomas Bohache, eds. *The Queer Bible Commentary*. London: SCM Press, 2006.
Mays, James Luther, and Joseph Blenkinsopp, eds. *The HarperCollins Bible Commentary*. Rev. ed. San Francisco: HarperSanFrancisco, 2000.
Newsom, Carol, Sharon H. Ringe, and Jacqueline E. Lapsley, eds. *Women's Bible Commentary*. 3rd ed. Louisville, KY: Westminster John Knox Press, 2012.
Page, Hugh R., Jr., Randall C. Bailey, Valerie Bridgeman, Cheryl A. Kirk-Duggan, et al., eds. *The Africana Bible: Reading Israel's Scriptures from Africa and the African Diaspora*. Minneapolis: Fortress Press, 2010.
Patte, Daniel, ed. *Global Bible Commentary*. Nashville: Abingdon Press, 2004.

Introductions to the Bible

Old Testament

Collins, John J. *Introduction to the Hebrew Bible*. 3rd ed. Minneapolis: Fortress Press, 2018.

Gertz, Jan Christian, Angelika Berlejung, Konrad Schmid, and Markus Witte. *T&T Clark Handbook of the Old Testament*. New York: T&T Clark, 2012.

Knight, Douglas A., and Amy-Jill Levine. *The Meaning of the Bible: What the Jewish Scriptures and Christian Old Testament Can Teach Us*. New York: HarperOne, 2011.

Sweeney, Marvin A. *Tanak: A Theological and Critical Introduction to the Jewish Bible*. Minneapolis: Fortress Press, 2012.

New Testament

Allen, Ronald J. *Reading the New Testament for the First Time*. Grand Rapids, MI: W. B. Eerdmans Publishing Co., 2012.

Boring, M. Eugene. *An Introduction to the New Testament: History, Literature, Theology*. Louisville, KY: Westminster John Knox Press, 2012.

Brown, Raymond E. *An Introduction to the New Testament: The Abridged Edition*. Edited and abridged by Marion L. Soards. New Haven, CT: Yale University Press, 2016.

Ehrman, Bart. D. *The New Testament: A Historical Introduction to the Early Christian Writings*. 6th ed. New York: Oxford University Press, 2016.

Index of People

Pharaoh
  daughter of, adopting Moses, 23, 26,
    29
  daughter of, married to Solomon,
    76–77
  Hebrews oppressed by, 23–24, 26, 27,
    28, 29
  Joseph and, 14, 16
Pharisees, 179–80, 183, 188, 191–92,
    194, 196, 198
  Jesus' meals with, 192, 196
Philemon, 238–39
Philip, 183, 189, 195, 200, 203, 204,
    206
Philistines, 57, 58–59, 60, 61
  judges and, 49, 50, 51, 52, 54
Phinehas, 36
Phoebe, 212, 213
Pilate, 180, 182, 183, 187, 193, 196, 198,
    200
poor, the, 117, 120, 159, 196, 244–45
Potiphar and his wife, 16, 18
Prisca, 212, 216
prophets of Baal, 74, 76, 77, 78, 84
Puah, 23, 26

Queen of Sheba, 73, 75, 77, 80, 94

Rachel, 6, 13, 16, 18, 20, 22
Rahab, 44, 46, 47, 242
Rebekah, 6, 13, 15–16, 17, 22
Rehoboam, 74, 76, 81, 82, 94, 95, 96
Reuben, 6, 18, 23
Reuel (Jethro), 23, 25, 27, 29
Ruth, 54–57

Sadducees, 180, 183
Samson, 50, 51, 52, 53, 54
Samuel, 57–64
Sanballat, 102, 104
Sapphira, 203, 204, 206
Sarah (Sarai), 6, 13, 15, 17, 20, 21
  in New Testament, 221, 222, 247
Satan
  cosmic war with, 253, 254, 255, 256
  Jesus tempted by, 179, 181, 183,
    186
  in Job, 111, 112, 113

Saul (apostle). *See* Paul
Saul (king), 91, 92
  anointing of, 58, 59, 62, 63
  David and, 58, 59–60, 63–64, 65, 68,
    69
  Samuel and, 57, 58, 59, 62–63
Sennacherib, 85, 88, 96, 132, 134, 136
Shadrach, 151, 153–54
Shallum of Israel, 81, 83, 85, 87
Shalmaneser III, 82, 88
Shamgar, 49, 51, 52, 54
Shaphan, 89, 90
Sheba (rebel against David), 65, 66, 67,
    71
Sheba, Queen of, 73, 75, 77, 80, 94
Shechem, 14, 16, 18
Shemaiah (exile), 139, 141, 143
Shemaiah (false prophet), 102, 104
Shimei, 71, 73, 76, 79
Shiphrah, 23, 26
Shunammite woman, 85, 88, 90
Silas, 203, 205, 207
Simeon (Jacob's son), 6, 16, 18, 23
Simeon (righteous man), 191, 195
Simon (Jesus' brother), 189
Simon (leper), 183
Simon of Cyrene, 183
Simon Peter. *See* Peter
Simon the Zealot (Simon the
    Cananaean), 183, 189, 195, 206
Sisera, 49, 51, 52
Solomon, 73–74, 75, 79–80, 94
  anointing of, 73, 76, 79
  birth of, 65, 66, 67, 70
  David and, 71
  Proverbs and, 124
  Psalms and, 123
  and Song of Songs, 128, 129
  Temple built by, 73, 75, 79, 80, 91,
    93–94
  wealth of, 73, 78–79, 80, 94
  wisdom of, 73, 75, 77, 78–79, 80, 94,
    124
  wives of, 73, 76, 80
son of man
  Ezekiel as, 150
  Jesus as, 180, 182, 184, 187, 190, 208,
    254

Index of Places

Page references in italics refer to maps.

Index of Themes

31994238R10160

Made in the USA
Lexington, KY
27 February 2019